THE EXPLORER RACE

EARTH HISTORY AND LOST CIVILIZATIONS

SPEAKS OF MANY TRUTHS, ZOOSH
and others through ROBERT SHAPIRO

THE EXPLORER RACE

EARTH HISTORY AND LOST CIVILIZATIONS

Speaks of Many Truths, Zoosh and others
through Robert Shapiro

Published by

Light Technology
PUBLISHING

ISBN 1-891824-20-1

Published by:
Light Technology Publishing
PO Box 3540
Flagstaff, Arizona 86003
(800) 450-0985
www.lighttechnology.com

Table of Contents

Chapter 27

Chapter 28

1

When Earth Was in Sirius

Speaks of Many Truths
July 9, 1998

All right, this is Speaks of Many Truths.

Welcome.

Thank you. Tonight I want to begin on our project and talk about the times when this planet was in the Sirius cluster of stars and planets. This book, being part of the *Explorer Race* series, will build upon premises established by the previous books.

Long ago, when this planet was still in the Sirius star system, the surface of the planet, its contours, was similar—not exactly the same, but similar. Some of the mountains you have here now were much taller; some were still growing. Perhaps the most striking difference was that much of the planet was covered by water.

Mountains would be that which emerged from the water. Generally speaking, anything below fifty-three hundred feet was immersed. This was not seasonal, but year-round. As a result, there was not much dry land, but there was some.

The civilizations established in such a place would have to acknowledge or incorporate water, or perhaps even live upon or within it. I'm going to stay focused tonight on civilizations that have some relevance to the Explorer Race souls and/or Earth society.

The Trilling Water People

The one I will begin with had to do with what I would call the fin people. These beings were at home both in the water and on the land. If you were to see them, they would be <u>humanoid</u>. They had <u>two arms and two legs and a body</u>, but their head looked like a separate appendage on the body. There was no noticeable neck, and the body had a fishlike quality. On the back (<u>they walked upright on land</u>), there was also what amounted to a fin. It was not a big fin; compared to that of a dolphin, it was about half that size in its extension from the body, but similar in length to the dolphin's fin, about halfway along the body.

Fig. 1. Dolphin.

The beings did not wear clothing, and the body was scaled like a fish's. They would venture on the land and could be out of the water for up to forty-eight hours, but their home was really in the water. <u>They had the capacity then to be air breathers and water breathers</u>. They knew where the warm currents were deep in the oceans, and they would gather about in those currents.

The culture had more to do with what one might think rather than with material objects. The planet was fairly idyllic in terms of temperature, moisture and food sources, which were not dissimilar to plankton, not unlike what whales consume here. Although they had scales and fins, they also had <u>gills and lungs</u>, so they were, you might say, unusually adaptable. <u>Their two lungs were for breathing air</u>. They were about half your size, but that was adequate for their purposes. Their lineage, although not directly connected with the porpoise, would be—if you could look at them and look at their auric field and understand the soul's resonance—more like cousins and not brothers or sisters in terms of appearance.

They had, I would say, a unique custom—and this is perhaps why they had access to the land: They could make a trilling sound, for reasons they did not clearly understand. For them it was a ceremony. They would come out of the waters up onto the land, a mountain that, for all intents and purposes, looked like an island to the casual eye. They would walk up partway until they ringed the entire mountain, the way you hold hands and can see one another. It would take time for enough of them to come out, so there would be a rough circle around the mountain, which might, depending on its size, take from forty to four hundred individuals.

One of them would start making this trilling sound, not always the same one, and pretty soon they would all make it. They would make that sound for about forty to fifty minutes, then gradually, one by one, they would stop. While they made the sound they would look away from the water. After they stopped, they would turn around and look at the water, contemplate its beauty and gradually return to the sea.

This went on for many generations without their culture grasping that there was more to it than custom. Their sounds were very closely spaced. It wasn't a harmony in the sense of different sounds blending together, but it was close to the same tone. Gradually, as other water worlds made contact, they were given, not exactly a wide berth, but they were considered sacred or holy people by other water worlds because of their custom of trilling in a very specific way on the mountains.

Thus very little was done to interfere with what they were doing, even though most of the other water-world societies were not fully cognizant of the reason for the custom. They simply thought of them as the holy people or the sacred people, and that was that.

Their trilling had started rather suddenly and became a custom within just a few years. Everyone could remember when it started or knew someone who could, but no one could give a satisfactory answer as to why.

The Visit by the Dolphin Progenitors

After a few hundred years of doing this, visitors came from water worlds who seemed to have a vast knowledge of wisdom available, if not necessarily their own. They traveled in ships that were so light in weight when unloaded that your typical five- or six-year-old child on Earth could move one or rock it if it were sitting on the ground. These ships were vast, easily 300 feet wide by 180 feet high, and rounded on the top and bottom. If empty, the shell was featherweight, although very strong. It would be filled, however, with saline water, like seawater but without quite so much in the way of life forms that are found in typical seawater. It was saline water such as might be found in an ocean not yet peopled by beings, a pure ocean.

There were beings inside who were at home in the water and who had the capacity to take different forms. The form they chose most often was _ribbonlike_. As for their lineage, these beings are the predecessors of what I now consider to be _dolphins_. They are the parent race of dolphins.

One day a ship with these beings came to this place. They had heard about the beings who came out of the sea and trilled and went back underwater, going on about their lives without really knowing why they did it but thinking that perhaps it was a ritual. The beings in the ship knew why they were doing it. They heard that these beings who trilled were dedicated and would do this as often as they got the urge, which, using the current calendar, was every week or two. The beings on the ship were very impressed that a race or culture would keep up such a custom for hundreds of years without fully grasping its true significance. They felt that the trilling beings deserved an explanation, if only to appreciate the full extent of what they were doing. So they decided to visit this society, observe for a short time and then communicate.

Their home was in another star system in Sirius, and for a time they watched from the outer atmosphere of the planet, looking through the hull of their ship. The ship itself had a color that looked almost beige with some gold mixed in, so you might have an impression of filmy gold over beige. But when they wished to see out of it, it would be entirely transparent.

They observed for about two and a half days, during which time a trilling took place. They were most impressed. They observed that the society was cultured and had deep reservoirs of thought, meaning that they could think consciously and could be aware of their deep thoughts. In that sense, the trilling culture did not have a subconscious. They had a conscious mind and stages of deeper consciousness, all of which they could be in touch with.

So the dolphin precursors very slowly approached one of the places where they felt the trilling would take place. They landed in the water, their ship bobbing in the water not unlike a seagoing vessel. The beings did the trilling, then afterward they turned around. (You understand that sometimes they would sit for a time and look at the ocean.) This time they sat and looked at the ship, and shortly afterward, a being emerged in the form of a gold disk.

These visitors could change their appearance. They were not concerned about being praised as deities and wished to be seen in this form for a time. This being looked very much like a small gold disk, maybe two feet across, with radiance around it, a spherical shape.

Trilling for the Future Explorer Race

The gold being approached the trilling beings and said, "We have been observing you for some time. We are from another star system in this galaxy, and we would like to speak to you about the larger nature of your ceremony. Would you like to know about it while doing things the way the trilling people did?" One would nod, and then gradually the others would nod, in very much the same way that they did the trilling. One would say, "Yes," by nodding, and then they would all gradually begin nodding.

The gold being waited until they were all nodding and then said, "I will tell you now what it is about, and then you can pass it on to the rest of your society should you choose." The being said, "A long time ago, a group of souls that was most cherished by the Creator of this universe had to wander all over the universe in order to understand their purpose and begin to have motivations and ultimately achieve their intent. This group of souls is the Explorer Race.

"In the beginning after their launch, they had much excitement exploring the universe, and this was some time before you began your trilling but before they came to Earth. Earth is a planet that is related to this one." (The gold being didn't tell them everything.) The being said, "Before they came to Earth, they went through a time when they needed to coordinate the total experience they'd had up to that point, so for a few hundred years, which coincides with the time you have been doing this ceremony, they needed to establish a means of communication that would also feed them and get them used to the idea of being nurtured, loved, fed and united by something seemingly external. This would prepare them for the type of physical lives they would be living on the Earth, where externals would be all-important.

"The system that was used was sound. You on this planet have been making a sound that would be stored until needed by these beings. From your frame of reference," said the gold lightbeing to the trilling society, "this sound you are making will be stored for millions of years," speaking to them, of course, in their own context of time, "and it will not be used or consumed by these souls," (referring to the Explorer Race) "until they have that need.

"You might reasonably ask, 'Why not have someone make that sound near them when they need it and why store this up?' Well," said the gold lightbeing, "because you are related to them, they will look similar to you. They won't be quite as adaptable to the water as you are and will be air breathers, although some will visit the waters as you do.

"They could be fed only by beings from this planet," (meaning in the time of the trilling people) "beings who had strong connections to the sea and the land, beings who were genetically related," (although, the gold being used a different term) "and beings who had an innate sense of the sacred, because that is what these beings will need in the future," the gold lightbeing said.

"So there must be all of these things. When you started making the trilling sound, it was felt by Creator that the sound itself—which Creator will save for a later use, to be broadcast to these beings—will have to ripen." (I'm feeling that another word is better; will have to age, let's say, not unlike the way a wine or liqueur ages.) "It will have to age, and by aging it will travel the length and breadth and depth of this universe, picking up bits and pieces that may in some way be associated with this Explorer Race."

Well, the trilling people were most impressed. They nodded, first one, then many and then all who were out of the water and present for that ceremony. Finally one of them said, "How long do you feel we might be continuing with our ceremony?"

The gold lightbeing said, "This is one of the reasons we are contacting you now. What you have done so far, including today, is enough. That is all that is required. However, as long as you wish to continue such a ceremony for your own purposes, you may do so, but from now on it will be only for you and for this planet. There is now no need for further accumulation for those others in the future." That's all the lightbeing said.

Gradually they all were nodding. One might wonder (in contemporary times now, speaking to the reader) why they did not ask the gold lightbeing, "Who are you and where are you from?" But in those times and in that place (where the trilling society was and in Sirius generally), one did not question a communication or contact with any being who felt good to you.

These beings, the trilling society, were largely instinctual, although they had a vast capacity for thought—and you can see how that relates to you. So no one even considered asking the gold lightbeing from the ship who they were or where they were from. What was said felt good.

"Well," the gold lightbeing said, "I will be going now and rejoining my people. Then we will return from whence we came." Before leaving, the lightbeing said, "I want to compliment you on your service and your unquestioning loyalty to life," meaning, of course, not only service to their own kind, but also to you in these times, or at least the precursor of you before you became physical on Earth in your time now.

The beings nodded and in their own way gradually smiled, one by one, until they were all smiling at the gold lightbeing. The gold lightbeing smiled in its own way and beamed back at them, then floated back to the ship. The ship rose off the surface of the water and went back from whence it came.

I'm mentioning this society because it is profound to consider how long before the arrival of the Explorer Race on Earth plans were in the works to support and sustain every aspect of what Earth people, Earth souls such as myself and you (speaking to you from my time), would need. Is this not interesting?

Absolutely.

The Whales' Song

That is one society. Any questions about that?

Is there any evidence of that now on this planet?

I'd have to say that even though those beings have some relationship to other species as indicated, the trilling done by whales is not dissimilar. So there are still residuals of such ceremonial soundings. Whales do not just make communicative sounds. They sing and make ceremonial sounds as well, not unlike yourselves. You have your conversation and your communication, yet you also sing—sometimes for entertainment and sometimes for ceremony. Whales are very much the same.

If we were to listen to the trilling and the whales' song would they sound similar?

[Publisher's note: Speaks of Many Truths speaks from the last time he was living as a human on Earth, which was in the 1600s in the western part of the Unites States. He was the mystical man for his tribe. He is also the author, through Robert Shapiro, of the *Shamanic Secrets* series.]

The trilling was all one note, whereas the whales' song has many notes and many different sounds. But there is one sound that whales do make that is very similar, although they make many different ones. I think a good whale researcher would be able to make an educated guess at the sound, as it tends to be not exactly a perfect pitch but maintained close to a perfect pitch, and it lasts for a time. It is not as long as the trilling beings' sound, but it is similar in its tonal structure.

It is interesting to note that the trilling beings never made these sounds in the water as whales do, but only on land, for this ceremony. In the water they communicated through instinct, what you would say would be a knowing.

Not telepathically?

Telepathy is a word in your time that is grossly misunderstood. It is often thought to be the transmission of words without speaking or even the transmission of pictures. But true telepathy, although it has the capacity to suggest images and pictures and so on, is more of what I would call a knowing, and worded communication is not part of it.

What happened to these beings?

Their life span in terms of time was several hundred thousand years. Their number was never very large. It was not rigidly maintained, but they had a naturally fixed number, never much more than three or four thousand. After several hundred thousand years they left the planet, though not in a vehicle of their own making. A vehicle came for them and offered to take them to a similar place that would be more stable. They were told about the future of their planet, which would move from one galaxy [system] to another and would, as a result, change radically.

[Publisher's Note: Beings who speak from other levels of reality can see all of the various realities and the dimensions of each planet or moon or star, which makes even a solar system look very complex. Some beings call a constellation a galaxy; some call a solar system a galaxy.]

The vehicle that came to pick them up was a water ship, but not from the precursor dolphin people. The beings who came with it said, "We have heard many good things about you from the dolphin people, and we would like it very much if you would come to our world, which is stable and will remain in the Sirius star system." They waited in the ship for about three months while the trilling society discussed it amongst themselves, not with talk but with felt telepathy.

When they all agreed, not just one but everyone (that is how they are), they swam to the ship. The ship welcomed them and they swam aboard. When the ship and everyone aboard it were sure they were all there, the vehicle traveled to the other planet, which remained in the Sirius star system. They are still there today, their descendants still numbering no more than three to four thousand.

The trilling ceremony, having become part of their culture, remained in practice for several thousand years beyond the point when they were picked up, but it has now ceased to be part of their ceremony. They are the sort of beings who do things as a group and gradually make changes.

The People of the Winter

Were there other civilizations on this planet when it was in Sirius?

Yes, they were not the only ones there. The planet was large and could accommodate others. You want to know about them?

Whatever you feel is important.

One of them was particularly interesting. It was a society that was slightly below the surface of a vast mountain that was above the water. The access to this inner world within the mountain, this vast inner cave, did not extend beyond the water line, but it was pretty big.

So it was dry?

Yes, inside the mountain. It was a winter world. It had snow and ice, and the beings who lived there were people of the winter. They chose to live there. They did not require clothing because they had very thick skin and because of the constituent makeup of their bodies. There was a thick layer of fat or tissue, so they did not suffer from the cold.

They were interesting beings. They never went to the surface. They were what I would call the great communicators. They had a most interesting capacity to live beyond their own time. In terms of the physical operation of their society, the duration of their physical being (of their entire society) was no more than five thousand years, but unlike the passage of beings from Earth as we know it now (if I might include my time with the Earth), they did not pass through the veils and go on elsewhere.

They would go through a change from their physical bodies, a transformation, becoming transparent lightbeings (occasionally with parts of them translucent) who had the same general form and shape they had when they were physical, and they remained right where they were. Taking into account then the five thousand years of the physical part of their society and the remains of their society in these lightbodies, they have existed for millions and millions of years. They are one of the few beings who rode the planet to its current position, where Earth is now.

These beings still exist on Earth, although over time they have changed their appearance. They had a sort of round appearance when they were physical, but now they have adapted their lightbodies to a shape that looks like a human being, and they have a very sacred society.

They have a unique capacity for communication. They do not, in their own right, have what you would call a culture or a communication or a cultural societal body of wisdom, but they are the link between all forms of life on this planet—all cultures, wisdom, ideas, even ideals that are reasonably benevolent (including benevolence with adventure and excitement but not discomfort)—from their beginning to some indefinite future. I am not able to say it ends, but it just seems to go on indefinitely.

They link to all societies in their time, including when they were physical in Sirius on this planet and now—all societies that existed then and have ever existed on this planet up to now. They do not take from societies, even our society, because human beings or any beings (a fly, an ant, a cow, a snake, a fish, a man, a girl), no matter who, have their own culture and wisdom, including what they can tap into should they need it. Beings will either receive energy, radiate energy or both, because beings essentially broadcast their own being at all times (human beings too, of course). Much of this broadcast energy is encoded with what you believe, what you feel and what your essence is. Your essence as a human being would not only be your essence in this life, but your essence in all your lives, wherever you've been, whatever you've done.

All this radiation from all these cultures and beliefs is siphoned through this culture as through a sieve, not because they want to know, but because they perform a seemingly vast service. When this energy passes through them, they link on to the physical basis of all life. That is why you might have a particular affection for an animal as a person or why one animal has an affection for you. Maybe you go to a place in your town where there are many cats. Although all the cats might glance at you, only some take a personal interest in you. Maybe you take one or two of the interested cats home according to which ones you are personally interested in.

This link appears to be established by what these beings are doing. As far as I can tell, this has nothing to do with the love one person or being might feel for another on a personal level, but rather with the love, connection and feeling of comradeship or even the feeling of honoring all life, the feeling that different life forms have experienced for one another. So it is broader rather than individualistic.

Is there a place on the planet now that you can identify as their home?

I'm going to have to ask permission. They have moved there. They will give one or two of their locations because they have moved about. Part of their society is, of course, at a higher dimension to protect them. It is in the Andes, and part is in, around and near Mount Everest.

Do other beings come in ships now to talk to them? Do lightbeings come to communicate with them?

No.

How high a dimension are they?

In terms as stated for these books, the dimension would be almost the thirty-third.

The Evidence Beings

We assume that some of the Sirian societies on this planet migrated somewhere else when the planet was going to move.

Yes. There is one last society that I would like to discuss. This particular society was established and is still on Sirius, on many planets. Though I call it a society, it is more like a calling. The beings who make up this society come from all different forms and walks of life on Sirius. It seems that their society predates Sirius as a place.

They are very ancient and different beings, and beings continually become initiated when other beings die out. It is generally passed down through lineage, through families, but occasionally other beings who are not of their lineage are inducted and welcomed into this society if they show any interest and talent for what the society does.

I am mentioning this one because it is so important to archaeology and other studies that have to do with understanding from your now time. They are precursors who might have influenced you, so this makes it a little broader than archaeology. The society is what could be described as "the evidence beings." They can travel in time and will at times move evidence from one time and place to another. They have been known to establish footprints where none had been.

They might appear to be a being who you'd not think anything of, but because of their initiation, they can travel in time. So imagine a time in our society on Earth when you are more interested in where you came from and less inclined to filter that through the restrictive images and dogmas of shortsighted religion.

Shortsighted religion would be, for instance, a religion that concerns itself only with the last few thousand years, whereas there are versions of science that will evolve into religions that do not put restrictions on time. Let's say that at some point in time these religious and philosophical scientific communities become more interested in where you came from. You might need evidence to support and sustain your curiosities. When that happens, one of these beings might, if the evidence is not available to you, go back in time and bring evidence from that time to your time, since sometimes evidence does not last. They will place it where it will be found, such as a footprint people find when excavating sites. There would be a footprint of something that might appear to be human, but it might be much larger or seemingly wearing something on its foot that was not in concordance with the understood evolution of the society that was then present—what you might call unexpected discordant evidence. The evidence placers are totally dedicated to helping different societies, your own and others, when these societies begin to wake up to the vaster context of their place in the universe.

Not too many years ago they brought some dinosaur footprints and placed them in an area where nomadic tribes would discover them. In time, stories passed on from one generation to another would come to the attention of archaeologists or social scientists of the later time, who would go there to explore and examine. These things are all designed to pique your curiosity to examine your own roots and heritage. Is this not a wonderful thing to do?

One might say, as an archaeologist (if you took the broad-minded, critical view), that this might be tampering with evidence, but they do not see it that way. From their perspective, it is providing evidence in an attempt to support you (not exactly lead you), by piquing your curiosity to discover more things about yourself and your connection with other beings, and ultimately open up your societies to communication with other worlds.

That is why it is necessary these days to provide your scientific community with ancient relics or evidence of ancient relics, meaning impressions in the soil and so on, that are clearly technological, as in the case of the footprint that appears to be a foot clad in something not unlike a boot. If it had to have a comparison, it would look not dissimilar to the boots the astronauts wore on the Moon.

Such evidence is hard to accept when found in an excavation where an ancient Earth society existed, yet it is present. More and more such things will be found in your time. In the past, such evidences were thought to be hoaxes and were blamed on workers or people who had somehow been observing and were playing a prank on the researchers. But more and more in your time such evidence will be considered, and though it is discordant with other evidence, it will accumulate.

Eventually, such footprints will be carefully cut out of the surrounding soil or rock, or there will be castings made or some effort made to preserve these discordant evidences and accumulate them in various places where they can be studied by broader-minded individuals. They might, after comparing this footprint with that footprint and examining an impression of something that looks technological, come to the conclusion that somehow these footprints and evidences were left by societies from some technically oriented place that visited these more ancient ancestors in that ancient time.

The ultimate conclusion will be that these people were from "some other place," and eventually the thought will be added "and some other time." That and its gradual acceptance in the scientific community, and more quickly by the general public, will be the final link that will prepare the intellectual community of your time to accept and then embrace contact with visitors from other worlds and times.

Say more about these beings. They were on the planet when it was in Sirius, and now they are here in lightbodies?

Lightbodies, yes. They seemed to have preexisted Sirius. I'm calling them "the evidence beings" for lack of a better term. I'm broadening the definition of a civilization for this particular society, if I may, because their society was not unlike the early days of the National Geographic Society, which was a group of like-minded individuals.

It's just some of them?

No, it's all of the beings of this civilization, but they did not live in a central place. It was more like something they did for a purpose. Wherever they are from, they always seem to leave evidence behind (if you can look through windows in time as I do), some of which has never been found, undiscovered evidence that gradually dissipated over time.

That is why they sometimes leave evidence in places where the scientific or the philosophical community would find it hard to believe that it had not been found before, because it is in such an accessible, though remote, place. It is certainly possible that it wasn't noticed before because it wasn't there before.

When they are installing evidence, they cover it with something or disguise it so there will be at least some casual reason why it wasn't noticed before, but not so much that part of it isn't visible or detectable. This is the case of the remains of a highly refined instrument or perhaps a machine, a piece of metal they would bring from a more advanced time to a place where eight thousand years ago there was a society. They might put it there, well-oxidized, so it would be found.

Here's an alloyed piece of oxidized machine metal found in an area that eight thousand years ago was exclusively peopled by a so-called primitive society (people who lived off the land), no matter how advanced their culture might have been. A little aside on my own: Native peoples were once considered primitive in this country. I think your anthropologists today recognize that when one is camping, one might appear to be primitive but might be advanced in other ways. In any event, it is hard to find such an object in an excavated site without its stimulating the mind. From time to time, such objects have been found and accumulated, and most are readily accessible; only some have been kept from the public eye.

Do they do this evidence planting only on Earth, or do they do it all over Sirius?

They did it all over Sirius and sometimes in other galaxies. Because this planet is connected to Sirius, they do it here as well. They do it to support certain societies more than others. Since the Explorer Race is well-known in this universe as being an experiment brought along very carefully, they are working with you more than they might with others, because you need to discover who you are gradually, at your own pace, rather than discovering it suddenly. A sudden discovery, for instance, might be when a person dies and goes through the veils in spirit form and suddenly discovers his or her vaster being or when a person meets a long-lost friend or relative and suddenly discovers so much about himself.

For your society and time, it is well-known and understood that although you consider yourselves in your time to be adaptable and to have the capacity to make fast changes, your society in fact is threatened by such fast change. You achieve group knowledge when something is learned, understood, largely disseminated and gradually accepted by everybody on the planet very, very slowly. So evidence must be planted carefully.

Are there specific pieces of evidence they would like to tell you about?

I think the ancient footprints and some of the bones discovered by the famous Dr. Leakey were planted by these evidence beings to suggest other races of beings, in order to encourage the human race and the scientific community to see that other races of humanoid beings exist. Unfortunately for Dr. Leakey, his evidence, although just as good as any other evidence, was not accepted and even today is considered highly suspect by the scientific community. This gives you an idea how slow the scientific community, with all of its discoveries and abilities to think in new ways, is to accept physical evidence of something that seems to be contrary to what is believed. That is why science has so many of the dogmatic functions of religion. At this time it has not found its God, but it will.

So they are soon going to plant more as we begin to wake up faster now?

Some evidences will come to light that will be very difficult to ignore, such as composite materials discovered in sites where it was impossible for these materials to have gotten there. The cold, hard reality is that these things are there and must be accepted. These discoveries have been happening for a time but have been kept quiet by researchers.

Because they didn't fit.

They didn't fit. It wasn't that the excavators were necessarily narrow-minded, but they understood that the scientific and the intellectual communities would not accept such things at this time. Therefore, much of this evidence has been accumulated or stuffed in little boxes and put on shelves that say "unknown" or "unaccountable" or "unaccounted for." But not far in the future, such evidences will be gathered in a more central spot.

Right now you are noticing that businesses are combining and corporations are merging, so it won't be long before educational communities start doing that. Universities will not only have links from one country to another, but they will actually combine and share materials, studies and exploration systems. All things will begin to combine, including governments, so there will be a lot of foot-dragging there, although in your time you can see the beginnings on the economic front.

I'm so glad that you are starting like this rather than going back only a few thousand years. I hoped you would do that, because Zoosh said we were going to uncreate the past, which would cause this planet to be from here and not from Sirius.

Although that is so, this is the way it is given to me to speak of these things. As I'm looking through these windows in time, this is how it is given to me and this is how I am presenting it, even though what Zoosh has said appears to be the case.

I don't usually have this problem. I'm usually very focused, but I've been almost out of my body or asleep or something.

The energy that has come through tonight has had this broadening, expanding effect. When I spoke of these different societies, their energies came through, and when a physical person is exposed to such energies, it is broadening.

Is there any way we can put a time as to when this planet was moved here?

Probably not. It would be easier to say millions of years ago and leave it at that. Otherwise, it would be literally throwing the gauntlet out and saying "prove us right" or "prove us wrong," and we don't want to do that.

[Publisher's note: In the Jesus book, book number nine in the *Explorer Race* series, Jesus said, "We want to add to the table and not sweep away what was there before."] I feel that is what you are doing here. I could not improve on those words.

Earth in Sirius

So, this planet in Sirius had the same consciousness inhabiting it that we call Mother Earth now?

The same, but more liquid, meaning that Mother Earth's true nature at that time was more fluid. Her waters were on the surface, whereas now many of her waters are under the surface. The demonstration of her personality is more masculine in your time than in those times in Sirius, when it was more feminine.

If she let all the waters out now, everything under fifty-three hundred feet would be flooded?

I cannot be certain of that, but it would be a number close to that.

So that's why we find seashells on top of the lower mountains. It's not so much that they've been thrust up, but that they have been underwater on Sirius.

Yes, sometimes they've been thrust up, but other times they were underwater here when Earth was in this position and the seas were greatly more peopled by different beings. Some of it might be from a previous world location.

Since the planet has been in this position [Earth], there have been different levels of water?

Some of the mountains have grown, some have shrunk. There has been some upthrusting, and the surface of the water has been higher at times and lower at times. A lot of that has happened in this solar system as well.

What about things we look on as wonders of the world, such as the Grand Canyon? Did that happen after the planet moved here?

I believe it happened after it moved here through erosion. As geologists are fond of saying, the force that has had more impact on Earth than anything else is water, moving water in one form or another.

Why was the planet moved here?

It was understood by those who have the capacity to move planets from one star system to another that the planet that had been here would not be here much longer. They would have such knowledge and could take thousands of years to make the move, although it didn't take that long. They knew that the planet that was here would be destroyed thousands of years beforehand.

Can you say how, or is that not something anybody wants to say?

I think not in the context of what I am doing now. I am back in time now.

Who or what decided to move the planet? Those involved with the Explorer Race, obviously?

I do not have this information at this time. Perhaps you could ask later. Maybe when we have gotten representatives of these societies to talk, perhaps some of them will know, but I do not have this information at this time. I think I am done.

2

Ancient Artifacts Explained

Speaks of Many Truths
July 10, 1998

All right, this is Speaks of Many Truths. Good evening.

Did you want me to show you this picture? Did you see it through Robert's eyes?

Yes, I saw the first one through Robert's eyes.

The Triassic Footprint in Nevada

Here is a partial shoe imprint in Triassic rock from Nevada 213 million years ago.

This was planted by the evidence people who placed it there with the intention, interestingly enough, that it be found by another group of beings who were visiting the Earth. As you know, people from the stars, especially fifty, sixty years ago in your time and before, were visiting the Earth regularly.

This particular group who was visiting the Earth

Fig. 2. Partial shoe imprint in Triassic rock from Nevada.

was scouting the planet for mining operations, which probably would have disrupted animals and people and possibly even the water system. It was intended that they discover this footprint and interpret it in the way I will describe. This particular group of ETs was not malevolent but what I would call business-oriented, if we might call it that.

Unscrupulous?

Well, not terribly unscrupulous, but looking to gather products that would be useful on their planets and the planets they traded with. The products would be used for important things there, but not really taking into account what those products might be doing.

Specifically, they were after rose quartz, and as you know, rose quartz is not always near the surface. There might be veins that run many miles, and they could therefore have created a vast mess. So this evidence was planted really for them, because there is another group that polices them, to put it in the context of your current language, and they leave footprints behind like that.

The intention was that they would see that footprint and believe that this planet was protected by these people and hence be scared away or feel that it wasn't safe. As it turned out, however, it wasn't necessary. The group does look out for your planet, or did for a time, and tries to keep things from being overly disrupted, but this time a vehicle from Zeta Reticuli shooed the miners away.

They didn't do anything malevolent or warlike. They just created an announcement in the center of the craft, the vehicle, that the planet was protected and that there was a valuable experiment taking place on the planet. Because the Zetas understand calmness, they directed them to another uninhabited planet that was not in the solar system but that they could go to and get what they needed. In this way no one is put out.

Can you say where those beings were from or who they were?

They were really more nomadic beings. They were from the ship they live on. Going way back, they may have been originally from Orion, but that would have been several generations previous to those beings, so I feel that they were from the vehicle rather than from a place.

Now, when they moved this shoe sole in rock, where did they move it from? Where had it been before they planted it in Nevada?

It hadn't been there. They just put it there.

I know, but did they just make it up, or did they actually move it from some other place? Was it there in 2 million B.C., or 213 million years ago?

They just placed it there. You understand that they can move through time. I don't know if I can grasp your question. You are saying, "Did they go back in time and bring it to another time?"

Yes.

No. They had the capacity to produce evidence and materials that would date, by your technology, to a previous time in such a way that it couldn't be questioned by current scientific methods. Ultimately, when you begin using what we call heart technology, it will be very easy to say, "Oh, this is not about us. This is about other people." One might even pick up object and say, "Oh, this isn't from here. There is a ball later on in the picture. That was from an ET." But I'm getting ahead of myself.

I'm glad you made this clear, because I thought in order for them to plant it, they had to take it forward from where it had been.

No; they can, but they usually don't.

So how long ago was this situation with these miners and the Zetas?

Oh, several hundred years ago.

It wasn't found until 1922.

A Metal Tube in France

Let's get the next one: a metallic tube found in France in a sixty-five-million-year-old chalk bed.

This has to do with an underground civilization that did not have its origin on this planet, in either of its locations. The underground civilization is no longer under the Earth in your time. Its origin was from the stars, I believe from one of the planets in the Orion constellation. They were on the planet during those times.

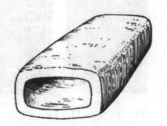

Fig. 3. Metal tube found in France.

They were here sixty-five million years ago?

They were here then.

Was the planet here then or in Sirius?

The planet, I believe, was in transition, so it is an object they left behind. It is a child's toy, and I am looking at it through my window in time. I can see a child who looks almost human, and the object is floating above the child's hand. The hand does not look exactly like our hand, but it is very similar, and the child is keeping the object in the air over its left hand. It is about this far [shows with hands] . . . How far is that?

About a foot.

. . . above the child's hand. Every time the child moves the hand to the left, the object tilts.

Can you describe how?

Vertically. Then the child moves the hand to the right and the object tilts back; then the child moves it to the middle and the object is in balance. It is intended that the object teach children about balance and the use of their physical bodies, not unlike children in our times and your times as well, who learn with their toys, with balls or blocks or objects or stones, yes? They learn how to stand up and sit down, sometimes unexpectedly, and other things—crawl around. In this civilization, children learn with tools that are responsive to them, so this is essentially a child's toy.

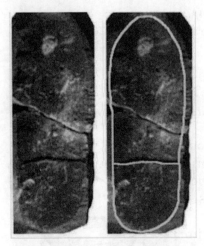

Fig. 4. Shoelike prints found in Utah.

A Footprint in Utah

Fascinating. The next one is the shoe-like print, five hundred million years old, found in Utah.

This is an actual print. It is not placed by the evidence people. It was, again, a visitor who was on the planet for a very short time, one individual. Where did you say it was found?

It was found in Utah.

Oh yes, so that confirms it. At the time, that area was under water and the visitor was under water exploring for relics of his civilization. His civilization comes from a star system, the Bear. The people from there had for a long time an underground civilization here, but this person, who was what I would call a social scientist, came to investigate for relics of a civilization that had been transferred back to their place of origin, not because of any threat but because they had completed what they had come to do, which was to study life on the planet.

So that person left a footprint. Advanced civilizations like that make every effort to leave no trace, but as scientists of your time know only too well, sometimes you leave a trace and didn't mean to.

Can you say if the Earth was in this position or in Sirius?

When was it?

It is dated at five hundred million years ago.

I believe it was in Sirius.

A Metal Sphere in South Africa

Okay, the next one—a metallic sphere from South Africa, with three parallel grooves around its equator, 2.8 billion years old.

Yes, this was also left by the extra-terrestrials whom I referred to before. The object once had within it a substance of a different density, and when struck lightly, as you might say . . . tap your fingernail or something like this . . . Describe what I'm doing for the sake of the reader.

Fig. 5. Metallic sphere found in South Africa.

You're snapping the index finger against the thumb, very gently.

You see, I snap it against the thumb and the vibration that would come from the object would produce a picture. The picture was more than an illustration, as you have in your times both permanent illustrations and fleeting ones on your technological devices. It would produce a picture that could be experienced; you could go into the picture. For example, if you were to use it in your time, you would strike the side if you were thirsty in the desert. You would need things like this.

The object, when it produces the picture, doesn't produce it according to what you think you need, but according to what you actually need. So it might be a form of liquid that appears there, for instance, as a picture you actually go into and use. It might be a form of liquid that is not only like water, but it would be a nutrient as well. Maybe you need food as well or nutrients in order to stay well. It would be there as long as you needed it, but if you moved from that location, it would quickly dissipate, leaving no permanent mark or evidence behind.

That particular object was unintentionally left behind when the person who was using it died a natural death. The flesh and bone structure has long since disintegrated, but the object remained.

Who was using it? You talked about an ET civilization?

Yes, a visitor from another civilization, I believe from a planet in Sirius.

Did they have these things? I mean, it is 2.8 billion years old?

Yes. That, of course, tells you that the planet was in the Sirius star system at the time. When this planet was moved, there was a very full sweep in order to remove all the objects that might have been left behind. But some were missed, as is often the case, and there are others yet to be found. Some will be found, and people won't know what they've found; they will just toss it aside and others will think it is something from the present. When an animal or a man is digging for some other purpose (for gold, for instance), he might toss aside something like that, thinking that it is nothing. But if it is a scientific expedition or something of that nature, it will be noted and logged and put away in a little box that says "Anomaly." Usually it will have a big question mark on its front: "What's this?"

So this thing is not functional right now?

No, the material on the inside has long since dissipated, so now I would call it a decorative object no longer capable of performing its originally intended function.

Extinct Bird Footprints in Belgium

Here's a picture of five partial foot impressions from a formation in Belgium, found in 1919.

I think that the foot is not exactly from a human being. It was found in 1919, but I think it is from an animal no longer on Earth. I take it

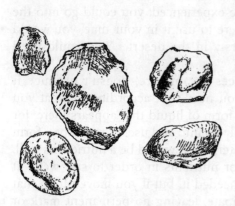

to be an animal. I believe it is very intelligent; however, I am feeling that it is an animal. It reminds me, looking at it, of a very big bird, yet it walks rather than flies.

But not anything that we have a name for, you're saying?

I do not think so. It might be reminiscent of the phoenix.

And was it on our planet here or in Sirius?

Go by the years. When was that age?

Fig. 6. Five partial foot impressions.

Early Pliocene to late Miocene. A lot of these artifacts are tools and skulls. What are you interested in talking about? Some of the tools? They look like chipped rocks that are very, very ancient.

Tools might be interesting.

They're not technological tools.

They're not? Then let's skip over that. I am most interested in anomalies that look technological or out of place—because visiting, especially

Era	Period	Start in Millions of Years Ago
Cenozoic	Holocene	0.4
	Pleistocene	3
	Pliocene	5
	Miocene	25
	Oligocene	38
	Eocene	55
	Paleocene	65
Mesozoic	Cretaceous	135
	Jurassic	215
	Triassic	250
Paleozoic	Permian	290
	Carboniferous	360
	Devonian	405
	Silurian	435
	Ordovician	505
	Cambrian	570

Fig. 7. The geological eras and periods.

through time, is still a function—things that are clearly of a different age, such as the child's toy.

What about this [Fig. 8]? This is a human skull taken from a very early time in Argentina, millions and millions of years ago. Is there anything you want to talk about?

No. I would comment on anything unusual. If it was a skull from an extraterrestrial, then I might say something, but not if it is obviously of a form of human.

Fig. 8. Human skull from Argentina.

A Piece of Wood Fetched from the Past

Here's a piece of wood from about 1.75 million years ago. It looks like it is sawed on one end.

It's from 1.75 million years ago?

Fig. 9. Piece of wood from 1.75 million years ago.

And appears to have been sawed with some kind of a tool.

Yes, it does appear that way. I would have to agree that it has experienced a machine. Let me see what it is. It looks like we have a traveler in time here. He is a person who has lived a life not too long ago, in terms of your current timing. I believe that he was well-known in his part of the country for moving huge stones about by putting a hand above them. He also had the capacity to travel in time and would sometimes travel into the past to a time and place where he would feel peaceful. He never felt quite comfortable around human beings in this age—the twentieth century.

Is this the man who lived near Miami, Florida, who built the coral castle?

The one who could move stones around. I believe so. He went back and brought a form of wood that was not readily available anymore. He cut what he needed and stayed for a time to thank the land and the trees. He was a spiritual man. He would often go back into the past just for peace. Oh, you could say, practically speaking, "Why didn't he go into the forest and cut these things in his own time?" He was, after all, someone who was trying to avoid being seen doing what he could do.

There was a time earlier in his life when he wanted to show some people how to do these things, but the times and the places weren't right, and people were shy of him. So he would go back in time and sometimes forward in time to find what he needed, what you would now say, peace of mind.

Just talk a little bit about your overall plan here. You said that sixty-five million years ago, the planet was in transition.

That is what I understand. Zoosh might see it differently, but that is what I understand. The planet existed for a time in both places. It is an interesting phenomenon that has been photographed in recent times by the famous Billy Meier, who has been allowed to take a photograph of a Pleiadian ship moving from one point in the sky to another, almost simultaneously being in two places at once.

The planet in one stage of its transition did that, so for a time there was an overlap. I believe that there is a technical reason for this, but Zoosh would be the better one to ask.

So the problem is, we're not going to find many things. Most of the things I have pictures of go back only a few thousand years. Perhaps we've misdated them, though.

No, I think that the dates are pretty accurate.

I'm very interested in The Vedanta's account of civilization, which is considered mythology. They had atom bombs and flying machines and things. Can I ask about mythological times, or is that a separate book?

What is considered myth today is referred to as such because there is no apparent evidence. Sometimes these things, especially what is referred to in *The Vedanta* and other great books, may refer to civilizations elsewhere. This does not mean that it is not profoundly important in your time, but I'm not at this time aware of any civilization on this planet before your own that developed and used atomic bombs.

Vywamus said in a workshop in 1990 that there was a city in Cornville, Arizona, six million years ago, that was destroyed by an atomic blast.

Please do not get caught up in right and wrong. Different spirits see things differently, and as a mystical man, I can only see through the windows I am given. If I do not see it, it does not mean that it isn't so, but I can only speak about what I see, and apparently what is shown to me is intended to be in the book.

3

Fire and Ice People and Multidimensional Lightbeings

Speaks of Many Truths

August 3, 1998

A ll right, this is Speaks of Many Truths. Let's touch on a few more civilizations and try to get closer to historical time references.

The Fire and Ice People of Iceland

I want to talk about a civilization that was here for about fifty thousand years. They were very active with the volcanoes. They were a civilization that had a very high degree of heat resistance. Although they couldn't be exposed to fire directly, they could in a uniform design protect themselves, and in that way, they could be quite close to lava and volcanic eruptions. They had, in other words, the capacity to resist heat.

With protective clothing?

Even naturally, because they had what is, I believe, called an exoskeleton. This is often found on Earth amongst the insect world. This kind of shell is very useful in protecting the being from extreme heat or extreme cold.

Until they existed on this planet, their civilization had never existed on any planet. They had been a civilization that existed entirely in space. They had an unusual beginning; they were a result of a genetic experiment that did not turn out the way the experimenters had hoped.

The experimenters were attempting to create a civilization essentially of laborers who would enjoy their work. This is not a slave labor situation, but rather laborers who would not have any desire for upward mobility, who would be happy and enjoy themselves doing physical work and who would be rewarded, supported and nurtured regardless of their performance. So it is not a Brave New World experience. But what occurred is that the minds of these beings became much more powerful than the experimenters planned, and as a result, the beings desired to travel and see things.

A few experiments down the line, and the experimenters did come up with what they wanted, but still they had the soul and the sense to know that the beings who were created could not simply be discarded like so much chattel. They needed to be given what they would need to survive if they chose to do so. This civilization, being distantly related to the experimenters, the Zeta Reticulans, had a very high degree of technical proficiency.

Over about twenty-five years of Earth experiential time, they manufactured a large vehicle that had the capacity to hold a civilization of eighty thousand to one hundred thousand in comfort. Once the vehicle was completely and thoroughly checked out to see that it would work for these beings, it was gifted to them. At that time, the beings numbered a total of about thirty-five.

They were told that because they had been created by these experimenters and didn't turn out exactly the way that was desired, the parent race (if I can call it that) felt obliged to give them what they would need in order to establish their own civilization, including an in-depth adviser.

They asked one of their teachers if the teacher would be available to these people and advise them about where to go, what to do, how to do it and so on. The teacher said, "I cannot go, but I will, when asked, make an appearance, at least temporarily." So a special chamber was built as an added feature so that the teacher could come from a distance and manifest sufficiently to be seen by the beings on the ship, yet not actually be there. That was the offer.

Meanwhile the people, the thirty-five of them, said, "But the ship is so large." The technical race said that it was a bit overwhelming, but this pod would be about 150 feet in diameter and would function as a primary living quarters and navigation area. The rest of the ship was in case their numbers grew over the years. Then the civilization-to-be said, "Oh, we see. That is very generous of you." Then they began to travel.

This was the shape of the universe [draws]. It evolves in shape, and at that time they were located about here in the vehicle. (I'll make the dot larger.) Of course, this was their path, recognizing that some of this represents directions. When you see lots of dots in one area, it means that they are going the other way.

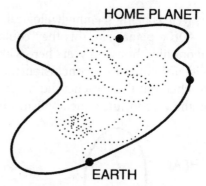

Fig. 10. The Home planet.

He's making lines so that it looks like they are going left. But they are going left/right and sometimes possibly up and down in dimensions and around, going to all these different places.

Yes, back and forth in this case, the paper being two-dimensional. I need the three dimensions going this way and this way. You understand?

The purpose of our talk tonight is where they wound up. You can see over time.

That is Earth, at the bottom right?

Yes, it is you at this point. (Remember, it's a different shape here.) So they wound up there and took this journey. This journey took them millions of years, and of course, by the time they got to Earth, they had stabilized their population at about eighty-three thousand. This gave them enough excess living quarters so that if they wished to take guests onboard or if they had a sudden boom in their population, they would be able to absorb it.

They got to Earth after traveling a great deal and were fascinated by volcanoes. In all the places they had been to, they had never seen volcanoes. They had almost exclusively gone to places that were cold. They found that they were very attracted to the cold and that they felt more invigorated and alive in the cold. Here, they discovered that not only was cold available, but also great heat, and much to their amazement, they thrived in the heat as well. So they established a civilization for the first time, a planet-based civilization that lasted about fifty thousand years. But being essentially nomads, after fifty thousand years they felt that they really must move on.

They managed to lodge their ship (through interdimensional methods) underneath the Earth and began their civilization's quest to discover the interrelatedness of great heat and great cold. They seemed to thrive in exposure to both, and such a polarity was fascinating to them as well as being seemingly illogical.

On a planet like this they could explore such things. They spent about fifty thousand years here with that as their primary intention but did not come to a conclusion they could accept. They asked their teacher, but their teacher did not know. However, I can access it. This is the reason: their metabolism [draws.] These may not be the best

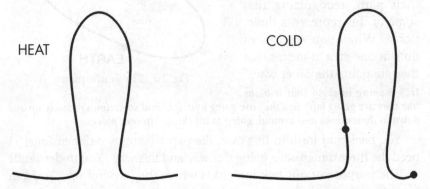

Fig. 11. Graph showing range of metabolism of Fire
and Ice People: heat and cold.

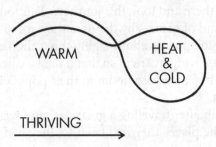

Fig. 12. How their
metabolism functions.

graphs, but they give you the idea.

Their metabolism functions within a very narrow range. It functions in either heat or cold. Yes, they knew that was the situation. The answer, however, is this [draws Fig. 12.], something like that. This is the actual answer. In terms of thriving, they needed both heat and cold.

In all these millions of years before they got to Earth, they had only experienced cold?

They had experienced only cold and had been doing fine as far as they could tell, but when they were suddenly exposed to heat and cold, they did much better. It took them a while to realize what was happening, because it was happening over thousands of years. But about 35 thousand years into their stay here, they discovered that their intelligence quotient, as you call it, had accelerated about 40 percent. They had not realized it because they are a civilization that did not keep records. They were always in the moment. They would consult memory only as recorded by the ship. The ship itself had the capacity to maintain some kind of general record or history, but they themselves in their culture did not ever live in the past. They would live only in the present, being primarily instinctual in their decision-making process.

When beings are instinctual, they are less likely to notice any great increase in mental power, because decisions do not come from the mind but from the body. As a result, it took them time to notice what you might say is the obvious. When they did recognize this incredible growth in their mental power, they began to realize that they were becoming more like their parent race, which had fantastic mental power but did not function in any sense in the instinctual body.

So they had both?

Yes, they suddenly realized that; this was quite sudden. The realization of this happened over a period of less than six days of experiential time. They suddenly realized that they had unexpectedly achieved the mental capacity (or close to it) of the parent race while exhibiting their personal capacity for instinct. It took them another ten thousand years to realize that it might be time to go back and visit the parent race to see if there might have been some intention to cause this.

They were too far away to communicate through space, so they went back. It took them much less time, because they took a direct route. The instinctual beings left some of their people on Earth. The parent race had not expected that this would take place, but they were essentially thrilled about it and asked them if they wouldn't stay in proximity to the parent race for a while so that the parent race could learn instinct from them.

When they decided to do that, they went back to Earth, picked up the rest of their people and returned to the place where the parent race was. I'm mentioning this because there is some connection here, some analogy to your context with the Zeta beings. The Zeta beings, of course, always wanted you to be more powerful mentally, but other teachers, guides and even other ETs felt it was essential that you not be too mental—or you might not find your instinctual place of function. I believe that this was the proper decision.

Instinct, after all, does not require great mental capacity. It only requires devotion or paying attention to one's physical self first. That is the civilization that I'm mentioning. Do you have any questions about them?

How did they experience both hot and cold on the planet? Was it just because the planet held those extremes? Did they go to the heat and to the cold?

I believe they did this by going to places where there was heat and cold in the same place, such as in the great North. In Iceland you could experience volcanic action, yet on the very next mountain over, say seventy or eighty miles away, you could experience ice and snow. They went to different places that had cold, and when they discovered the volcano, they were astonished to realize that they actually liked it.

What was their life span?

Very long. That's why they are careful about maintaining their population. Their life span runs anywhere from fifteen to fifty thousand years, so they are careful.

But over millions of years they had a massive number of generations. They had to have some understanding of history, or they wouldn't have even known they had a place to go back to.

Yes, the ship had the capacity to automatically store those records. The ship would not only observe what was happening inside it, but also what happened externally. It even had the capacity to observe the thoughts of the individuals, and because these people did not feel comfortable with that, they did not interact in any great sense with the ship. They just felt that it would be better not to think about it.

It's like having someone eavesdropping on you without your feeling really good about it. Nevertheless, the parent race felt that it was essential, because they were conscious of the fact that the beings themselves were less likely to keep any formal historical frame of reference and might therefore make the same mistake over and over again. That did not occur because the beings were instinctual, but from the parent race's point of view, it might have.

The parents were not Zetas but were a relative of the Zetas?

Distantly related to Zetas. Quite a bit taller. If you were to see them, they would be seven to eight feet tall. They had very spindly arms and legs that had an unusual appearance. They were not exactly like an insect, but they had very long arms and legs in proportion to the body. And they had a head that was not always fully at the surface. Sometimes it would retract, so if you looked at them quickly and casually, it would look like they had a very small head. But in fact, they could retract their heads. They would do this, apparently, when they were thinking deeply or felt the need to protect themselves.

What is the result now? How long ago, roughly, did these beings leave the Earth?

Again, I'm unable to provide that. I'm sorry that we won't be able to give you too much of a timeline, but I will give you this—human beings were not here yet.

Has the parent race kept its mental abilities and learned to be instinctual from these beings? Has the parent race by now achieved this combination?

It has taken them a very long time to even grasp the function of instinct. They are not yet instinctual, but they now understand how it works.

Have these created ones stayed around the parent race all this time?

Yes, to help them, because the parent race had made a few serious mistakes, the kind of mistakes that can be made by a mental being who obeys logic, but for whom simple knowingness within the body itself would be foreign; therefore, they could follow a path logically yet stumble many times. So the offspring, if we can call them that, have stayed around to help them.

With great love, because they are nomads?

Yes, but they take trips sometimes. It is in their nature and their hearts to be nomads, and they will travel sometimes. They can't just stay in one place.

What dimension are they in?

It looks like the offspring are naturally in the dimension roughly about 4.5 or 4.8 and the parent race is actually in dimension about 7, but they can communicate with each other. Those of the parent race can easily accommodate themselves, at least in transport, at the offspring's rate of vibration, the third dimension, but the offspring cannot. If you are in a dimension, you can go to a higher dimension only if you are very thoroughly shielded. If you are at a higher dimension, you can more easily come to a lower dimension.

Fig. 13. Mark left in Iceland to indicate that the Fire and Ice People went somewhere.

They didn't leave a drawing or a relic on this planet?

Yes, they did. They left some signs. I think most of them are under snow and ice right now in Iceland, but they left these signs, these marks [draws].

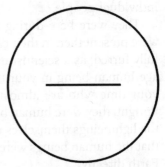

Fig. 14. Sign for the ship left in Iceland by the Fire and Ice People.

They are not exclusively responsible for them, but it is a mark they would leave if they went somewhere.

Like on a rock or underground or anyplace?

Usually in a cave, someplace obscure. Occasionally they would leave this sign as well [draws]. That sign is the sign for their ship.

Will it be a while before we discover that?

I think quite a while, because at that time, the volcanoes were very powerfully erupting all over Iceland, and since then there have not been so many eruptions. As a result, a great many areas that were once exposed are now iced over. But someday it will be found in a cave. The cave itself will probably remain intact for some time, and there may even be other artifacts found.

I hope the people who find them find these Explorer Race *books.*

They might by that time.

The Multidimensional Lightbeings

The next civilization was most unusual. I mention these beings to you because it is important for you to know how different some beings could be. These beings were profoundly into dimensionality. They could access anything from the second to the fifteenth dimension. They came for only about fifteen years to this place, but that was a long time for them to spend anywhere.

They could not touch anything without leaving a mark. They were lightbeings. If you were to see them, they would look like abstract light forms or like a line in light. They are very unusual. They were almost totally here for the exploration of Earth as a planet. They recognized Earth as someone, a being. They also recognized the other planets in the solar system as individuals. They lived on such a massive scale that they related to planets as equals but did not relate to individual people.

They were here during the time of human beings. Human beings were present then in their early formation; they had more body hair—not fully furred, as a scientist might say, but more body hair than the average human being in your time. (Yet there are some human beings in your time who are almost as hairy as these people.) They walked upright; they were human beings. Their faces were human. But as I say, the lightbeings themselves did not interact with them because they felt that the human beings were a portion of Earth, and they interacted with Earth directly.

I'm making an exception by mentioning this civilization, because it is important for you to realize that not always do beings who come here from afar come to see you. Sometimes they might be coming to speak to somebody else entirely, such as Earth in this case. There will be other visitors who will come from time to time to speak specifically to various animals and even insects, but not to human beings, although they might possibly be seen by human beings.

What did they want to talk to Mother Earth about?

They wanted to ask her if she was satisfied being here, because they had the capacity to do anything. Truly, they had no limits. They had the capacity to do anything, and they offered to assist her. She thought about it for almost fifteen years, then said she felt that she was all right. Then they thanked each other and the beings left.

These beings were from this universe?

No, from well beyond this universe.

From Love's creation?

Well beyond that.

How did they happen to get to this planet, and why?

They came here because they heard of the experiment here, and they have a profound sense of self-identity with planetary bodies. They see themselves, although they are light, as being the souls of planetary bodies everywhere. So they wished to come to speak to this planet because they had such respect for it.

And how are they connected to the souls of planetary bodies?

They see planetary soul bodies as light. I might add that the soul bodies of human beings are also light, and a sensitive person can see that if he or she is sensitive visually or on a feeling level. So in order for them to feel connected with the planetary body, compared to the individual on the planet, the lightbody of the planet would have to be at the same density of light as their own, which it was. It was identical. Therefore, the only reason they would travel into this universe or creation was to commune with something like themselves.

Have they ever come back since then?

No. They asked Mother Earth and she considered it. She gave it the full attention that it deserved, plus she had to do other things, existing and hosting species on her, so it took her about fifteen years to decide.

Were these the first humans?

I do not think they were, but they were the first ones you would definitely recognize as human beings, the first human beings you could look at and say, "Oh, these are people of today." They had very little hair on their bodies, but if you looked at them, you'd say, "Well, they are pretty hairy, but they are obviously people."

So there was an evolution of humans?

This isn't any evolution. Evolution does not exist in physical terms.

Was there a change in the DNA that somebody tinkered with?

Different races of beings, no tinkering. As far as I can tell, the hairy human beings were dropped off here.

By whom?

I see them coming up from underground.

How did they get underground?

I do not know.

Do you see what area of the planet they lived on?

Canada—North America, but very far north. I don't think in terms of your present map that they ever got much more than fifty miles into the northern United States. Mostly they were in Canada.

Did their lineage survive?

I believe for a time they went back under the surface of the planet and have left the planet now.

4

Sirian Olfactory Healers in Africa and Immortal Core Personalities of Earth

Speaks of Many Truths

August 3, 1998

L et's see what's next. There was a civilization for a time in Africa. This civilization slightly predated the African people of your and my time. The people were humanoids, but not from Earth. They were from Sirius and were all female beings. There were no masculine beings at all and they had the capacity to give birth on their own, but only to female beings. So it was an all-female race.

They were somewhat delicate in stature, meaning that none of them was more than five feet tall. The occasional person was five-foot one or two. They were delicate in the sense that they had refined features, the kind of features you have today—articulated fingers and toes and so on. They had a profound desire to know. They lived on Earth for about twelve hundred to fifteen hundred years in what I would call an encampment.

Because they did not require food or drink, they could travel at all times. They did not sleep, and they enjoyed their visit here. I think their civilization had an unusual lifespan compared to the ones we've been talking about. Their lifespan was never any more than seventy-five years, so they turned over many generations here.

They were particularly interested in flowers and, using their olfactory sense, they could smell a flower and assimilate its healing and nourishing qualities without consuming it. It is through their sense of smell, then, that they were nourished. They would also store, through some kind of box (they see it as a box that doesn't appear to have anything inside it), the smell of things; they would breathe out into the box and close the box. Then the box would be sent back to their home planet on Sirius and be available, should the people on Sirius require that essential fragrance for some nourishment or healing that might be necessary for their or another race.

They were very devoted to the healing of their own, although they didn't need much healing. But the other races did. You might say that they were nurselike or doctorlike in that sense, but everything was done with a sense of smell. If they came across an animal or a person who was injured, they would recall the smell that they had assimilated from a flower and would breathe that smell onto the person, and the person would be healed.

I believe that one of these being's bones was discovered in the South African region. I think there was some controversy because the skull structure was not human and also not apelike, and there was confusion about what it was. Your science is, unfortunately, perhaps more dogmatic in the narrow sense than truly exploratory, but this is a fleeting thing.

Within twelve to fifteen years of your time, your science will become much more open, broad and accepting of exploring and examining all life in a benevolent way. One can't truly examine and explore a being if there is some destruction of that being or any member of its species by science; then, of course, the being—say, an animal—will exhibit as many false signs as possible, as a prisoner of war might do so as to mislead the enemy. Not because animals would normally consider human beings as an enemy, but if human beings behave like enemies, then animals will make every effort to mislead them, and this includes their biological and physiological actions and reactions.

Were they sent here with a leader? For a purpose?

They were sent here with the idea that it was known that this planet had an almost infinite variety of flowers and scents, and because these are people of scent, they came here to assimilate these scents.

But were they here at the same time as other races of humans?

Yes, early humans and other beings, meaning animals. They remained almost entirely in central Africa. This was a space where they felt most welcome. At that time, it was sufficiently isolated so that if they were found by local beings, they would just be considered different, but they would not be considered spectacularly different. They were discreet.

Central Africa is a desert at this time.

It was not then.

Were there mountains or other features that would identify this garden area?

Yes, it was a rain forest then.

In central Africa?

Yes. Most of Earth was at one time a rain forest.

What happened to it? Did people cut the trees down?

Some of it was natural. In the northern areas there was snow and ice, and in the volcanic areas there would be fire. In the case of strong storms, there would be lightning, and to some extent there was a natural clearance of the forest. Ultimately, at some point there were too many people, and people will consume. It is interesting to note that people, such as in your Bible, have great fear and loathing for the jumping creatures, insects that jump and eat . . . what do you call them? . . . hoppers, grasshoppers. There is great fear and loathing, and they were considered a plague. There was much suspicion and superstition about these beings, but in fact, to some extent they exhibited the traits of overpopulation.

When human beings overpopulate an area, they also tend to defoliate it. So when the animals sometimes do this, it is because there are too many of them. But also, when they do it, they will sometimes be exhibiting to you, saying, "Look, see—this could be you."

At some point these Sirian healers were picked up and returned to their own planet?

Yes, they were here for a short time, and once they had smelled all there was to smell in that area, they returned. There are many rain-forest planets in Sirius, but this particular area in central Africa had at that time plants and flowers that did not exist anywhere on Sirius. That is why they were there and stayed there.

And we don't have them anywhere on Earth now?

I think that those flowers are gone for the moment, but their seeds are still there. If the beings feel welcome—and that requires not only the feeling but enough people saying, "Welcome!"—they will return. Perhaps one of the advantages, should they return, is that their way of smelling the fragrance of the flowers—not by cutting them and putting them in a jar but by going there and having people smell the flowers as they grow—will cure almost all brain diseases.

Of course, to welcome them, you'd have to welcome the rain forest, and it would come. You must welcome it and mean it, and you must cut nothing in the area, for any reason. All plants have the same feelings as people, and when they are cut, they are frightened and hurt and it takes them a while to heal. If they are cut badly enough, they never heal and they die just like people. But when the plants are loved and appreciated, they thrive just like people.

Is it really wise just to let lawns and everything grow and not cut or trim?

It is up to you. If you feel at some time that you need to cut, then walk through the lawn and various places and apologize. Don't say, "I'm sorry"; it is meaningless. Say, "Please excuse me." That is something you can say without feeling ashamed. Most important, when people talk to plants and animals and they say, "I'm sorry," it does not work because there is shame associated with that term. But when you say, "Please excuse me," that works better for animals. Usually there is no shame there.

When you say, "Please excuse me. Someone is going to come and cut," take two or three days (meaning days and nights), and on the fourth day the person comes to cut. By the third day they will be desensitized, and after the cutting on the fourth day, they will remain desensitized for another three days. Then when they start to resensitize, they will have pain, but it will not be excruciating. When you do this, it is also more likely that most of them will survive. If you have the cut taking place, try to make sure that what is left is at least four inches high, not cut down to the nub. That is one of the purposes of our book, is it not? We want to inform.

You will go to a place that is wild, where the grasses come and go and nobody cuts them. They are happy. They are human in their own consciousness. They don't think of themselves as human, but they think and feel no different than any human being. If you can understand this one thing only—that every being everywhere feels the same way you feel—you will be well on your way to spiritual advancement.

So these Sirian healers probably didn't leave any signs or symbols or artifacts?

No, they did not. They left no mark at all. They were disinclined to damage anything. They liked to walk lightly on the Earth, and they did so.

And they didn't have to eat? They were higher-dimensional beings?

Well, not so much higher, maybe fourth. Maybe they could exist in the fifth in a slightly altered state. They could exist in the third in a slightly altered state.

So their descendants exist now on Sirius?

Yes, their civilizations existed before this on Sirius and after. It is ongoing. Now, however, they are the richer for the scents. Scents were not needed there for the healing of other beings or the enriching of their own beings. They would put them at the bottom of a pool of water. Then they would open the boxes and let the scents distribute in the water. The water of a planet always knows what the beings who are there or who may visit there need. If the water felt that those plants or flowers were needed, they could reproduce them on the planet just through the scent.

Without seeds?

Yes. In that way the beings, who had a strong sense of honoring, would not take a seed because that would be removing something that was happy to be on Earth. They could not take a seed because maybe that plant would be needed on its planet. They would not function that way, but they felt free to absorb the scents because those were freely offered by the flowers. If circumstances existed that such flowers would be needed, the scent would be sufficient.

Everywhere and anywhere I know of where water is, water is the first and the last; it is the first to know and the last to let go of its knowledge. In this way, sometimes through evaporation, knowledge is spread around the planet. Water evaporates and goes into clouds, then clouds move on and go someplace where the water is needed. The water comes down with the knowledge and nurtures different forms and plants—and possibly, as in the case of Sirius, stimulates, supports and nurtures those plants to grow there.

It is the same on Earth. On Earth one has many lakes, and in the lake bottoms sometimes there are seeds. These being deep down makes no difference to the water, and if certain plants are needed, sometimes the water can assimilate the essence of the seed. Then one has plants growing elsewhere where they are needed.

It is divinely beautiful, isn't it?

It is divine. Yes, it is divinely beautiful. All beings are living in the temple of Earth, whether you realize it or not. But the sooner one realizes it, the more likely one is to appreciate its value and be more gentle with it.

I think we are just about at the end of these civilizations for which there is no evidence. Soon you will have to ask questions about civilizations for which there is evidence. But I will see if we can get one more.

Immortal Core Personalities of Earth

There is a civilization that has been on Earth for as long as it existed in Sirius and as long as it has existed in this galaxy. It is, as far as I can tell, immortal and will be here indefinitely. These beings have been available over the years to holy men and women, Tibetan monks and others. They are often seen wearing white robes and can appear in the form of any type of being, including animals—although as animals, of course, they will not wear garments.

They live inside the Earth at dimension seven, but they can reveal themselves in a slightly less than physical, but almost physical, sense to those who seek out wisdom. They seem to be, as much as we can understand them, the immortal aspects of Earth's personality. As such there are never any more than ten to twelve of them.

They can show themselves as the many or the few. They are profound beings and rarely come to the surface. But sometimes they do, and they usually come to the surface only in the form of an animal—a rabbit, a robin, an earthworm, an octopus, a jellyfish, a sea turtle; sometimes in the form of a night bird, an owl or even a mockingbird—but I do not think they come to the surface in the form of human beings.

They are here to consult with beings who seek out wisdom, and when they are not interacting with beings on Earth, they will return to the seventh-dimensional core of existence of Mother Earth's personality.

Do humans see them in their white robes in dreams or visions?

If there are people such as monks or visionaries or shamans, they will sometimes see them in form. If these people want to consult these beings, they will sometimes see them in visions or dreams, but there have been people on Earth who have seen them in form.

Recently?

Yes.

Has the information given by these beings been put into books and printed, or is it guidance for the individual seeker?

I think that a lot of New Age material has much of what they have said in it. People will say that they had visions and so on, that they saw a beautiful being wearing a white robe.

Do the beings identify themselves or give a name?

In my experience, usually they do not. Putting a name on them is rare. When you see someone like this, although you might think you would immediately say, "Who are you?" more often you think, "What are you? How did you get here and how did you come through that wall?" The being might respond to that, or he might more likely respond to the immediate needs of that person or being.

Say it is an animal. A rabbit will accept a being coming through stone without any question, and it will perhaps say, "Are you here to help or 1

"What's your name?" appears to be a friendly gesture, but do you know that it is not based in friendliness? It is based in authoritarianism, meaning, "Tell me your name so that I can grant you equal citizenship." I am not saying that you should not ask for names, but that the urgent need for names is not about friendliness. It is about "Tell me your name so that then I can classify you."

Many ancient teachers would refuse to give their names to the students, and if a student pressed a teacher for his or her name, the teacher would go away and not return. This is the teacher's way of saying, "*Feel* whether I am right for you; don't *think* about it."

So these are parts of the core personality of Mother Earth?

Yes, and she will often send these parts of herself to beings who are most receptive. That's why I say they will go to animals or go to, as I've called them, holy people, people who are in touch with all life and honor it. These people will gauge the value of another being on the basis of their heart reaction, not their mind.

The mind can only go on what it has learned, but it does not have a capacity to be in the present. The mind references everything from the past. Only the physical senses and the physical body can be in the present. Your body knows what is good for it. The mind can only gauge what is good for the body on the basis of what it has learned so far, and that, of course, is limited.

So even now, with all the mining and population and aggravation that Mother Earth is facing, she can still send out these personalities?

Yes.

There's a being called Sanat Kumara, who is supposed to be a soul of the Earth. Is he involved with this?

Yes.

He's one of the personalities of Mother Earth?

The being who has been identified in that way is one of these beings.

But there aren't any other names we'd recognize?

Most of them will not say a name. This identity has announced itself as a name, but that is an exception. I do not know why it has done so, but it has.

Is there anything they'd like to say through you for the book?

No, I don't think so. I think when we get communications from beings, it will have to do with civilizations for which there is evidence. The next time we meet, pick a civilization you wish to ask about, and we will begin with evidentiary civilizations.

But there is nothing I can find that goes back more than ten to twelve thousand years.

That's good enough. I have mentioned civilizations that I feel are important to mention, and if I feel that there are any others, I will bring them up.

There seems to be a gap between the introduction of the prototype humans on the planet and the first archaeological evidence at about twelve thousand years ago.

We cannot speak of everything in one volume.

Early Civilizations on Earth: Mongolians and Desert People

Speaks of Many Truths
August 6, 1998

I am going to talk a little bit tonight about a few other civilizations.

The Visitors of the Paler Skin and the Land of Ice

When the planet was moved here from Sirius, one of the first things that occurred was something unknown on Sirius, and that is ice. In my visions I am not aware of any ice planets in Sirius—they all have liquid water, but not ice. One of the almost immediate circumstances, then, was that the life forms who came with the planet had to go underground for a time. That is why there are such elaborate and extensive underground facilities, you might say—to support and sustain many different multicultural and varied civilizations of all types of beings under the Earth's crust so they would be relatively safe.

Safe from the cold and ice?

Yes, and safe even until recent times from strife on the surface of the planet. Of course, in those days, they were safe from the cold. At the same time, messages were transmitted throughout this galaxy, especially nearby, inviting beings who lived in cold or who were adapted to it to come to the surface and participate by establishing an Earth environment that would cater to beings who could well tolerate the cold.

That is when you got your first visitors of the paler skin. They did not stay long enough to be considered a culture or a civilization, but they visited for about fifty years. They explored the entire surface of the planet and measured the depth of the ice. They were somewhat surprised to find a planet here, since their civilization had monitored the absence of one, then all of a sudden there was one.

They brought with them many hardy, cold-weather species of beings, although they themselves knew they would not stay. They brought with them a precursor to what is now known as the polar bear, but this particular bear (I think we can call it a bear) was much larger than the current polar bear. It was fully eighteen feet long in its well-developed stage, although nineteen- and twenty-foot-long bears were not so rare.

They also brought other species you now see and experience in a cold-weather climate, such as penguins and other forms of sea creatures. You've also seen ones who swim and catch fish and come up on the ice and are often considered amusing. [Publisher's note: There is a chapter by Penguins in ET Visitors Speaks number eleven in the Explorer Race series.]

Yes, seals.

Those seals were also volunteers and were precursors of your current seals, although they were prepared for a much colder climate. There were the penguins who were much smaller, but they had very, very thick hides and a thick layer of fat, not unlike what one finds in a whale, and so the outer appearance of these sea birds was slightly smaller than today's species.

There was another species of penguinlike creatures who were entirely white and slightly larger than today's species. The seals were also white. All the animals who were brought were in fact white, which allowed them to be safe from any potential threat. Over time they developed the dark fur they have now, but originally all the species were white.

During the fifty years or so that these light-skinned people were here, they were documenting the surface of the planet. They created, in some places, artificial hot mineral springs so there would be water available for the animals to drink.

At this time, the ice spread very far over the Earth, well down over almost all of the United States and farther south as well. There was not that much land that was not iced over. The planet remained this way for quite a while.

This culture, then, was largely responsible for the initial seeding of strong species of beings who could survive bitter cold. They were from a distant galaxy that has ice on almost all the planets, some of which have water and oxygen but there is more carbon dioxide. So they had to wear breathing gear on Earth. Their home planet is entirely frozen over with about three-hundred-mile-thick frozen carbon dioxide. Their ships can pass through this with light beams, into the interior of their planet, which is not hollow but has a lot of holes in it that come from lava rock. They have been able to carve out some of those holes and make very pleasant living quarters.

Did the animals come from different planets?

They were brought. Yes, remember that a message went out, so the animals were picked up by these species of people. They were picked up on planets that had at least some oxygen, because when the planet came here and iced over, its oxygen was greatly diminished for a time. So they didn't look for animals who needed a lot of oxygen, just animals who could tolerate oxygen and who would have the capacity to tolerate more oxygen over time.

What caused the planet to freeze over?

One of the phenomena associated with long travel in this sort of light diffusion was that when the planet was re-created in this space, it had to take on some of the qualities of planets in this solar system in order to adapt (not unlike an immunization shot that you have today for diseases), and one of the most acceptable qualities was ice. Many of the other planets in this solar system have some form of ice, if not water ice.

The planet Earth was not comfortable taking on other aspects of the planets—such as extreme heat as in Venus, or gases that would later be unacceptable to plant and animal life. Understand? So the least destructive and most benign adaptation was ice. Earth immediately went into a very profound ice age in order to accustom itself to such a thing. Since that predominant ice age, there have been other times when the ice has spread, but never that far.

Ice was on the planet for quite a long time; it started receding very slowly after about 80,000 years. It receded all the way back so that there wasn't any ice. During this time of the retracting ice, which took about 120,000 more years, the generations of animals who were comfortable with the cold evolved a bit and changed colors to adapt to the surroundings as they changed. The animals learned to stay to the extreme north where it was still cool, but not cold enough to freeze the water.

The Initial Populating of Earth

During this time, both the North and South Poles were open and the worlds inside the Earth were freely accessible to the surface populations (at that point, animals) and subsurface populations (other animals and other beings). So what occurred for a time was what I would call a cultural renaissance.

The surface of the planet had more water on it than at any other time since it had been in this position; much of the land that is now exposed was covered with water. Generally speaking, altitudes above three thousand to thirty-two hundred feet were exposed to air, but below that were frequently very wet areas, like lakes or swamps. What occurred was a great gathering of beings associated with water planets. And for about forty years, beings who lived on water planets in Sirius and other places, including beyond this universe, would come to visit planet Earth to talk and hold discussions in boats on the surface. (The water was very calm.)

They would discuss how they foresaw the development of this planet and the gentle usage of it (at that time they did not know its ultimate intention as a school for the Explorer Race). So the consensus was born—because this planet was from Sirius—that there ought to be lots of opportunities for beings from Sirius to come here to visit and to start their own cultures if they wished.

They also decided that any cultures from water planets anywhere ought to be allowed to come here and see if they could foster and nurture a culture. These were not rules so much as guidelines. This was the true beginning of all sea life and some of the land life you now know here.

Some of the land life, after all, is quite adept and comfortable in water, such as ducks and geese and beings like this, who you think of as water beings but are freshwater beings. This is when the freshwater fish cultures and the sea life you know began to come, often transported in ships and sometimes in light, if they were sufficiently advanced to be adaptable to such transport.

Some people also began to arrive. Some of the people began to arrive who are now known as the dark-skinned African peoples and some of the native peoples (some whose descendants are still alive today and some who are no longer present). There was a people in Siberia who was the precursor to what we call in our time "Moon-faced people." Moon-faced is a compliment, not in any way looking down on them, because to our culture the Moon is sacred.

But these people who have this beautiful face . . .

Do we call them Mongolians?

Yes, the precursors to the native peoples of what is now known as Mongolia and Siberia began to live in those areas. Some of these areas were under a lot of water, but these were people who were comfortable with water and who later also proved to be very adaptable to snow and ice.

The precursor people to those who are now known as the Eskimos also came right about that time. A tribe of people who were partly the precursors of the Hopi, Navajo and Cree nations also began to be distributed on the higher spots in the land, coming, again, on ships.

The dark-skinned races in Africa initially peopled what is now South America. They were there for many years and even today there are still remnants of those people there, but the darker-skinned peoples discovered that they were more comfortable on that continent now known as Africa. They were able to define and build more profound cultures, educational systems and methods of higher learning devoted to the arts and so on in Africa rather than in South America, because South America was at that time largely what I would call a port and there was a great deal of coming and going.

South America became a kind of a landing ground, a receiving area for cultures coming and going, and the dark-skinned African peoples felt that this was too much distraction for them. They did not withdraw from South America, but they did not promote the culture there too much; as I say, there are some remnants still there today.

For quite some time, animals, fishes, birds, even insects and human beings (if not the human beings you have today, at least the precursors to them) were arriving. There began to be, after some time, a feeling in the cultures who were inside the planet that the surface cultures needed to evolve on their own because they were beginning to lose the native threads from their native planets. They were losing those and adapting more to the inner world's culture. The people in the inner world felt that the surface cultures were going to lose too much, so the people in the inner world decided that they would close the poles for one thousand to fifteen hundred years. They did this, not by icing them over, but by closing them using magnetic disguises.

The surface cultures then started adapting more to the environment and restructuring the old ways from their native planets. Essentially, they began to work into or dig into the planet itself. After fifteen hundred years or so went by, the poles were again opened and people were allowed to come and go freely, but they didn't come and go as much because by then they had reestablished their central ties to their native planets and cultures and had gotten going on their own. This is what the people inside the Earth had always wanted. This was the initial peopling of the Earth.

Can you say where the new arrivals came from? How close is this to the sixty-five-million-year point when the planet arrived here? Are you coming greatly forward in time?

I'm still talking well back in the past, because civilizations came and went, but we're coming forward quite a bit because we are talking now about the initial life forms brought to Earth. We're talking about life forms that would now be found as fossils, such as certain fishes. But we have to remember that many of the fossils of the human beings and the initial beings arriving from these distant planets are not to be found because of the burial techniques of the time. This is something that is largely unknown in your time.

The burial techniques of the time did not involve burial in the Earth. The races who came here believed that this wondrous water planet, found in a place where water planets were least likely, should be left as pristine as possible. Seeds for plants could be placed upon the ground, water could be asked for or brought and with a finger the seeds could be gently shoved slightly below the surface, but *under no circumstances* could anybody dig. Digging was unknown. The idea of leaving some-one underground or digging underground or even building a funeral pyre that would require cutting and burning and destroying other life forms was out of the question.

So in early burials all bodies were transported either to home planets or taken to places where the bodies were discharged, as they call it. The components—once the soul had left the body, of course— were just redistributed. Occasionally, among some of the species who were more attached to their home planets, the bodies would be returned there.

But for many, many years of culture after culture and civilization after civilization, no two-legged person was ever buried in the Earth. This is why it is uncommon to find really ancient bones of any peo-ple. When you do find ancient bones, such as the ones found by Dr. Leakey, this would be a visitor who came here and was stranded in some part of the planet when it was not widely peopled and therefore died a natural death.

These cultural customs, then, largely explain why one finds fossils of animals and not people. It doesn't make sense, if you think about it— why aren't there more fossils of people?

The Mongolian People

What is the time of the first people on this planet in this location?

For many millions of years before that, you started having fishes and birds and so on, but right around forty million years ago you started get-ting the first people who walked around and established cultures, as I said. Especially prominent in these cultures were the precursors to the peoples in Mongolia and Siberia. <u>These peoples are largely responsible</u> today for fully half of the genetic base on Earth, not because they traveled so far and wide, but because they were so durable.

When other races came and went, they were still there. Once that race arrived, there has almost always been some version of those beings there, and that durability has led to their predominant influence. Of the genetics on Earth, 47 percent are traced directly back to them and another 30 to 35 percent to the dark-skinned peoples in Africa.

Although the lighter-skinned peoples were the first to come and begin distributing species, in terms of an established and lasting culture, they were really the last major culture to arrive here. They did not arrive until about a million years ago (your time), but those cultures did not last. The people did not have the durability—and most importantly, they did not know how to communicate with the more durable races of people here, notably the dark-skinned peoples, whom I'm going to call the Mongolian peoples. They did not know how to communicate with them in ways that were compatible to everybody. They were trying to survive entirely on their own, without having had millions of years of adaptation. So the civilization was very tenuous at first and really did not get a foothold for some time.

Where did the Mongolians come from? Where was their home planet?

Their home planet is in this universe [draws].

I'll draw the universe shape as it exists now, roughly. If this is Earth and its galaxy, then this is where the Mongolian races came from. The dark-skinned African peoples came from Sirius, so they came from much closer.

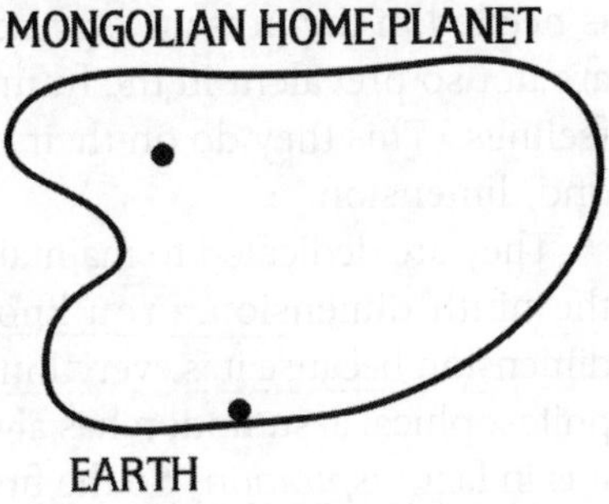

MONGOLIAN HOME PLANET

EARTH

Fig. 15. The Mongolian's home planet in this universe.

The Mongolian peoples came from much farther away, and they became even stronger on the journey, because on the journey, they were led to believe that life on this planet would be much harsher than it really was. They were led to believe that extremes of temperature were the norm. This was a minor error, but it actually allowed them to become much more durable in their form by the time they arrived, and the temperatures were cold enough and extreme enough that they were able to maintain that durability of physical form.

This is interesting. We've been told that the bodies were basically Sirian proto-
types. No one ever talked about Mongolians before.

The bodies, you could say, are that, but this is what I am being told
now. On this planet, one has to account for its variety.

What was their home planet like? Do they still exist? Do they still communicate
with their mystical people here?

Yes, they have a very advanced civilization, and "advanced civilization" means not just a very high dimension, but a high dimension with
the intention of focusing on the denser dimensions in order to create
absolute and permanent balance. So their focus is balance—not a tenuous one, but a permanent balance. In this way they are able to achieve
a sense of inner calm and peace that can be projected into that future so
that when they arrive in that future, it is waiting for them, even if something has agitated them in the moment. Therefore, this calm tends to
create a perpetual state of calm.

It is not an artificial thing, however. When they have more calm
and strength and love or reverie, it will spread with them—not just
around their planets (because at some point it has done that), but into
other times they might be evolving into. It is in this way that these
predominant feelings (when they exist in an abundance beyond what
is needed in the present) spread into the future, in case those feelings
are not so prevalent in the future to support the perpetuation of those
feelings. This they do on their home planet, from the ninth to the second dimension.

They are dedicated to maintaining this balance from the first through
the ninth dimension. You know, little has been said about the first
dimension because it is everything that exists before anything exists. The
philosophical assumption has always been that this must be thought, but
it is in fact inspiration. So the first dimension is inspiration, and entirely
that. Nevertheless, it is inspiration that is released on what I would call
a timely basis; picture it as a pool, then suddenly it is shooting up.

What they are trying to do on their planet is to attempt to synchro-
nize the first balance that I discussed, from the ninth through the first
dimension at all times, even allowing the first dimension's inspiration to
function in the way it normally does. They are attempting to do something in complete harmony that actually seems to be in disharmony.
This can only be done by very advanced peoples.

So they answered a call to bring bodies here that would provide a durable physical
genetic structure for the Explorer Race?

No, they came as immigrants. They lived here because they were
told that this place needed durable people who could provide physio-

logical balance—bodies that would function and tend to seek out balance. At the same time they brought an abundance of curiosity along with them. Fully 67 percent of the energy of curiosity that exists today is due to them.

Curiosity was not as profound a function in the dark-skinned African peoples because they had a very peaceful and calm culture, and self-discovery was considered more than something that took place with one's immediate self. Self-discovery had to do with one's entire world, culture and environment, and it was expected rather than unexpected. Since it was expected, curiosity was less necessary.

So the Mongolians lived for millions of years on this planet?

The pre-Mongolians, really. Remember that these peoples did not know about the Explorer Race, so they came on the basis of the invitations. They did not come because this planet was going to be this or that; they came because of the invitations of the moment. It just so happens (not coincidentally, of course) that these circumstances ultimately led to a very satisfactory physiological potential for the Explorer Race people.

How do they feel now on the home planet? Are they aware of what is going on now?

Oh yes, they are fully aware. They do consider the native peoples of Mongolia and northern Siberia to be their descendants, just as the people on Sirius consider the dark-skinned African races, wherever they live, to be *their* descendants.

The Desert People and the Experience of Individuality

Now that these individuals were beginning to people the Earth, you began to have more visitors from space, extraterrestrials arriving in ships who were interested in this place. For a long time the only people who came had water as a function of the organization of their structure or culture, but after a while other ETs started to come.

Initially, these ETs were contacted to say that the agreement was that only so-and-so would come to this planet. For a while that was honored, but after a while it began to break down, as things often do.

Only water beings? What do you mean by only so-and-so?

Only cultures who were exposed to, lived with and were otherwise adaptable to some form of water were encouraged to come to Earth for a time. But after a time this began to break down, and you started to get peoples of the desert. In those days, the desert was unknown. There was no desert anywhere on the Earth, but these desert peoples felt that there was a value in the desert. They came and got their start on the planet. Then they went to the various peoples who had talked about the populations of Earth to discuss with them the values of the desert, in terms of what it could do and how it might be benevolent for the planet.

For a long time there was great resistance to deserts. Those who considered this to be primarily a water planet could not see the value of establishing any portion of the Earth that was largely devoid of water. So there was kind of a standoff. The people who were desert people wanted to establish an outpost, but they did not want to offend anyone, so they waited.

Eventually, there came a time when the water peoples of other planets said, "We cannot be rigid about this. We must allow you to show us the value of desert cultures and desert people"—on this planet, of course. So these desert people established a very small desert in the area now known as the Sahara and said, "We will keep it to just this small place and show you what it's good for."

They drained the water? How did they create a desert?

Initially, they created a very high mesa where the Sahara now is. It was like they elevated the area, more than it is now. At the top of this very large mesa was a desert, and the rain that came to all parts of the planet would be deflected from there, with occasional exceptions.

Artificially?

Yes, artificially. What the desert people from space said is, "We will leave a few of our people here. Then if any of the peoples on Earth wish to visit this place, we will make it easy. We will accommodate them and give them all they need. We will let them visit and see if they get anything out of it."

They were very accommodating, and they did this. Visitors would first come for curiosity, and then that passed. Then other visitors with more of a philosophical bent would come and study, staying longer to see if there wasn't some value. They discovered that the value for them was in the ability to become more personally involved with themselves as individuals.

This is when individuality began to be a more profound experience. Up until this point, one had cultures and societies that one was a portion of, but one was not a man alone or a woman alone. That did not exist. But in the desert—even today, if you go there by yourself, even with everything you need—it is possible to become very focused because of the great heat and your immediate physical needs. These tend to turn into being your immediate needs in general. So this was the beginning of the experience of the individual. Because of that, the other peoples from the water planets said, "We can see the value in this, especially in coming times when cultures become more complicated and there will be a need for individual self-examination."

It sounds like there was sort of a United Nations of planets, like a council of people who brought civilizations and seed cultures here.

I cannot call it a council or a United Nations of planets because it was more of a friendly organization, not a structure. It was not even an organization. It was more what I would call a club. If we called it a club, then we'd understand that it didn't have many rules, but the rules it did have were honored.

Shamanic Technologies

Since they came in spaceships, what was their technology? These weren't people wandering around the planet. These were high-technology civilizations, right?

Technology in those early days had nothing to do with it. The peoples who were living on the Earth had nothing to do with hammers and nails. Remember that all life was considered sacred. A tree, a fish, a bird, a man, a rock, water, all of that was considered sacred, and to interfere with anything—such as cutting down a tree to make a board and build a house—would be considered just as bad as killing someone. It was a crime of consciousness and philosophy and of the heart, and it was not considered for even a moment. No one would even think of it. The technology was what I would consider more of the mystical or the shamanic kind. If people needed something—say it was raining all the time in a place—instead of asking for shelter, people would ask that where they live the rain be lessened and that the Sun would sometimes shine; then they wouldn't need the shelter.

So spacecraft came and went, and they were totally aware of that type of technology?

Yes, but they decided not to use most of that. Remember, they were thinking of Earth as being a pristine place, a place to start anew, a place to maintain as it is and not changing it any more than they had to. They didn't want to bring technology. They would rather use cultural and mystical arts, also known as divine spiritual magic. They would use that for anything they needed to eat, anything they needed to change, as long as it did not interfere with other life forms. If there was a problem and their solution would interfere with other life forms, then the solution would not be applied. That was the first time people started living with problems as a daily experience. Rather than change something that would cause damage to other life forms, they learned to live with problems.

Give me an example.

For instance, let's say that the water was too high and they would have to keep moving their camp up and up and up. Perhaps they would get tired of doing that. They would get settled and like where they were, then it would rain and the water would come up and they'd have to move. Even if the water wasn't raining on them, it would be raining nearby. They didn't ask the rain to go away completely, only above them so they would not have to move.

In order for the water not to rise and fall as it did seasonally, they would have to literally change the seasons or cycles, which would interfere with other life forms, to say nothing of the way Mother Earth was adapting her climate. So they learned to live with it.

So they lived, from our point of view, a simple, mystical native life?

No, no. You must understand that *they had what they needed.* They just didn't use machines to create it.

Think of today. A person is sick and goes to the doctor and gets help from the doctor. Well, in those days if somebody started feeling uncomfortable, he would immediately do mystical cures, shamanic cures, and then it would be resolved. They did not cut a single leaf to do that. That came much later.

What about the interaction between the home planet and the colonists, in terms of spaceships coming back and forth? They didn't feel cut off? They were still connected to their own planet during all the time you are talking about now?

Yes. The ships came and went from time to time. When the ships arrived, the people went onto the ships and experienced fun things of the planet that they might not experience on Earth, but they still returned to this planet. However, they always had the option to return home to their native planet should they wish it, if they felt complete here. Some did just that as others continued to arrive.

New arrivals?

New arrivals, then some of the original arrivals would go home.

Did they feel abandoned, separated or cut off?

No.

That is the case with all the different cultures all over the planet? Where are you now? How many millions of years ago?

I really can't say too much. I know you want me to say those things, but I'm not allowed to say too much. I can give you an occasional reference and that's all. I can only say to you that right around the time . . . about five hundred thousand years before the light-skinned peoples arrived and began to get their cultures established was about the time that ships were coming less often, once a month instead of once every few days. By that time the cultures had established foods that were happy to be eaten. You see, there is a big difference between foods that are eaten and foods that are *happy* to be eaten. When a food is consumed that is happy to be eaten, it gives you a great amount of energy for a very small amount of consumption.

There are still some foods like that today, but very few, and they are happy to be eaten only if they are grown in very special ways by people who know how to grow them and do special things with them—honor them, love them, sing to them, tell them stories, treat them just like another beloved member of the family. These plants will produce whatever they produce to eat, and a little bit will be very nurturing. They are filled with love and life force. They've been cherished. They have been nourished and are happy to return such nourishment to those who nurtured them, not unlike the way a child is happy to take care of his or her parents or grandparents because those people nurtured and cherished him or her. It's also, of course, a pleasure to have someone around to tell stories with and look after the children when you want a day off.

These kinds of well-established civilizations were here for a long time. During the beginnings of those well-established civilizations, other peoples came and went, a large variety of people. If you looked at them, you would say, "These people are from another planet." They came and tried to establish civilizations here.

Most of them did not go past a couple of years, including peoples from Zeta Reticuli. They tried it, but they had to live in a domelike structure. Since they could not adapt to a water planet, they lived in a desert community under a dome. Because they could not adapt to the planet sufficiently, they decided that they were out of place on the planet and it was not good for the planet. So they retired to their ships and to their communities elsewhere.

You had such a variety of peoples that one could say it was almost zoolike, but a zoo for people. Most of them came for only a short time. Initially, of course, like other cultures, the philosophers or the scientists came in first, then their families, to see if it would be comfortable. But most of them did not want to stay.

However, some of them met and had interactions with other cultures. Then you started getting different genetics, but certain cultures came and stayed. This was the case for a long time, until you started to get the more recent arrivals, such as the light-skinned people, which is about a million years ago.

6

The Arrival of the Light-Skinned Peoples and Lucifer Introduces Tools

Speaks of Many Truths

August 6, 1998

When the light-skinned peoples came, it was getting closer to the arrival of the Explorer Race. It was right around the time or a little before the arrival of the light-skinned peoples that the energy of discomfort began to rise a little bit, because Creator felt that in order for the Explorer Race to function and learn, there would need to be enough discomfort so that learning would be prompted. As a result, by the time the light-skinned peoples began to arrive and establish civilizations, there was about 1 or 1.50 percent discomfort.

This began to build momentum quite a while later. In the beginning, for the first quarter of a million years or so, it increased very slowly. As it turned out, just having light skin was a problem because of the sunshine, the reflection off the water, the intensity of the seasons and the fragility of the body. The bodies of the light-skinned people who initially arrived were from the Pleiades, Orion and Andromeda. These civilizations were less likely to become permanent. They would stay for ten, forty, fifty years, but they felt that they needed to become too artificial— they had to wear things to protect themselves, they had to be in buildings. They felt that they did not fit into the circumstances on the Earth. So the cultures would often not stay past forty or fifty years because they kept having to fall back on the creation of what they felt was (to Earth, anyway) artificial technology, which they created from materials brought from their native planets so as not to damage anything on Earth.

Nevertheless, the feeling by the various races of beings was that the light-skinned peoples ought to maintain some significant effort to be here. It was about this time that the ice had come down again somewhat. The light-skinned peoples were urged to try living in more snow and icy environments because the need for body coverings would naturally protect them more from the Sun. This was what they began to do.

In these areas were already established peoples of Mongolian-type races and the now-Eskimo races, so there were peoples there who could help them and guide them on the magic they needed to utilize in order to survive and thrive. Nevertheless, it still took quite a while for them to establish themselves.

Ultimately, they started to get a strong foothold and toehold in the northern areas of Europe, which are now Finland, Sweden and the Nordic countries. They were able to establish themselves there, but they had to break a cardinal rule, which was that in order to survive they would need to be able to utilize things around them.

At first, they did what the Eskimo people showed them, which was to make a shelter out of ice. In those days the Eskimo people were not making shelters out of ice, but they knew how to do it. They showed them how to do it, but only with ice that wished to be used that way. As contact between the Eskimo people and the light-skinned people diminished because of the distances involved, the light-skinned people began to simply cut out pieces of ice to make their version of ice houses, without asking the ice if it wished to participate. That was the beginning of utilizing things against their desire.

Now we are catching up to more recent times.

That must have been incredibly difficult. They were encouraged to do it just to maintain a presence here? What was their motivation?

Their motivation was that this was a pristine planet and a chance to do something new. It was exciting, it was an adventure and it was something unavailable to them on their home planet. In other words, it was a great adventure that could only be done here, and if it got to be too much, they could always go home. There were always people who wanted to come and be here.

The other peoples on the planet, including peoples who largely had an organization that was supporting the gradual population of Earth with human beings, welcomed them. They wanted them to be there and felt that they ought to be there. Because of this welcome, they were more inclined to make a greater effort to be on Earth than the other peoples seemed to need.

Of course, you have to understand that the other peoples had been here for so long and had adapted so well over time that it didn't seem like they were working hard to stay here. But they had history in their favor, as it is with any long-existing culture. The light-skinned peoples understood this mentally, yet it did not make it easier for them to establish their culture. They weren't jealous, but they felt that they were initially in an uphill battle to stay here. That's how they justified cutting the ice to build the ice houses. When it was heard that they had done this, the original Eskimo people and other ice civilizations for a time withdrew their long-distance consulting with the light-skinned peoples and admonished them for doing this.

Then the light-skinned peoples reestablished their sacred relationship with the ice, which of course supported them, and went back to the sacred way of making ice houses for a time. But because of that initial building of ice houses without the ice's permission and desire to be utilized in this way, it was the establishment of an alternative method. The alternative, seemingly more convenient than the sacred method, began to catch on with some of these explorers or adventurers. That was really the beginning of the fragmentation of society, from being universally spiritual to being partly technological in the conventional now.

They had long-distance communication using radios or telepathy or what?

The same kind of telepathy that exists now and in this function. Instead of channeling, as is being done here, you would hear, see and know; there would be pictures and you would convert the pictures into understanding and knowing.

If you had a language, the pictures would be converted into words like this, but it wasn't mental telepathy. It was more along the feeling line, which is, of course, real *physical* telepathy. Physical telepathy is always associated with feelings transmitted throughout the body. They stimulate actions when a person is more conscious or stimulate subconscious realizations that become gradually known to the conscious mind.

Would the mystical person do this or did everybody do this?

Everybody. It was not yet the age of specialization. Everybody did everything.

Although, without knowing it, they were preparing for the Explorer Race, these were not Explorer Race souls yet?

No.

They were still basically functioning for their own society's benefit?

They were functioning for, as they saw it, the mutual benefit of this beautiful and bountiful planet, just as you would experience pristine areas of the planet today, in your time, as a mystical retreat. That's largely how they saw it, because people did not come here with the idea of emigrating. They came to experience it as long as they wished. Some stayed, but they didn't come here with the idea of emigrating. They came because they were welcomed, especially as a different variety of peoples, and because they had some exposure to water planets.

Lucifer Introduces the Tool

Over time other ships and vehicles began to show up. Some had technological societies not dissimilar to the technology you have today, only more advanced, meaning less moving parts but still something you might consider a machine or a tool. These beings began to visit the planet. Some beings on these ships began to offer this technology (from their point of view, in a generous way) to surface dwellers if they wished to partake of it.

This relates back to the original Explorer Race material, to Jehovah and Lucifer and all of this business. But what occurred was that none of the people were interested in tools except the people who had already started.

The white people?

Yes, the white people who had already started that experience and still had that splinter group who felt, "Let's just use the ice and let's not ask it if it wants to be used"—that attitude. Even though it was really a latent experience by then, it was still there. So those people did accept these tools, which were really crystals from Lucifer, who was at that time a much more benevolent being. He did not realize that he was unintentionally stimulating (if not really beginning) separation on this planet. They began using crystals to amplify their desires, or amplify in general, in order to create things. That was the first tool.

So now we learn for the first time that when Lucifer and Jehovah came with their ship, there were Mongolians and white people and Africans and others living on Earth.

Yes, by that time there were many peoples all over. There were quite a few peoples in China and other places. Certainly the present Australian Aborigines were present. There were lots of peoples all over the Earth, but they were all living in that mystical fashion, even though some of them had very light skin. For example, there was a light-skinned race of people in New Zealand and in portions of Australia who were of a slightly higher dimension. They would make forays or trips into the third dimension and sometimes live in the fourth or fifth dimension, which they still do in that area. These people preceded the present native peoples of New Zealand and Australia, and they are a very advanced race and are a light-skinned people. These people were never fully engaged in the third-dimensional experience on Earth, but they were engaged part-time.

The only peoples who would accept the things that Lucifer offered (from his point of view, generously) were the people in these Nordic countries. That was a problem, and soon it was stopped by the leader of that ship and Lucifer was admonished, not unkindly, and was sent to the planet in order to recover the instruments. Lucifer did this, but the complications that ensued from using tools separate from oneself had already made an impact, which was the desire by the former Nordic civilizations to have more and more tools. Those peoples were then essentially lifted off the planet and new immigrants were allowed to settle and reestablish those Nordic ways. The peoples who had been here were not punished by being lifted off; it was just understood that they were becoming too involved with the idea of tools. The idea was still to keep the planet pure and mystical.

But you know, even if you try to change things by removing people, you cannot change the interaction between physical bodies, some of whom were made up of Earth and her lands. You cannot remove those ideas and desires just by removing the people, but they did not know that. Thus the desire for tools was in the land there, and it spread.

Human beings at that time were born like they are now? Nothing's changed?

Yes.

So some of the bodies that had been born on Earth were removed from the planet?

Yes, because it wasn't considered right or proper, when they lifted off that culture, to leave anybody here. They took everybody because there were families, and even if there weren't families, they were a united group. It was either everyone or no one, so they took everyone. Then they asked other people if they wished to settle, and they did. It was an attempt to re-create a pure thing, but you know, once things are changed, they are changed.

If all the experience on the Earth is in the Earth because the bodies go back to the Earth, then this early experience is not represented in the particles on Earth?

Well, that's not really the case, because the physical bodies (I'm trying to be discreet here) eat or consume and eliminate waste. The food that wants to be eaten is eaten, and that which is released is released. In this way, things passing through the body are left on the Earth.

The Sirians from Jehovah's Ship Come to Earth

No one ever talked about what happened to those beings from the negative planet in Sirius who were on Jehovah's ship, only that Lucifer brought tools. But what happened to all those beings? Did they live and die on the ship, or did they come down onto the planet?

I think they did not come to the planet until later. I see beings coming from that ship to the planet, but they don't seem to be the same beings who got on the ship, so it must be later generations. It doesn't make any sense that they would come on the planet then, because their experience of discomfort would have been too much for the planet.

Oh, that's how more discomfort is brought to the planet for the Explorer Race?

That's right. When succeeding generations, which had less discomfort but still significantly more than the planet was expressing, did emigrate to the surface, that's how more discomfort was unintentionally deposited here.

Unintentionally by them, but as far as the grand scheme goes, that's how it got here.

Yes, that's right.

These beings on the ship were from Sirius, but if they looked like the negative beings who came here in the past half century, they didn't look like the human race prototype. So what happened when they finally came onto the planet?

When they came onto the planet, they looked enough like the human race so that they were accepted. Some of these people just weren't comfortable here, especially because of the format of living here. They couldn't come onto the planet. They just knew that they couldn't (or didn't want to, but to them, they couldn't).

So they essentially lived on the ship. The ship had the capacity to keep many people very happy and comfortable for a long time, if in a somewhat confined environment, so they chose to stay on the ship. When they finally sent immigrants to the surface, the ones who emigrated looked pretty much like people here.

How did they change? How did they go from what the negative Sirians looked like to the human prototype?

You're talking about negative Sirians. Explain.

There was a planet on Sirius that blew up recently that you are going to go work with. They will be on 3.0 dimension Earth.

Yes.

These are the beings.

No. This planet on Sirius blew up only recently. This ship you are talking about was way, way back.

Right, but that's the planet the beings on that ship came from.

Yes, but they did not look like those beings who are now on 3.0 Earth–who came after the destruction of their planet. They looked more like human beings. I don't want to talk too much about that, because this book is not about that at all, but there used to be, in the distant past on the so-called negative Sirius planet, a different race of beings. The race of beings who is coming to 3.0 Earth, those I'm going to work with, looked one way, and the race of beings who left and came here in that ship looked another way. The race of beings I'm going to be working with came to be the predominant race of beings and the ruling class on that planet in Sirius. The others, who left on Jehovah's ship and came to Earth in these ancient times, were the ones who were put upon or the ones who were not being treated the way they wished to be treated, with a few exceptions, as it always is with races. There are always a few exceptions who are treated well.

Naturally, that race of beings wanted to leave in order to escape not only the unpleasantness there, but the way they were treated as outcasts. They looked more human, except that they had three nipples. This is still considered a recessive trait. Occasionally, people show up with this trait. This does not mean that they are negative beings, but that their genetics can be traced back to the arrival of Jehovah's ship.

Did they settle down in a particular place on the planet?

They settled in areas we are calling the Nordic areas; they were allowed to cover much of their skin because of the cold, and this protected them.

Their skin?

Yes, they were light-skinned, and their skin did not have what many light-skinned people have today; it did not have the capacity to accustom itself to the sun and gradually get darker as a result. They were more like the light-skinned people you still have today in your time, whose skin just burns in exposure to the sun and does not get darker. That's what they were like; they needed to be covered, and in order to be covered they had to be somewhere cold. It was very practical.

I think that we might best continue tomorrow.

7

The Long Journey of Jehovah's Ship from Orion to Sirius to Earth

The Ship Physician and Zoosh
August 8, 1998

The Underground Escape

I am the chief physician onboard the ship you are concerned with [the Vee, Jehovah's ship]. I was in the curious position of being onboard the ship before it was taken over by those of the underground who came onto your planet. When those days in my career existed, they were very difficult. In those days, the people who ran the ship [the government of the Orion planet] wanted me to come up with physiological ways to control the crew—the antithesis of a physician's intention.

They wanted me to explain how the physiology of the bodies worked so that they could put little electrical things in chairs where the people sat and near where they did their duties in order to make them work faster and punish them if they were thinking or saying anything against the government. So the best thing I could do was to give them false information.

They had enough information so that I could not fool them about the physiology, but I fooled them about the voltage. I made the voltage something that would be annoying but not really damaging. Jehovah was at that time a leading philosopher of the planet in the Orion system, and he was involved in many discussions about genetics and the re-creation of the race.

Of course, the rulers wished to use his knowledge to control, so he could see that there was no future in being there. The underground movement (we did not use these terms that have become popularized, but I can see their value in your culture) was quite strong, but it was not organized so that everybody knew about everybody else. It was more a loose-knit organization.

We made a plan and took a year (the equal to one of your years) in which to spread the word that on a certain day we would have control of the ship. Jehovah planted in the ship a series of genetic controls that would cause the ship to break down and temporarily go (as computer talk says) off-line. When that would happen, the ship would have to return to the planet. That would be allowed. The ship would be out of action for about forty-five days, during which time the people in the underground would make their way to the ship. Jehovah said that he would create a diversion, and he and several others did just that, and almost four-fifths of the underground were able to make it onto the ship. The rest of them stayed to battle in the diversion, allowing us to get away.

The Benevolent Planet in Orion

Then we considered where to go. We had control of the ship. The rulers attempted to destroy us, but Jehovah had planted several devices in their communication chamber that scrambled the signals to the enforcers, and the ship was able to get away. For a while we just went far away from the planet to a region of Orion that was more benevolent.

People from other planets told us that this planet was known about in Orion, and that it was sequestered—or perhaps the word is segregated. No one from the outside would go there. They said there was an energy field set up to look like an asteroid belt that blocked any great violence coming from that place to the rest of Orion. That's what they told us. But I had time to think about it, and I realized that they were not entirely candid with us, so maybe they didn't trust us. They told us that story, though. We did not really care, because we were so happy to be around people who were cheerful and benevolent. They did not allow us to mix in their societies on their planets, but they sent many ships with supplies and help and food, and they encouraged us to stay in that area as long as we wanted while we recouped from our great suffering. This we did.

We stayed around twenty-five Earth years, during which time we recouped sufficiently, and Jehovah was elected to lead the ship. He had always been interested in cultural genetics, or as he called it, social genetics. He said that his dream was to establish a benevolent spiritual population someplace on a planet where we could attain access.

He spoke to the scholars of the planet that we were near, and they recommended that a trip to this galaxy would be warranted, but not yet. We were told (I was with him) that it would take time for the planet they recommended he work on to be ready. They didn't tell us that the planet wasn't there yet. Looking back on it, I think they probably thought that we could not understand. They might have thought that. Of course, I think we could have understood, but my recollections might be perhaps a little bit more in our favor than we deserved. We were, after all, coming from a planet that was hostile, and although we were an underground fighting for freedom, we were not exactly benevolent beings. We were pretty edgy most of the time.

They recommended that we explore the rest of Orion and then go on to Sirius. They also gave Jehovah something he did not have before. By that time he was old, getting on, and they gave him the capacity to either reengineer his own body so that it could live for a long time or else clone himself. The cloning process was a little different than your process, but similar.

Anyway, we all discussed with Jehovah whether we should all use this process. Some of us just wanted to pass over in the usual way, but others were interested in this form of physical immortality. Jehovah told us that if anyone was interested, he would discuss it with them and they would decide. We would all decide, because we all meant so much to each other. Jehovah and several others decided to do the physical immortality with their own bodies. No one chose the cloning method at that time. The rest of the people decided that they would just go through their natural cycles and raise their children.

Over those twenty-five years near the benevolent Orion planet, the ship was converted to house and maintain—culturally, ethically and physically—about one hundred thousand people, although there were nowhere near that many on the ship. But people on that Orion planet said that we would have children and that someday we might need the room. Even if we didn't, we would have it. They convinced us that the ship would be like a portable planet in some ways.

We resisted because we liked the idea of its being a warlike instrument in case we came across the rulers of that Orion planet. We liked the idea of having powerful battle instruments—you would say guns, but they weren't quite guns. We hung on for about twenty years, but we let these benevolent people talk us out of it. They promised that they would give us defensive instruments instead that would make the ship invisible—not only physically, but invisible to any detection. And they would give us whatever we needed so that we could safely escape any attack.

They promised us, and they did build it into the ship. They made the ship into a living being so that the ship itself would move through different dimensions if it felt under threat, if it was in imminent danger of being totally destroyed, with everyone on it. And in transit through dimensions it would repair itself had there been any damage, including repairs to any people or beings onboard.

They were secretive and would not tell us how this worked. Several of the leaders were infuriated; they wanted to know. Remember that we came from a society that was warlike and aggressive, and even though we had escaped and wanted a better world, we were pretty aggressive-looking as I look back on it. They felt that we weren't ready to know, and with what I know now, I'd have to say that it is true, we weren't ready to know. Therefore we really didn't know how many of the defensive systems they gave us worked; they worked automatically.

What could we say? We wanted the systems, while at the same time we did not want to give up our weapons. But they drew a line in the sand, as you say, and would not budge an inch. (I like your sayings very much.) Eventually we said, like children, "All right, you promise that this will work?" They said, "Yes, yes, we promise," like they were talking to children—and we really were children, spiritually speaking. To this day we think of them very benignly, because they tried to bring us along gently, as one would bring along an incorrigible child, which we really were.

They fixed us up nicely and then said, "Now it's fine. Fly around Orion, and when you are ready to leave, come back and we'll visit again. We'll give you other things and we'll talk more about things to you. We'll send a couple of people with you to have discussions and tell stories and sing songs and teach you things when you want to know." Isn't that nice? "When we want to know," rather than saying, "When you're ready." In this way they were trying to keep from offending us and at the same time trying to keep us from stumbling about the galaxy and doing harm.

We flew around the galaxy for about four to five generations. Most of the beings decided not to become physical immortals, but most of the leaders on the ship did. I did. Jehovah convinced many of us that we were essential. He said, "Let's do this," so we did. I can't say that I regret it, but sometimes I do.

Anyway, it was all right, and we flew around, as I say, for four or five generations. When we felt that we were done examining Orion and came back to the planet, we found out, much to our amazement, that the beings we had left there were still there. The two beings on the ship were also there, but we had thought that they had taken the immortal stuff. It turned out that they are all immortals on that planet, physical immortals. They were all still there and were happy to see us. We stayed there another two and a half Earth years.

Rescuing the Sirian Underground

Their two people who'd been with us got off, and they installed a very complex communication device that would allow us to communicate with them—not only mentally, but utilizing all the senses, even touch—from a distance so that we could access their advice and wisdom wherever we went. They suggested that we go to Sirius, because there was a planet there that also had an underground, and there would be people who would want to escape. When those people would escape, they would do something, and we could do something, too.

They gave us a meditation that was like a prayer to prepare the people for us to come and rescue them. So we went there. I must tell you that when we got close to the planet, even though we were using the devices so that they could not see us, the energy from the planet was so awful that a lot of our children and the gentle people (a lot of our people had by then changed over generations and had become very gentle and vulnerable) had to be put to sleep temporarily and encased in cylinders so that they would not be harmed.

Those of us who ran the ship automatically would then function within similar shields. The people were assembling in a spot; they didn't quite know why. We thought maybe the beings on Orion had something to do with it. So then the ship (this is another thing the ship did—we did not know how, but we didn't question it) sent something down in that part of the planet that masked these people. You understand?

Made them invisible?

Yes, and then the ship itself flew down into this terrible energy and took these people onboard. There were several thousand. They were segregated for a long time because the energy was so terrible. We spoke to them through an intercom system, using very gentle voices. We had several beings onboard the ship not unlike robots, but they weren't made of metal, who could go in and talk to the people. They were very gentle and the people thought that those beings were the ones who were talking to them. For the first five years they had no idea that we were onboard the ship. They just thought that these living machines were running the ship. We didn't say anything, because it took five years to clear them of this terrible energy.

One person at a time, they would be put on a table that had light underneath it and above it. The cover above it would not close completely so that they would not be frightened, but when it was within about a foot of the person's face, the light would function. It would take about four hours.

The first thing that happened is that they would fall asleep, and four hours later they would be cleared of all but their deepest scarring memories. Those would take several years to process out with therapy, and once that happened, they would go into a separate compartment. Of course, families were done first—husband, wife, children, not just randomly. Single individuals came last.

After they were cleared, after about five years, we began to reveal ourselves. They were very startled to find that there were thousands of people on this ship. They had had no idea; they just knew that they couldn't go past a certain point. But they weren't angry. They were just thrilled to be rescued. So when we revealed ourselves, they were thrilled to find other people. It was really like a homecoming.

Then the ship was guided by our Orion friends. We asked about going to this galaxy, to Earth. They said it wasn't quite ready yet, but that it would be ready in about ten years. They said, "Take your time." So we went around Sirius like we did on Orion, with our new Sirius friends, and explored other planets there. Our Sirius friends were thrilled, because they of course had no idea that all the other planets on Sirius were benevolent. A similar thing occurred that had occurred for us on Orion, in that other beings from benevolent Sirius worlds came aboard and talked with these people. They encouraged them and even sent some of their diplomats and philosophers to be with us for a while. It was wonderful.

That happened for quite a while, but none of those people from these other Sirius planets came with us. Of course, we wanted them to come with us, just like we wanted the Orion teachers to come with us, but they didn't. They put in a similar device for communication, though not quite as exotic, and said that sometime they would send a ship maybe with people onboard, but they couldn't come with us right now. They were so gentle. They didn't say why, because they knew that we were going to start something major on Earth. But we did not know that yet; we just thought it was a place we were going to go to live. We had no idea about all that would be done.

The Domed City on Earth

After that time allotment went by, we were all guided then that it was time to go to Earth. So we flew to Earth and found the Earth really beautiful. As your astronauts know, it is quite stunning to see this planet from Sirius, this water planet, in this kind of solar system. It's just amazing! It's a jewel in space, as people say. It's true.

When we got to the planet and landed, many people got out and walked around, saying, "Could we live here? Do we want to create a society here?" We stayed about a generation and a half, with the ship on the ground all this time, thinking that we would build our city to incorporate the ship. But others, including Jehovah, suggested that we keep the ship next to the city in case we wished to use it to travel somewhere. It was good that he chose that.

We built the city. It was something that we decided because we weren't sure whether we had any vestigial remains of discomfort in us. We built a city enclosed in what would appear to be a glass dome, but it was something more akin to quartz than glass. We had a very benevolent society there for about a generation and a half, but after a while people started wanting to explore. After all, the Orions amongst us had explored Orion and Sirius and the Sirians had explored Sirius, and we liked it. Grandfathers were telling grandchildren of these great adventures, and the succeeding generations wanted to do that, too.

So we talked for a long time. Jehovah suggested that perhaps there was a way to do both, but that we would probably have to remove the city from the surface. It took about ten years to make that decision, because some people liked it there and didn't want to go back on the ship unless everything that was in the city, including all the entertainments, was duplicated in the ship. That took about ten years, and when that was done, everybody said okay and they all went back on the ship, removing all traces as best we could.

Then Jehovah said that he would like to experiment a bit. We had seen the city we had created. We could see out but others couldn't see in. He said that was probably an inheritance from our years of fear, so we probably had some discomfort when we were here and we saw these benevolent beings on the planet Earth.

Jehovah wanted to experiment on them and maybe create a race of beings, but while he was talking to us, there was a voice in the room that said, "We are happy being what we are." We were all quite startled, because we had not realized that these beings were fully realized and conscious. "We are all quite happy being what we are. If you wish to create a benevolent race of beings, we have no objection, but please give us about three or four years to get our people to our underground city. Would that be acceptable?"

And of course we all sort of stammered, "Yes, yes, that's fine," being quite startled. Not even the benevolent people on Sirius and the people on Orion had those powers, so we were quite amazed.

Anyway, we waited a few years and looked around the Milky Way (as you call it) for a while, then came back and checked the surface of the planet. We couldn't see any of these beings who had apparently all gone underground, and that's when Jehovah started creating human beings. I think you have the rest of it.

No, not really. Were there other beings on the planet?

No. There were lots of animals, but no humans. We asked our Sirian and Orion friends where the animals came from, and we were told that other ships had come and brought them, and in some cases the animals (I'm calling them animals because that's what you call them) had come in light, incarnated in bodies made of Earth substance. Some of the animals are very advanced. That's why they can come here in light and begin incarnating in Earth bodies.

I thought that Speaks of Many Truths said that the Mongolians were already here all over the planet. Was his time a little mixed up? You got here before any other humans are here?

We did not see any others. I don't think his time is mixed up. We just have different points of view.

I'm causing harm to this body and I must stop. It is a requirement.

Zoosh

All right, Zoosh present. I didn't know how long the connection would be able to be held because the energy of those beings is incompatible with Robert's. I was able to screen some of it, but not all. You probably won't be able to talk to that being again. It's not worth the damage.

No, absolutely not.

It might be worth mentioning in the book why this session ended abruptly, because when people who channel read this, it is important for them to know that if there is a physiological disruption, it must stop right then regardless of how benevolent the being might be or how benevolent everyone is.

I just have a lust to ask so many questions.

You can ask me, and I will do my best. I cannot give you the personal answer that this being would give, but I'll give you the best that I can.

All right. At the beginning, was this a warship they commandeered?

Yes. Jehovah and a few of the others were crew members. Jehovah was a regular crew member—middle management, a lieutenant, but he was very smart (he was always very smart). He was on the ship for many years. Then he went to the surface of the planet, because it was recognized how smart he was and the rulers wanted to swing him to their way of thinking. He was being inspired with great philosophies, yet did not reveal too much to them; but he revealed some in an attempt to persuade them.

When he attempted to persuade them, he wasn't just using mental logic; he would use energies. Sometimes they would be confounded and agree with him, but when he left their presence, they would get back to what they were before they had been transformed by Jehovah (being again in discomfiture) and would forget their agreement with him. So he learned the hard way, as a wise being must, what works and what doesn't.

Is this the time of the Senate, of the league of warrior beings and the Black League?

I have only used the term Black League because it is popularized. People think of it as the Black League, the Empire, this whole business, but let's just say that it was the time of struggle, not unlike the struggles you've had here between one side and another.

The warriors were basically in power?

No, the warriors were never in power. The warriors served those in power. That's a very important distinction, because it is usually the case, even on Earth now. Sometimes warriors will temporarily take power, but they soon become politicians, being only warriors in uniform but not true warriors. True warriors do not merely have knowledge of war, they have inner strength. There is a good word for this, *shibumi.* It is a Japanese term, a good term. It is an integrity; it is very special.

When the physician started, he was also an officer on this ship. The ones who were in power wanted him to install these electrodes to control the ship members?

Yes, they wanted to use him as sort of an antidoctor.

Much of the underground then got off the planet by themselves? I thought they were evicted, but they chose to leave?

They escaped. Some didn't, and they died bravely in battle.

During the diversion?

Yes.

Are the scholars on Orion the same immortals that the Warrior of Light talked about last night?

[Publisher's note: See "A Warrior of Light–The Ultimate Ally" in the October 1998 issue of the *Sedona Journal of Emergence* and also the book *ET Visitors Speak*.]

It's possible.

Let's go to the negative planet on Sirius. We learned from Speaks of Many Truths that these were human-looking beings who were the underground or the oppressed there. Where did they come from originally?

I believe they came from other planets in Sirius, émigrés. Some of them were sent to this planet originally; they came to study it in hopes of transforming it. That's enough for tonight. Good night.

Good night.

8

Andazi Teach Jehovah How to Create Human Beings

Zoosh

August 8, 1998

Zoosh, Speaks of Many Truths said that when Jehovah's ship got here, there had been millions of years of Mongolians and Africans and others. Were they here when the ship got here?

I think that this is a superimposition, meaning that Speaks of Many Truths' timeline is a little different, just as your timeline now is a little different than his. His timeline is a little different than theirs, so we're talking about timelines again, graphs [draws Fig. 16].

Timelines are different. Picture a skeleton, then overlay musculature and tissues. It's like that. They are superimposed. Where these timelines might intersect would be here [draws Fig. 17], if you were to view

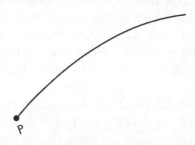

Fig. 16. Speaks of Many Truths' timeline.

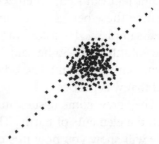

Fig. 17. A moment viewed through three timelines.

that moment through these three timelines.

I know you mean the civilization here now.

Anybody, yes. If you were to view that at this precise moment, you'd be seeing three superimposed timelines, but there might be many others. I am showing just these three so that you will get the idea of the complexities involved here. That is why Speaks of Many Truths sees one thing and the Jehovah person sees another thing and you might see something else. There are lots of complexities in between, above and beyond and so on. I don't want to confuse you too much.

The Creation Process

When Jehovah started creating humans, what was his process? What was his basic material? Did he use animals or did he clone the beings on the ship?

He did not use animals. He was prepared to use animals, but he was sternly warned by beings inside the planet that animals were to be considered sacrosanct, that animals needed to remain purely of their own being. He was told that they were here to teach human beings and any other beings he cared to make, and they must be allowed to be who they were.

He was told that this was also true of plants and that the only exception might be the soil and minerals of Earth, if Earth cooperated. These things were all new to Jehovah, so they were actually educating him spiritually. They were largely responsible for his spirituality in the beginning.

And these are those we call the Andazi [see **The Explorer Race,** *chapter 3]?*

Yes.

Continue as if the doctor had been able to talk. Can you tell more of the story?

I'm not sure if I can. I'll do what I can. They initially asked for volunteers from the ship to provide tissue samples. People said, "Give up parts of our bodies? We're not sure if we want to do that."

But Jehovah said, "Well, we need something as a base structure for creating these beings. We can grow tissue from tissue samples, but we need samples." He asked for volunteers, and interestingly enough, no one volunteered. So he said, "Okay, I'll volunteer." He provided some tissue samples, then a few others stepped forward. But he had to lead, and that was proper.

They grew some tissues and were considering how to animate them with the elements of Earth. That's when the Andazis stepped in to say, "We will show you how it is done." They would not come aboard the ship, but one of their number came to the surface of the planet and asked for Jehovah and several of the crew to come with him, but the doctor was not amongst them. There were several people onboard who were nearing their transition, so the doctor had to be with them. He was very disappointed that he couldn't go. The rest of the physiological team, biologists, this kind of people and so on, went down there and saw it done, but they had no idea how.

They brought a tissue sample, something so small that it would barely be noticeable in a petri dish. They put it on the ground and the being pointed, not saying a word. (Even though these beings were very articulate.) He motioned them to stand back, then he pointed to the soil around it, like this [gestures].

He circled with his arms.

He made circles, then he made circles the other way around the dish that contained the tissue sample. Then parts of the soil came up and formed something like a fountain, a tunnel or a rod above the tissue sample. It absorbed the tissue sample and light was around it. Then from above came a soul, and from below came part of the soul of Earth into that body, forming this beautiful Earth human, a woman's body. Of course, everybody jumped back, thinking that they were in the company of God or someone like God. But the Andazis said to Jehovah, "I will show you how to do this, but you can show no one else except your successor."

He made Jehovah take a sacred oath. I think it was not because he didn't trust Jehovah, but because he wanted Jehovah to feel how serious it was. He showed Jehovah in a fold of time. It's as if he said, "I will show you," and in the next moment Jehovah knew, but there was a fold of time that I believe took three or four years. If you slowed it down on film, you would see Jehovah disappear and then reappear. But to the crew members, the being said, "I will show you how to do it," and in the next moment Jehovah knew how to do it, so they thought it had been instantaneous.

But he had the memory of the event?

Oh yes, he had the memory. So that's how he began, and to this day (although you have not been told this) the soul of the human being comes in through the top and part of Mother Earth's soul comes in from the bottom. This is another reason why it is difficult for Mother Earth right now, because with five and a half [now six] billion people, a lot of herself is invested in you.

When you are at the end of your natural cycle and your soul departs, then your body goes back to the Earth and her soul returns to her. The body is the vessel of her portion of her soul, and that does not go with you. In that way, the body is ensouled on its own but functioning the way Mother Earth functions. You can sometimes have a crisis—for instance, a plane crash in which the souls of people, the immortal part, leave before the plane hits the ground, as happens very often in fatal plane crashes so that the immortal personality does not suffer. The soul of Earth in those people will still be in them, experiencing all the fear and so on. The function of the crash will be physical, and nothing will happen in the crash that isn't a part of Mother Earth's natural function—such as flames and disruption, as in earthquakes. It is not always the case, but it is frequently the case that the soul will leave the body just before death.

So it doesn't feel the physical suffering.

That's right. The immortal soul does not learn anything from physical suffering that causes death, so it is allowed to step out.

The reason they created human bodies was that the people on the ship couldn't just live on the Earth and reproduce?

It was really much simpler than that. They had heard of these adventurous things, and they wanted to go and do them. They didn't want to hang around and live on Earth in a city when Grandfather had gone off to this planet and Grandmother had gone off to that planet. They had heard these wonderful stories and wanted to do it, too.

But they knew they had to people the Earth? Was there some mandate?

No, there was no mandate. It's just that Orion and Sirian people had been told that this would be a planet they could go to and create a race on and live on, too. They were looking forward to it. Remember that their original motivation was to escape and find someplace to live where they would be safe and happy.

Why did they have to create a race? Why couldn't they just travel around the planets and land when they wanted?

Because ultimately their bodies would not be durable enough. They created this dome in which to live because they were afraid of the atmosphere of the Earth, which was not like their own. They could breathe it, but it would greatly shorten their life span. In those days, there was significantly more oxygen than there is now, and although some people can benefit from that (depending on their range of genetics), most of those people could not, and it would greatly reduce their life span.

That's why they knew it was essential to create a race of beings here. They hoped that the race would somehow assimilate them on a reincarnational level, although they did not at that time know how to do that.

Did they in fact do that?

No. They decided that it was more important to go elsewhere.

Where did they go?

All over, but Jehovah wanted to stay here for a time, so he did. He supervised the creation of some of these human beings, and it happened significantly farther back than your Bible indicates.

Are these beings a tribe that we know now? Is there a lineage or something we would call them?

No, they've emigrated to the fifth dimension, and they can sometimes image themselves in the fourth dimension. They're still on Earth, but not third-dimensionalized. So they are in various places. I think it would be discreet not to say where they are.

Everything he created is gone, or is there a lineage that resulted?

No.

There is no remnant of physical humans who are connected to them at all?

No, which is perhaps as well.

Because?

Because you have to remember that the tissue samples were primarily from Orion beings. Think about your history. When the corrupters came from Orion, if your genetics had been more Orion, you would have been infinitely more susceptible to what they were trying to do, because you would not have been able to resist them physically. You have some Orion genetics in you, but not an overpowering amount.

Lucifer and Jehovah

The story is that they contributed tools and brought energy.

Well, I wouldn't want to say that they did that necessarily. Once Jehovah was working to create that race, that's about the time Lucifer and Jehovah started to have a falling-out.

Back up a minute. What about Lucifer?

He was on the ship.

As what?

He was a philosophy teacher, and philosophy teachers (that's really what Jehovah was in many ways) were held in high regard. He was a benevolent being who had certain philosophies in which he adamantly believed. One of them was that for people to succeed and make a life for themselves, they would have to control the means of creation for themselves, not necessarily control other beings. They needed a hammer and a saw to be able to create a house, all this kind of stuff, which was perfectly reasonable on other planets.

Jehovah tried to explain that all beings on this Earth, including trees and animals and so on, were sacred and would somehow be involved in teaching the race of beings he was creating. (It turned out not to be that exact race, but we'll get to that.) So Jehovah and Lucifer went at it hammer and tongs there for a while, and they, as you say, agreed to disagree.

Jehovah created this race and was very careful with the beings. He carefully gave them spiritual guidelines to follow and they followed them. These beings were really very benevolent; they were gentle and heart-centered and mystical in their natures and abilities. He initiated them to many things he knew, but not everything, in the hope that they would develop, from their own experiences with each other and their world, a mystical ceremonial existence of their own, which they did.

Ultimately, they discovered that they could move from the dimensions of about five down to three and up to seven. When they discovered that, they decided that they preferred to be in dimension five. He asked them if they would stay for a while in dimension three, but they politely refused.

They didn't have much effect on the planet at all?

Oh, I wouldn't say that. They're still here.

In Lemuria?

No, but they have been greatly involved with many of the older tribal peoples as guides and teachers who are often seen in dreams and sometimes in visions. They are occasionally seen physically, although rarely.

Then Jehovah said, "Well, that was a success." He felt that it was successful because the beings did exactly what he hoped they would do. They developed their own philosophy and lived by it.

Hundreds? Thousands? Millions?

Oh, thousands.

A particular part of the planet?

I'm not going to say. Do you know why?

I have no idea.

I am being discreet since they are still here, but at the fourth and occasionally fifth dimension. Why should I open them to detection? They know how to remain undetected, but they have to work at it.

Physically on the planet but not in this dimension?

Right. They are still here. In any event, Jehovah then said that he would like to create beings who were more in love with the third dimension, more physical. He asked his Andazi teacher how that would be done. The teacher said that it would be necessary to ask Earth to give more of her soul to these beings so that they would be more physical, more attached to the third dimension. So Jehovah did this, and Earth said, "All right."

And that's when he created the prototype race that was the basis for human beings here. (This race was created in what is now Africa) He created the dark-skinned African peoples, and they were the first beings from his point of view who were here.

Jehovah wasn't from Sirius, but Africans have the Sirian energy. How did that happen?

They have Sirian connections because eventually the benevolent beings from Sirius came to visit them. They talked at length with the mystical people and trained them somewhat. This happened later. They taught them how to connect with Sirians and so on, and dark-skinned people are sourced in Sirius.

So Jehovah made some effort to connect them to Sirius. He was then using tissue samples only from the most evolved beings from Sirius that he could find. It was after the creation of this race that Lucifer finally said, ("That's it) I'm not okay with these people having an allegiance to you and you being their God. I'm going to go down there and approach some of them and offer them tools."

Jehovah said, "If you do that, you are not going to be welcome to come back here."

Lucifer replied, "Is there anybody who wants to come with me?"

A couple of people did, and that's about it. He introduced tools to some of the people. At first the people weren't interested, but eventually some of the younger people became interested and tried them. It came to no good with those people, and eventually they threw down the tools and went back to do things the other way. But the seed had been planted. It was in their memories, and of course it became part of their stories, how tools were a bad thing, how they were tried. But you know how it is with people. Succeeding generations hear their parents say that this is a bad thing, so then they want to try it.

Lucifer tried to empower the people, from his point of view, and in the process he gave them separation. He knows this now, of course, but he did not know it then. Jehovah did not know how to say it to him that way. You know how you will often say, "If I had only said such-and-such." But he did not have those words until later.

He felt that it was bad, but he couldn't explain it.

That's right, he couldn't say why. He didn't have the words, and when the words came to him, it was too late.

Did Lucifer live on the planet?

Lucifer didn't live on the planet, but he had his ship and he had two friends, and they stayed near the planet. They felt badly about things for a while, but then they just got caught up. We've gone over a lot of this before.

Jehovah stuck around, but for people who wanted to go adventuring, they had other ships so that these people could go adventuring. He told them that he really needed to keep the ship near Earth because of its capacities and in case anything came up. He convinced them, so they spent time manufacturing other ships so the people who wanted to go adventuring could leave for a long time. They couldn't all go at once, but they would take turns. Jehovah's still here.

How long was he here in the physical?

About a million years. The connection is getting thin. We're going to have to stop soon.

What is the most important thing? Is that the only group he created—the people in Africa?

No, he then went on to create the people in Mongolia and the Eskimo people and many of the Native American races. But many of those races were greatly supplemented by beings from other planets. The Native American races he created are no longer in existence, but he created others. We're going to have to stop now.

Thank you.

9

The Academy of All Peoples: Cave Paintings, Symbols and Crop Circles

Speaks of Many Truths

August 14, 1998

All right, this is Speaks of Many Truths. I'd like to talk a little bit about the cave painters and wall painters. When you think about it, it is really fascinating. All over the world one finds these things, and there is some difference in style. Some beings chipped it in stone and other beings found other ways to create a long-lasting drawing—and all of this was done without people comparing notes. I'm not going to pick out one civilization and say that this one did this and this one did that, because this is just an overview. Then we will go on to a civilization, perhaps tonight. Perhaps Sumer.

Visitors to Earth Communicate with Pictures

For a time there were visitors to this planet from far away. These visitors scattered about all over the planet. Some of them were here as far back as a million years, but they continued to come to the planet up to about ten thousand years ago. They would go here and there, to various civilizations that lasted.

Ordinarily, when visitors would come from different planets and so on, they would communicate in some form to the people they visited. These people, although they could communicate verbally and understand the verbal communications of others, would for the first three visits speak only in pictures. They would not dazzle the people with pictures floating in space; they would hunker down, the way anybody would, and draw pictures on the ground. They would use basic sign language. They would point to themselves and then point to the stars. They would draw a diagram of the stars they were from, then point to the people they were visiting and draw a diagram of the planets there. So the communication would be with basic sign language, then it would be with pictures.

This was actually quite a common way for different groups of people to communicate in ancient days and even today, in your time. It still goes on to some extent. What street corner has not seen the frantic sign language of people of different languages who have to do all different things? It is a natural thing.

For a time, the people of Earth would just assume that it was a friendly visit and no more, but after a while the drawings the visitors made would become more elaborate. They would have different signs and symbols for different things. Because they spread out all over the Earth and were communicating the same way to peoples all over the Earth, this is how certain signs and symbols (not all, because some were accounted for by travelers of Earth origin), petroglyphs and ultimately pictographs came to be.

There are certain cave paintings, even paintings I've seen in remote places on the land that are in the open or sometimes in ravines, that have a particular otherworldly aspect to them. (They used to say "ghostly" aspect, but now they say "otherworldly.") These are typical of the signs taught by these visitors.

The visitors would not themselves make permanent pictures, but they would guide those who did not know how. They indicated to those whom they were teaching this style of communication that the pictures were intended as messages for future generations who would not know how to talk to one another or who would have lost the ability to communicate easily with visitors.

Of course, this refers in large part to the year 1900 up to your time, when the age of reading and writing became popularized in many places in the world. The new symbolic system tended to discount the value of pictures, and for a time communicating in pictures was considered childish or silly, or there were other ways of casting aspersions on it.

It is really in this time now that these messages are important. Because you have people who are particularly interested in such messages from the past and who go about digging things up and exploring for things, these messages are guaranteed to come to you. It is true, of course, that touching the message with the hand or some part of your body is the best way to learn it, but with so many people in your time, not everyone can touch it. The message remains.

That was the ultimate intention of petroglyphs, which are, I believe, pounded into the rock itself and left as part of the memory of the rock. Those rocks that were decorated in this fashion were always asked first if they would accept such a picture that would impact their surfaces. If they said no or if the practitioner felt that the rock was not comfortable with that, apologies would be made, and thank-yous, and the artist would move on to another place.

After all, if the rock were to be used without its permission, the picture or sculpture would not last very long. But if the rock is used with its permission, it will embrace the picture as one might embrace a loved one, holding it for a very long time. In this way the stone itself becomes part of the message as well as the picture in it. You understand?

The visitors taught this method, although they did not teach the acceptance by the stone. But the people they taught it to already knew that. These were people who had been given profound mystical training by their own people but were not needed most of the time as mystical people or medicine people, because others in their group or time or clan did that. Thus they could dedicate themselves to this project.

The pictures that are most interesting, that reflect actual language taught by the visitors, are the more ghostly or unusual images. Contrary to what is thought by some people in your time, these images do not represent the appearance of the visitors, but rather the actual language or symbolic meanings of the visitors. Of course, the technique evolved over time through other typical petroglyphs and pictographs and so on.

I'd like to give you an example of such a picture. This picture may not be available today just like this, but it gives you an idea [draws]. This is an example of a basic symbol for a beetle. And this [draws] is the symbol for universal man, meaning universal person. You can see how some of these have survived. There is a rock in Colorado that is famous for such unusual designs, most of which were used by visitors to teach the basic language of pictures.

This rock in Colorado, I believe, is in the southwestern area. It should be easier to find that way. There is a name—I think it is called Telegraph Rock. It represents the only remaining example I know of the visitors' primary sym-

Fig. 18. Basic symbol for a beetle.

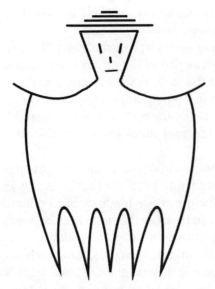

Fig. 19. Symbol for a universal person.

bols and meanings for different things. (If you can obtain a good picture of that, I will define some of the symbols, not all.) Some of the marks on the rock, as archaeologists have discovered, were not made at the same time. Other marks were made by individuals trying to learn the language of pictures. [Publisher's note: If any of our readers can send us photos of this rock, we will get the symbols defined and publish them in the next edition of this book.]

The Message of the Cave Paintings

What does it all mean? These pictures are intended to be a constant reminder that there is life elsewhere that cares about Earth life and that will be back to help you when you have made the basic steps to incorporate the meaning of the message. The meaning is simply to *honor all life as it is.* Granted, the visitors did not encounter life that would hurt them, and they were of an evolved state so that all animals, be they very large or the smallest, would have a very benign and loving reaction to them just as the visitors had to all beings. So one must grant that the visitors did not understand the idea of a mosquito bite. For that matter, they did not understand a snake bite or an animal defending itself or its young and hurting a person. We must allow for that. Even so, the visitors' message to you is ultimately, "When you have honored the other life forms on Earth," (to them that meant animals, insects, fish and so on), "then you will be ready to receive us."

When these visitors would say "us," it would mean not only them, but also the place they were from or visitors from any star systems or even closer. This, then, was not a message for the times of the people. It was more a message given to the people of those times to talk to *you.* That is why sometimes they have added other things. They have added pictures of animals; sometimes this had to do with asking the animal spirit to provide animals for food, but that is less often the case than a commentary on the gift of animals to the human being.

So these messages are really quite profound. Nowadays you communicate to one another for your times, and the only people who are really communicating to future beings for the future are those who work in stone. I might mention to these people that if you wish your art and your message to survive in stone, you must ask the stone, just like the ancient peoples did. You must ask the stone, "Would you embrace this message?" If you get a good feeling in your solar plexus area, in your chest, as I have talked about before (especially in the *Shamanic Secrets* series), then the stone will embrace it.

Don't assume that the whole stone feels that way. Ask all the stone, if it is big, "Will you embrace this?" If different sides of the stone have different answers, then carve only the side or area that has said it would embrace it, and be gentle with the stone. Don't use tools of great destruction, such as automatic tools. Use your hands and your chisels and hammers. The stone can accept this, but automatic tools are threatening to the stone. The stone is afraid it will fracture and will immediately repel the message. Even if you as the artist do not feel this message because you are involved in your message to future or present generations, the stone will reject it and will do everything in its power to eliminate it, just the opposite of what you want. So just be gentle. Some artists from several hundred years ago understood stone and knew that the gentler they were with it, the more likely the stone would embrace their messages, even though most of them did not know how to ask the stone, "Would you like this message?"

I'm not admonishing you; rather, I am making the suggestion. I'm sure there are many of you who would like to leave a message for the future, and there are stones out there that would be happy to receive such a message. Look for them, and when you find them, make sure it is all right before you proceed. Try to leave a message that heartens and inspires, because the overriding theme of all time with any message has to do with heart.

I don't use the word love, because you understand love more as a thought in your time than as a feeling; so let's call it heart. When you call it heart, then you can understand completely. You know what feels good and nurturing to your heart and what is strictly a passing pleasing moment. You all know the difference.

What about the cave paintings dated thirty or forty thousand years ago that have been found in deep caves in France and other places?

As indicated, these have to do with images often associated with honoring the animals and so on, honoring the animal spirits. Yet some symbolic messages come from the time of the instruction of the visitors.

You can tell the difference, because these messages are associated with what the people would call, in their time, the old language.

These pictures are different and are not easily recognizable as life forms of their time, much less your time. They are not just a happenstance, a mystical picture, but a mystical picture associated with the old picture language from either the visitors or from visionaries of their own people who received inspirations. This is also a factor among certain clans and tribes.

You're saying that the pictures in those really deep caves, the magnificent bisons and animals, were done by the visitors?

None of those were done by the visitors.

They were all done by humans?

Yes. Anything that is clearly recognizable as an animal is done by humans.

Beetles Link the Past and Future Timelines

The visitors only did symbolic drawings?

Yes. The difference is that the visitors would draw symbolic pictures like the one I drew for you of beetles. Obviously, it does not look exactly like a beetle, but it has a similarity. Many beetles look one way or another way. The visitors felt that <u>beetles</u> were essential, because <u>they repre-</u> <u>sented the link from the past to the future along any timeline</u>. That is why they must survive; <u>they carry the timeline link with them</u>.

This is why one of the very first illustrations given to Earth people by the visitors was the symbol for beetles and why great love was shown. A visitor might encounter a beetle, or a beetle might come up to a visitor because it would feel safe with the visitor. The visitor would never pick up the beetle just by itself, but would take note of the earth the beetle had walked over, scoop up some of that soil and then let the beetle stand on it. The visitor would then hold the beetle up to his heart area and indicate with a basic sign [points with the other hand toward the heart area] that the beetle was a profoundly loved being who affected the coming times for all Earth people wherever and when-ever beetles existed. This could be done through some symbolic use of the people's language. Then the visitor would very gently set the beetle back down on the earth, keeping the dirt under the beetle.

This was done partly for the beetle's comfort so that the beetle would be safe, but it was also done to indicate to those who would receive the message of the beetle that <u>its job</u>, aside from taking care of its own fam-ily and surviving and living as best it could, was to <u>touch the earth</u>. Beetles would sometimes walk around in places they do not have to go in order to touch the earth for the sake of mankind. This is why beetles do things that are really dangerous for them, such as crossing roads when there are cars there. They know that they must touch things that human beings will touch. In this way the timeline and all timelines that beetles support will be passed on to the human beings of their time so that the human beings will support timelines in general. This is how futures are guaranteed, even in the most tumultuous of times.

Such teaching by the visitors to the people of the time was typical. Most of these mystical Earth people whom they taught had already developed an appreciation and understanding for all animals, be they the very smallest to the very largest, yet such explanations were very helpful.

Sometimes, after the visitors had come more than three times, they would begin to communicate verbally or in thought pictures or heart pictures. These are two different things. Heart pictures arrive in the listener with feeling and the picture and the sensation and the understanding of the meaning, whereas thought pictures are strictly illustrations that carry no feeling—an important difference, especially in your time.

In this way the visitors were very thorough. They wanted to impress the importance of their art upon the people they were meeting and working with. That is why you will see in some tribal art or ancient designs things that are clearly beetles, because the message of the beetle is profound for all time, and the purpose of such art, even though it may not last forever, is that people touch it.

It is not always safe to touch the beetle because the beetle is fragile. If the beetle touches you, then it is a blessing, but if the beetle comes near you, it is not always good to pick it up because it is delicate. So the substitute was devised that a symbol, a drawing that looked like a beetle, would be put on things that people would touch anyway. In this way they would be reminded of the sacredness of all beetles everywhere.

What does that have to do with the Egyptians, who had scarabs everywhere?

The ancient Egyptians were initiated into this knowledge as well. Also, in their time, the Egyptians were taught by their teachers how to communicate with such beetles and that these beetles could bring messages that would save them, such as warnings or even messages of the future. The beetles were known and understood to be sacred messengers, and such artworks as have survived depict the great value and high esteem that such beetles held for the ancient Egyptian wise people.

Symbols for Our Time

The crop circles of today have many of the same symbols as pictographs and petroglyphs. I'm assuming that there is a reason for this.

Yes, because it is understood in your time that what is visual is more likely to reach many, many people and that most people do not have the opportunity to touch these ancient artworks we have been discussing. The next best thing is to give you a visual picture you can be struck by and feel its meaning. The intention, when such a picture is given, is not that you would simply look at it and think about it.

But walk around in it.

Only a few can walk around in it. No, the intention is that you yourself make the symbol, and when you reproduce it (it does not have to be perfect), you are then acknowledging the gift of the symbol. You also have the opportunity, when you are done, to touch it. Artists who make items that people might touch, such as plates and cups and bowls, give you not only the opportunity to touch them, but also the necessity. That is the real meaning of these crop circles. You are reminded and your artists are often stimulated.

If you give artists a beautiful symbol, they don't just look at it. They think, "What can I do with this, where can I put it and how can I incorporate it in my work?"

That idea about dishes is wonderful. You may have started a new industry.

Not so very new. Look at tribal cultures, and you will often see such symbols in the things they make. The idea of having touchable dishes in general release is useful, but what I recommend is that it is better to use symbols rather than actual pictures, because actual pictures will cause other feelings.

One looks at the symbol and feels the spirituality of it. One looks at the actual picture and might feel other things. I also recommend that the symbol be made in such a way (in the things you handle, like dishes and so on) that there is contour. You can touch it. It has depth. You can feel it rather than simply look at something that is painted. What can be felt with the fingers or with any part of the body as a distinctly different physical feeling has an impact much, much greater than that which is simply seen.

This is the difference between a heart message and a thought message. What can be felt, in its symbolic picture, transfers to the heart in a benevolent way. One knows that one is experiencing the best that the spirit of these beings has to offer in such a symbol. If one sees a scientific picture of a type of being, one might have other reactions.

The original purpose for a sculpture of any type was always to be touched. Even artists of a few hundred years ago knew this. Because antiquities are highly valued in your time and because the symbolic language of letters and numbers has become much more popular, the great value of touching has been temporarily lost by many people.

Look at any baby. What does it want? Babies are not interested in reading. They want to touch, and even if you show them a picture book, they want to touch it. They want to taste it. They want to hit it and see how it sounds. These basic messages are intended so that anyone can see what is basically true for all beings here.

There is a process called embossing. It's possible that we could put some of these symbols on a book cover and have them embossed, giving them depth. Then they could be touched. Do you think this is a good idea?

Yes, very good. And perhaps a symbol from Telegraph Rock. I will show you the exact symbol to use. I'm sure that there is a picture of Telegraph Rock in books, but you will find it afterward and then I will show you the one to use.

Beings from the Future Academy

Now I would like to speak for a time on where the visitors came from, because that is important. Remember that they were easily accepted by the people they met. They were not glowing with light. They knew that the people they met would think they were gods or something special—or worse, they would be frightened of them. They knew that they had to look as much as possible like the people they were meeting without interfering by usurping clan symbols and other personal identities of the group.

These visitors are from the future. They are associated with a time. It is a different timeline from your time now, but to give you an idea, it would be around the time 3500.

In their time, there will be a very special place on Earth called the Academy of All Peoples. This is a place that welcomes all peoples from all over the universe and beyond, and creates a place for cultural sharing and comparing of stories, which is so very important. It is also a place where people and tribes and clans and cultures of the past can be temporarily re-created in the spiritual feeling of that moment, 3500.

What would occur would be this: Perhaps there would be a study of the peoples of the ancient Nile, for instance, like the Egyptians. In order to study them, they could not just stand back and look at pictures reproduced of this past. They would study the people by being amongst them, in a gentle way for the people of the time—not studying them as scientists of your time would do, but more the way an anthropologist might do, by living with the people. They would not become initiated into being one of them, but would keep enough difference so that the people would recognize that the individual is a temporary visitor, yet also that the visitor clearly wants to put them at ease.

This is the exact method used by the visitors I have been speaking about tonight. They all came from this Academy. They were, by the year 3500's standards, the most spiritual examples of the people of their time. They had something to teach and could understand the communications of those people of that early time, because they would already have the mystical teachings of those people.

The visitors could in this way meet the people on an equal footing, looking similar to them in outward appearance, but most importantly (which is not fully understood in your time), have the same general feelings. They would react in the same general way as the people of those times, so if the people of those times were to greatly honor the sunrise and the sunset, for example, loving the beauty, the visitors would have those same feelings come up for those ceremonies. The people of the time would embrace them as friends and recognize the common bond between them.

This is a very important lesson for the people of your time, because sometimes when you try to make friends with someone from another culture, you do not know how they will react. You feel a gulf of difference between you when you react to the same event in very different ways. When such things happen, it tends to create a separation between peoples attempting to get together. It gives them, at least for the moment, the feeling that maybe they can never truly communicate.

This is understood in 3500, and therefore the visitors who came from that time were temporarily in existence. They were not what you would call robots or artificial people.

As I can understand, looking at the process, the people who wished to provide this service would lie down in something that resembles a bed. It is surrounded by blocks of what looks like marble to me, very beautiful stone. It is highly polished and looks like if you touched it, your fingers would sink in. I feel that the stone has absorbed much of the experience of these travelers.

So they would lie down in this thing and then their soul personality would temporarily depart the body, just as it does during deep sleep. Traveling through time, they would pick up the general appearance of the people they were visiting, using benevolent magic. The travelers' experience, lying in this soft bed but surrounded by these rock forms, would be that of a dream, and when the visit was over (lasting perhaps a few days or sometimes less), they would leave. Visitors would always walk away from the people they were visiting and walk around something. They would never disappear in front of the people so as to avoid shocking them.

They would then return in spirit form with all the pieces falling away, as it were. The soul would never be entirely disconnected from the person; there would always be that cord, just as there is in dreaming. So the soul coming back to its body would remember everything in complete detail.

Now, the reason they would lie in this bed was that the finer details, the infinitesimal details, could not be retained, as you know when you wake up from a dream. But the stone itself has a capacity to absorb the details. So after the dreamer would wake up, he or she would put his hands out like this—can you see?

About shoulder height, palms out.

The returned visitors would touch the slabs of rock and talk while they did so. When they needed to rest, they would relax and rest for a time or eat, but still remain in this bedchamber. Then they would talk again, sometimes using illustrative talk, which exists in that time in such a way that whatever the speaker is talking about is seen by those present—not on a screen like you have in your time, but seen in the mind's eye as a thought picture or, if the feeling is benevolent, as a heart picture, which it almost always was. Those who were listening and learning would thus get the full experience. So all the needs of all the people, both the people of the future and the people of the past, would be served in the most benevolent way.

Many symbols taught to the people of the past had to do with the shared communication of the Academy of All Peoples. People would visit from the stars, from all over, and would bring their pictured communications. So you had something that came to be a combination of the pictures of many different races that could be recognized by all races in a general way, knowing that it represented a certain type of being, action or message, a universal pictorial language in that sense.

How far back did they go?

They would go back about a million and a half years on this particular project, but sometimes they went way back, over a million years. Sometimes there would just be greetings, sort of preparing the people for the coming communications of friends from far away so that succeeding generations would be prepared to greet these people and recognize that they were friends—preparing the ground, as you say.

But there were many, many other ETs visiting the planet in addition to the ones from the future you are talking about?

Oh yes, but the difference was that when other ETs would come, they would look significantly different from Earth people. They would go about in their usual garb, not making any effort to look like them to put the people at ease. They would actually choose to look like themselves for their own reasons or because they were not there to teach Earth people of such things that the future visitors were teaching.

The people of the time thus clearly understood the difference. A lot of this has to do with diplomacy and being careful not to offend those you are visiting, and also with making every effort to put those you are visiting at ease. In any relationship, the more at ease the people you are visiting are, the more they are likely to communicate their true thoughts and feelings to you, which binds the friendship [gestures]. Describe, please.

Your hands are clasped together, thumbs crossing, palm to palm.

Yes, thank you. It binds the friendship in a lasting way. Someday . . . more of the running photographic form. You understand? The running pictures . . .

Video. They don't come to our time? They go back farther?

Yes, they only go to times where the vast majority of people have been initiated in some form of embracing the mystical nature of life. Largely because of the rigidity of the printed word, in your time the mystical is not trusted because it cannot be clearly defined and reproduced time after time, in rigid letters and numbers.

Remember that the mystical is a constantly changing cycle. The feeling that a flower has in one moment might be different in the next moment, just like a human being's. It will not always be predictable according to what happens around the flower or the human. This is something that the rigid language of your time has difficulty with, and that is why words such as "love" and "feelings" have long descriptions in your book of words. It is difficult to apply thought meanings to heart communications.

Ultimately, your scholars will recognize the limits to such exclusive thought communications and begin embracing the more universal heart language. This is, of course, the language of the people. People do not have to know how to read and write in order to communicate with their heart. This does not mean that reading and writing are wrong; it is just that it is good only up to a point. But it is the prevailing system of your time.

You and I adapt to it and do our best to use this system to communicate. With the running pictures we will be able to add something to it just as we have made some attempt with the single pictures. In time we'll be able to do more as the communications between us will come to be more acceptable by your industry that shows running pictures.

Oh, you mean that someday you may be on television.

Yes, and I will not be alone.

Should we look at any particular pictures? What about some of the cave paintings or some of the petroglyphs?

I do not think that's necessary. I've attempted to explain that. Remember always that if the pictures are more symbolic, they probably have to do with contact with the visitors. Certainly some symbolic pictures were present before the visitors came, but these would often be of tribal significance, meaning that this tribe has these pictures and that tribe has those pictures and this clan has these pictures and so on.

If they are exclusively tribal or clan pictures, their people themselves devised those things. But when something is found in Scotland and is also found in Egypt and in Iceland and so on, one has to consider that there is some unifying factor—and it wasn't television.

The Crop Circle Makers

Are these beings from the future putting down the crop circles?

Yes.

Really? No one would ever tell us before who was doing it.

They are from the future, and although they are not directly associated with the Academy of All Peoples, they are working in concert with them. Many races of beings work on projects in concert with universities in your own time. All these beings are from the future and send either their instruments, their vehicles or their technology, some of which can be sent through time without bringing the instrumentality itself. Others are done in other ways.

All this happens from future beings who have visited or are involved in some way with the Academy of All Peoples and believe in the work that the Academy is doing with peoples of your time and your predecessors on Earth.

So this Academy is directly connected with the Explorer Race then? These are Explorer Race people?

I would not say that they are *all* Explorer Race people. I would be more inclined to say that there are some, but they understand the Explorer Race project and are working in concert with it. Yet their ultimate purpose is to improve the quality of life for all Earth peoples and all peoples everywhere. That is the purpose of the Academy.

But they are in a higher dimension?

Yes. As I said, it was in a slightly different timeline. This is the timeline you are moving toward, because you have changed timelines even in the past thirty to forty years, and you continue to change timelines. Sometimes you will change timelines even without changing your dimension one bit. This is because the velocity of time equals the circle of life [draws].

As you know, there has been some misunderstanding about the so-called zero in your number system. <u>The zero is not really a number but is a symbol for the circle of life.</u> In that sense, then, it is often attached to your numbers for your own purposes. But every time it is attached to a number, it gives that number greater spirituality, because it draws it into the circle of life. That's why the circle follows the nine rather than precedes it. It is used as zero, nil, nothing; but in fact, it is one, two, three, four, five, six, seven, eight, nine, circle. Not zero.

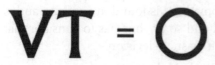

Fig. 20. The velocity of time
equals the circle of life.

Your numbers people will come to understand that soon. I'm referring to the numbers people who understand the mystical function of numbers. In time they will be making all numbers utilizing circles. Think about it. You could make a one with lots of little circles. Not too difficult. You could, instead of drawing a line to equal a one, make lots of teeny circles, and if you stepped back at a distance, it would look just like a line.

What does it do to the one, then?

It makes the one more spiritual because it acknowledges all things, even symbols of transient meaning, as part of the circle of life.

The Academy's main project is to come to planet Earth?

Yes, it is understood in those times that the profound project you have going on here is not just to restore Earth and the hearts of the people. It is also to incorporate all the factors that have not worked in other civilizations in such a way that they can be embraced for what they are and then utilized either as growth mechanisms (such as discomfort) or transformed by being loved for what they are.

In this way it is recognized that these times on Earth are intended to perform the unifying factor. No matter how beautiful you create a world—and worlds on other planets are beautiful beyond your imagination—those who created and maintained that beauty did so through exclusion as well as inclusion.

Earth in your time is attempting to incarnate a world that finds beauty in all things and manages to allow those things to be what they are rather than forcing them to be something else. You can use the theater masks, the one that smiles and the one that is sad, as an example. If the actor puts the smiling mask on her face and she is sad, it does not alter her feelings, even though she might be able to portray a happy person in that moment. When she walks off her stage, her sadness is there.

This example means only that the ultimate purpose of these communications is to unify. On Earth, even the difficult is embraced so that the union of all things in their intended purpose can bring happiness, growth, benevolence and ultimately total fulfillment to all beings.

It is understood by the Academy that that is what you are doing here. That's why they help you without interfering. One can teach the language of pictures without interfering. It is simply a sharing, not unlike sharings that occur other places.

Who was just talking to you?

Oh, who was touching me from time to time?

Yes.

Spirit friends passing by. They will sometimes touch this body, and I must acknowledge them, you know. The occasional thank-you that I will say incongruously when I am talking about something else means that someone has stopped by and touched me to say either hello or good-bye.

I see. I thought someone was telling you something like, don't forget to say this or that. You have expanded into a much greater beingness than before, it seems, into more of your total being.

Thank you.

Isn't that true?

Perhaps. I will certainly take it as a compliment.

I thought that you had deliberately moved farther out from that life of Speaks of Many Truths.

Oh no, I must be in that life or I would not be able to talk to people. Remember that my job is to talk to people *in their bodies as they are living now* with the frame of reference of a person, whereas Zoosh and others (perhaps other versions of myself also) could talk from a broader perspective. Yet as wonderful as Zoosh is, he cannot personally identify with the human life, which I can do. That is why Zoosh and myself are complementary.

Yet one can appear to be less and yet be more. When you face a person, you see the person's face. When he turns to the side, you see more. When he turns away from you, you see more yet. When you see something at a distance . . . let's say you are walking up a road and you see in the distance a very small tree. Where you are walking aren't many trees, and you think, "Oh, wonderful, perhaps there is water and people!" You look forward to getting there. The farther you walk up the road, the more you can see of the tree, and what started out as a small tree becomes very big. The Earth is round. Physical experience sometimes reveals more as you come closer and know more.

Let's start with the oldest. As you said, the oldest village was Sumer. Let's start with the oldest first. As far as your people know—and then work our way to the present as we have been doing.

There is such a great leap from even the forty thousand or fifty thousand years ago when you say the Explorer Race started to the oldest traces of civilization I can find.

Don't worry, we will make the connection.

All right, I'll get everything about what was called Sumer and the area that suddenly seemed to just spring to life. This great civilization was there, but it didn't seem to have anything before it.

We will have a good time with that.

Very good.

10

Sumer, an Art Colony from Sirius

Speaks of Many Truths
August 21, 1998

All right, this is Speaks of Many Truths. Good evening. Tonight we are going to discuss the civilization referred to as <u>Sumer.</u> I believe that this name has been given to it more <u>because of its geographic location</u> than some translation, is that not so?

I have no idea. It's called Sumeria or Sumer. Our archaeological history goes back only about six to ten thousand years, but the Sumerians have king lists that go back hundreds of thousands of years.

Who has king lists?

The Sumerian people.

Hundreds of thousands, you're saying?

Yes, person by person.

This is part of the documentation?

Yes.

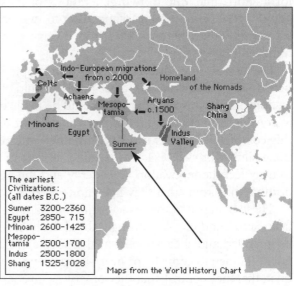

The earliest Civilizations:
(all dates B.C.)

Sumer	3200–2360
Egypt	2850– 715
Minoan	2600–1425
Mesopotamia	2500–1700
Indus	2500–1800
Shang	1525–1028

Maps from the World History Chart

Site of ancient Sumer

I see. So why do archaeologists feel that it is a civilization?

Because they look at pots and the excavations. They can trace all the Sumerian artifacts.

From the physical evidence?

From the physical evidence, yes. When they dug to the bottom of Eridu, it was dated at something like 6000 B.C.

Good explanation. Now, this civilization is (unusually) not built on another and was not established through conquering. Oftentimes when one finds a civilization built on top of another, it is because of the conquering of one over another. This is not the case. In this case it had to do with proximity to water and, as a result, resources.

An Artist Colony from Sirius

When the civilization referred to as Sumer established itself, it was establishing truly not a civilization of warriors but a civilization of artists, which was surprisingly common. That which is referred to as previous kings, which is the best interpretation available, really has more to do with teachers. But in that civilization as well as many others, teachers were considered profound and valuable beings—cultural treasures, as civilizations of today might say. That is the nature of the lineage you mentioned.

Now, this is not a colony that ever intended to be on Earth for very long. Rather, it was an artist's colony, with the intention of being here for a short time, one to two generations of these people. Since the people were from another planet, one to two generations by today's standards would be anywhere from twelve hundred to twenty-four hundred years.

Because of their interactions with the people in the area who happened to be passing nearby, these people would often discuss their philosophy. Their artwork, they felt, could be made only here. I want you to consider something, and those of you who are artists will understand this completely: Artists can study another culture and produce something similar or even exactly the same, at least in image; but for artists to truly feel the motivation, the energy and the inspiration of that civilization, they know that they must go to the place that inspires.

These beings had that exact same motivation. They were originally from Sirius, and they felt strongly about the lineage of their artwork and its intended audience, which was the people of Earth at that time who might happen to come by or near. It was never intended that they conquer, that they control, that they otherwise invade; rather that they go to the place where they would be inspired—the Earth planet.

They came to visit this solar system in order to create artworks and visit with people who were passing nearby, to tell their stories and show their artwork and often make gifts of their artwork to passersby. Some of these original discussions prepared the people of the area—it did not establish the Islam religion—but it prepared the people of the area to accept it.

Some visions were shared about a beautiful new philosophy that would come to the people, and as it would gain strength over the years, it would go through a brief period of polarity to the masculine. Soon it would reach its balance by an opposite polarity—shortly into what is now (in terms of your calendar) the year 2012. It would then have the opposite polarity, almost the extreme polarity of the feminine, but by 2025 it would be in balance.

There is a small artwork that has no head. The illustration refers to the fact that the body of the sculpture is complete, but there seems to have been a peg on which the head was placed. The original thought was that this would be changeable from person to person, but in fact, this was made to be given away to people as they came and went. I think just one was found in the civilization's remains, and it showed what would become of Islam.

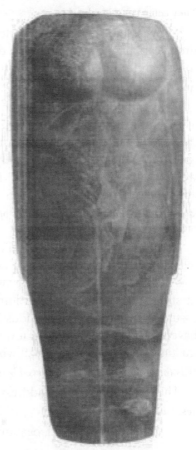

Fig. 21. Sumerian alabaster sculpture with no head.

The statue was given with four heads. The first head was masculine but it was a gentle and beautiful masculine. The second head was a fierce masculine. The third head was profoundly, gently feminine, and the fourth head was a perfect balance of masculine and feminine features. This statue was often given to leaders of groups that passed by, and sometimes what would survive would be the particular head the leader or that leader's descendants found most attractive.

So we have, then, a society based almost entirely on art. Of course, where there is art, there is the artisan and the craftsperson—craftsman and craftswoman.

You find that their techniques for building were sometimes copied but were mostly unique. Most of the structures have not survived very well, but some of the foundations are still apparent. This is who these people were.

They came consciously, then.

Oh yes, and then they departed. They stayed about eighteen hundred years or, calculating for the difference in time in your years, closer to sixteen hundred years.

And they taught?

They did not proselytize in the sense of sending people out to teach. They simply maintained their civilization. Those who happened to pass by and wished to stop to drink and eat and just share what was available, they would teach individually and never in a strident way but in a way that had to do with stories. I might add that they made no secret about being from another planet.

We must have hundreds of thousands of clay tablets from the Sumerians, but nothing on them says anything about that.

Perhaps it is because they believed more in the spoken word. They felt that what was said between people was sacred. What was written was intended to be a story. They would speak their wisdom in the form of stories and adapt their wisdom to stories. This might be why it is assumed that they had previous kings, because they very well might have used the word "king" if it was a word used by the local people of the time. But in their reality, it would have referred to teachers.

Was this gold mogul or king carved by one of them?

This is a helmet or a headdress?

Yes, made of gold.

The intricately detailed, beautiful sculptures and artwork that would

Fig. 22. Gold ceremonial helmet.

easily be appreciated in any art studio or gallery today are almost guaranteed to have been made by the Sirian artist colony.

I think this was intended to be a gift, but the occasion did not come to pass. I am surprised that they did not take it with them when they left, but perhaps they felt that anything created on Earth by them with Earth materials ought to remain on Earth. When they returned to Sirius, of course, they would remember how to make these things, and on arriving on their home planet after their long voyage, they would be able to reproduce the artwork they were inspired to do but use materials from their home planet.

Fig. 23. Princess of Lagash.

How about this one [Fig. 23]?

Yes.

That's one of the Sirians.

You notice the face.

Beautiful expression.

The expression. You can recognize their work, because either the head will be missing (the idea of the different heads) or the expressions will be very uplifting, like that. You won't have a sitting portrait.

Fig. 24. Gold feeding cup.

What about something like this gold feeding cup [Fig. 24]?

That would come later. You can see how much rougher it is, not as fine.

That's a good way to tell one from the other. So let's concentrate on these people. They were here eighteen hundred years. The city suddenly sprang up. It had agriculture, it had commerce, it had writing, it had art, it had literature—it had everything. The fact that it came from another planet makes total sense.

Yes. As you would do when you go to the Moon—you'd bring your technology and leave some stuff behind. If an archaeologist came along, she would say, "What is this? How did they get started? How could they have gone so quickly?" As you would say, they arrived and unpacked.

The Earth has been blessed because so much of what they brought is still used today—ideas of commerce and society and stories and art.

It is curious that it was never their fault or intention, but simply a by-product, a benefit that happened to occur. You know, it is not so very unusual, this idea of artists landing here and staying for a time. I believe that this has happened quite a bit. It is also, as you might imagine, common in other places where planets are benevolent to certain species.

Artists are, after all, restless to some extent. Ask any artist who has stopped working on a project. Most often he or she will not be completely satisfied but will have simply stopped. Restlessness is part of the nature of artists because they know they are always revealing something that is unseen to others. When one is doing this, there is a feeling deep within that there is more to be revealed, which is why artists are restless and why one very often finds them flying about from place to place for inspiration and such works as we see here.

This one is called one of the most beautiful Sumerian objects ever recovered. It is a marble cylinder seal. Would that be theirs [Fig. 25]?

This was brought. It is not of their making. I think it might have been left behind by accident.

There is so much in these books about Sumer. Did they have a goddess called Inanna?

Yes. That was their name for the idea of what you would call God, which is, of course, a nongender being, but which has now come to describe a masculine being. Inanna was the word for God in the form

Fig. 25 Marble cylinder seal.

of the feminine. I might add that many cultures from off the planet have difficulty with Earth cultures creating a masculine God, an authoritarian God. In reality, of course, if you are going to have a God, the feminine makes more sense because the feminine delivers creation.

This is a five-thousand-year-old alabaster vase. Is this one one of their works?

No.

That came later. Are we still not doing dates? Can you say what years they came, if they were here for eighteen hundred years?

I have difficulty with that, I am sorry. I am not withholding from you.

All right. Are there any stories? They built temples to Inanna, and that's come down to us. What about Ur's royal tombs? Did they have royal tombs, or were those the Sumerians? Did they bury their people?

An important question. They did not. If a generation passed over, they would wrap them in a certain way and place them in something like a casket. This would preserve them. They didn't leave anybody here. So no, they did not bury anybody. If bones were found, they were not those people's.

Fig. 26. Alabaster vase.

They would not leave anything like that, because there were skeletal differences between them and Earth people. For instance, in the area where the heart is, the ribs were not the same; whereas ribs protect the human heart, their ribs are softer over their hearts, a clear sign that the being was not an Earth person.

Some of these gold things they left behind, whether deliberately or not, that were found in the tombs, were picked up and used later by the people who moved in when the Sirians moved out?

Yes, plus the gold cup [Fig. 24] was not created by them. You can tell that when something is rough. I'm looking at it again now. Let's revise that gold helmet thing [Fig. 22]; I think they only created the part that indicates the ears, and it isn't finished. I think they created the helmet partly, but it represented an unfinished project and was never finished. Generally speaking, what they did was technical, beautiful, intricate, subtle, special, even modern art, but not rough; nothing coarse. If you find something rough and coarse, it was originating in some other civilization.

The gold helmet is very delicate on the top, but not on the bottom. Is that what you mean?

Yes, I think it represents an unfinished piece.

Look at the incredible detail! You can see every hair.

Yes, but it is not finished.

Who did they teach writing to? Did people who worked for them learn it?

They would tell the stories. If people wished to remember the stories, because the stories were very complex, they would create these tablets. Most of the tablets were given away. Even with all that were found, most were given away. Also, some were taken back to their home planet, but those that were left, I believe, were left because of the ship's capacity. They couldn't take everything. I think perhaps their original intention was to not leave the tablets except those that were given to individuals.

So they had scribes who did the bookkeeping, the trade, who kept records and everything? Those scribes were taught their language then . . . their system of writing?

Those scribes were themselves They did not have slaves or people who worked for them. They were complete unto themselves. They would perhaps have visitors, as I say, but they were their own people.

Okay, but did they take people in and teach them? They taught this language to somebody? Because it goes down for thousands of years after they left.

They must have done this if they gave the tablets to others. I think that when they gave the tablets to others, perhaps they explained the alphabet, how it worked, so that the people who took the tablets could read them. Maybe that is how it happened.

So they didn't build. They just used mud brick; they didn't seem to build for eternity. They built something to house them only while they were there.

Yes, to create simple shelter and, when you think about it, to create as little an impact on the planet as possible and leave only beauty behind. If something was for shelter only, then creating something that would not last is not unlike what you do today.

So they were dropped off and then picked up later, or did they keep their ships here?

They were dropped off and then picked up. It was felt by the colony (and they had much equipment) that if the ship was available to them, no one would come to visit them. People would be frightened by it. It was also felt that if the ship was there, people would not make much of an effort to make this place their home, even for a short time. It wasn't, however, intended to be a prison. It wasn't a prison colony. If people wanted or needed to leave, the ship would come and pick them up.

So they had communications?

Yes.

How was that explained to anyone who visited them? As nomads or travelers would come through, they would be welcomed. Would the Sumerians talk about where they came from?

Yes, they would wave or catch their attention from a distance. Because they could master languages very easily, they would call to the people in their language and say, "Come and eat, drink." They made people welcome and comfortable. If people were passing by or there was a trade route not far from there, they would let everyone know. They would say, "Tell everyone. We have plenty for everyone. Always know that you are welcome to stop here and spend the night if you wish." They were wonderful hosts, so of course everyone wanted to stop. They were there for a time and the people who traveled those trade routes during their lifetime thought it was wonderful. It was a gift. The only thing that people on the trade routes could really offer these people from time to time was unusual materials that they could work with or stories from afar, "what is happening on the other side of the mountain" kind of stories.

Didn't the people who visited them realize . . . to them the Sirians must have looked immortal if they lived twelve hundred years?

You have to remember that the people would say, for instance, "Well, we live a long time." They wouldn't say that they lived twelve hundred years, because that would be a little frightening to the average person. They would say, "We live a long time." The average person on the trade route did not come by very often, and they lived only thirty or thirty-five years. If you told the next generation that these people were there, they wouldn't know they were the same people. They didn't take photographs.

This information must have traveled all over the planet then, because the people on the trade route told stories to other people who went to other countries.

As people know even in your time, it is the salespeople who inevitably spread culture. One likes to think that it is the teachers and artists, but in reality it is the tradesmen.

Was there intermarrying?

No.

Did they enter the gene pool of the planet, or did they only stay to themselves?

They were very careful not to do that. They were just different enough to not be too attractive as mates. After all, you would want your daughters or sons to marry within your own clan or group, and the idea of marrying outside it would not occur to you in those times. The only circumstance where such a thing might take place would be an occasional orphan who might have been serving one of the tradespeople on the trade route. But they would not want to stay with these unusual people, although they would enjoy visiting. The people were very careful not to intermarry.

Akkadian seems to be close to Sumerian. Here is this incredible carving in a cliff several hundred feet high. It has words in old Persian, Elamite and Akkadian. Contemporary archaeologists in the last hundred years were able to read Sumerian because Akkadian was so similar. I'm trying to get the connection.

It does not seem to be carved by the Sirius people.

The Sirian Artists Return Home

The Sumerians left. Did other people move into the area where the Sumerians had lived?

Yes.

Who came in?

The people from Sirius left, then there was quite a gap, about a hundred years or so, maybe more. Then someone settled in. Of course, people would continue to stop and get water and so on, but before the Sirius people left, they told their friends. For about one generation Earth time, about thirty-five years, they said, "We are leaving soon." That's when they were giving lots of gifts. "We are leaving soon, so please take this to remember us."

"Oh, don't go."

"We have to go, but we will remember you and we will share your

Fig. 27. Akkadian carving in cliff.

stories with our people so that you will be remembered in the stars."

What a good gift to be told that. When people were told that, they were thrilled. Of course, it was true. They told the people before they left and then it was about 100 to 120 years before somebody else came. They left some things and the next civilization built on top of their civilization. Of course, the things they left were things that were more long-lasting. The huts, of course, did not last very long, but some of the artworks, the tablets and so on, lasted a long time.

But someone had to be able to read them and continue writing on tablets.

This must have been accomplished by those who came and were given the tablets. This is the only thing that makes sense to me. That is the best I have to offer.

These people returned to their home planet. It took a while, because even though the ship could travel very quickly, it traveled slow. Again, one understands artists—they want to see. Nevertheless, it managed to get to its planet in about five years of Earth time. When it arrived, the people were greeted with great joy and celebration. The dead were taken off with great ceremony and fanfare and given beautiful celebrations.

Then after a time of rest (about 112 days or so), the travelers gathered to talk and sing about what they had done and seen. They showed the art and so on. Sometimes two or three would tell stories from the Earth people who had passed by, the tradespeople, people traveling. Sometimes these would be personal stories and sometimes they would be stories of the culture. Sometimes there would be songs or dances. So there was a tremendous time, about a year, maybe a little more, when they showed Earth culture. This is how—you don't know it now but you will—museums came to be established on Sirius showing Earth culture and arts. These museums are still present today, and the culture of the time is well preserved.

Nothing was taken from the Earth except what was seen and sensed, so things were reproduced. You could see a complete reproduction of a trade group as an artwork—animals and people and foods and everything— in terms of your now measurements, almost three hundred feet long. It is a great hall, but there is no roof. It is an open building, and this huge sculpture is in the hall. On the opposite wall there are paintings and other sculptures of that voyage here.

It is a building laid out like this from an overhead view [draws]. Here's the three-hundred-foot sculpture. Here are other works and there are all artworks along this way. One enters here and exits. This is the Museum of Earth Culture.

Sumerian Life on Earth

How did they first get the idea to go to Earth?

They knew that Earth was once in Sirius, and they wanted to go to Earth as Sirius people. They were artists and thought they would be inspired to produce art beyond anything they had ever produced on Sirius by visiting a Sirius planet in a faraway galaxy.

It was entirely for artistic reasons, not because they had heard about anything. They had no idea what they would find, which is why they tended to bring more material than they needed, just in case.

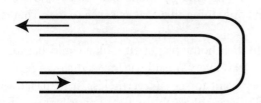

What did they bring? Did they make huts to live in? We know they grew food.

Fig. 28. The Museum of Earth Culture on Sirius.

They made huts. They could have created highly technical shelters, but remember, they wanted people to come and visit them and feel comfortable. If they had produced something very technical, it would have been frightening, so they produced something simple and welcoming and acceptable to the people of the time. They were very careful to be different, but not so different that they would be frightening. They were very gentle that way. So they brought everything they would need in terms of food. They were vegetarians, which is typical for extraterrestrials.

Then anything in the tablets about livestock and agriculture is definitely later.

Yes, and also anything to do with fabric. They brought their own fabrics. They had a method by which they could create beautiful fabric colors, not unlike what was being produced in the Far East and what one might see in Eastern artifacts today—beautiful old kimono garments, for example. They could produce things like that, so their garments were beautiful. The draping of the garments was done similar to the times. It was not exactly the same, but the head was covered. The fabric was beautiful, and they would sometimes give a small fragment to someone, but only if the fragment would not last. They did not want to disturb the culture. It would last four or five years, and the person who received the gift would treasure it for that time.

Did they have a family grouping such as we have now?

They were very communal. They did not have a family with a mother, father, children. There were males and females, yes, and there were children. But children were considered sacred beings. There was a great honoring, but there was no class separation between the sexes or even between the ages. They did not have families like you have today and like we have in my time. It was more of a commune, not as in your recent "make love, not war" communes, but it was more communal.

How many of them were there?

At no time were there more than six hundred.

Did the people come and go in the interim, or did they all come and stay?

The ship came from time to time to pick people up. Sometimes people did not want to die on Earth when they were getting older; other times, when children were born, they would prefer to be on their home planet. So the ship came and went a lot, and it would come and go quickly. It wouldn't take five years. It would be a small ship that would come and go quickly, but it was always nearby during the visitation in case someone wished to leave. When someone wished to go home, people from Sirius did not come and join later. Only the people who originally came were here and only the people born here who wished to stay. You could go home, but you couldn't come here once the original colony was established.

Were they able to breathe the air and eat the food?

The air was a little rich in oxygen for them, so they would have to use these tablets. They would put tablets in their mouths that apparently contained minerals that one might find in the atmosphere of their home planet. I think their planet contained a little more carbon dioxide. At that time, Earth had quite a bit of oxygen in the atmosphere.

Do you know what percentage of oxygen was in the air on Earth at that time?

It was 18 to 22 percent. It was too much for them.

Oxygen in the air is between 12 and 14 percent now with the pollutants?

Yes, a dangerous level for you all. That's probably why you are having trouble with memory and diseases that affect the brain. I would say, though, that this is what they used. They used these tablets, giving them more carbon dioxide, which would counter the effects of so much oxygen.

As the children were born, they would tell them who they were and where they were from and tell them their stories?

Yes, they would sing to them, have ceremonies. They would welcome them into the artists' colony. It would be what would be said in tribal culture today in your time, perhaps this clan or that clan within a culture: They would welcome the children into the clan of the artist, and when they later returned home, they would meet the clan of the artist on their home planet. The home planet is at least half the artists' clan; the rest of them, I think, were various other clans—some diplomacy, some enterprise, some agriculture. I think that's about it.

They don't have a government as you have now because they have peace with their neighbors. They do not need regulations. They have shared philosophies, so they do not require governments. The clan of diplomacy would have to do with interacting with other planets, I assume.

They started a lot of the institutions that we have today?

Well, I'm not prepared to give them credit for starting government the way the Greeks, for instance, have been given credit for. Remember, they came from a place with no government, so they did not start that.

What was their effect on the planet?

I would say it was artistic and cultural, but not governmental. There were no diplomats amongst them.

The people who stopped by learned from them, didn't they? They learned how they did things?

How they did things, how they lived, how they lived for one another, how they were devoted to one another. This, of course, prepared the people for Islam, which has a great deal to do with devotion to one another, supporting one another. Anybody who is familiar with this religion today knows that this is the core of the religion, even though this is greatly misunderstood in the Christian world. That is unfortunate.

I am hopeful in your time that you will be able to glean the best from all your religions and eventually come to what I believe is the natural religion, which is the honoring of all life through the feeling that is mutual and shared between all beings. The blade of grass, the dog, the horse, the child, the mother, the father—all these beings have exactly the same feelings, the same emotions, but they are physical feelings, without a word to describe a thought. Physical feelings are shared and physical life is largely shared.

I grant that the plants need water and minerals to grow and the human also needs water and minerals and other things to grow, but in time you will all live by the rule of heart, which is the understanding that all beings feel the same about everything.

The challenge for you today is that you are still operating under the delusion that all beings *think* the same. In reality, you all *feel* the same. The reason I say this is that I know you would say, "Oh well, people think differently." But there is confusion about what is physically felt compared to how people think.

Your teachers of today (I realize that this is off the subject, but I will finish quickly) tend to talk about how all people have similar thoughts—they want to succeed, they want to be happy, they think about what to do to be successful and so on. But in reality, all people have the same *feelings*. They need to be loved and accepted for who they are.

These are not thoughts; they are core feelings. You all have the same physical feelings—what feels good, what does not feel good, what is frightening, what is nurturing. The blade of grass is frightened of the lawn mower. You are frightened of the big vehicle that might hit you when you are out walking. The fear, though, is the same. The blade of grass feels fear in the same way as the human.

If you remember this, it will give you the key to how to honor all life. All life feels the same way you feel. You may not share the same feeling in the same moment, but the function of feeling works the same for all life. In my experience, this applies to all life everywhere, not only on Earth.

How did they react to other forms of life? Did they have any animals as pets or companions? They grew all their own vegetables, right?

Yes, and if necessary they could synthesize food for times when there might not be enough or when there were more visitors than they expected. They had machines that could create and generate what they needed.

They did not bring animals, but they treated them as equals. When people would come from their trade route, if they brought their animals, the animal would be honored. This one would bring them food and water or lead them to water, then someone else would sing to the animals and another would perhaps brush them or pet them or make the animals as comfortable as they could be. They were treated with the same welcome as the human beings.

Those on the trade route thought this was kind of funny or eccentric, yet they did not see any harm, so they allowed it. If you had an animal on the trade route with you and you were with this animal a lot, sometimes you would have a name for it. When you left, you would say to it, "Well, you are also looking forward to coming back here again." It was the same then, you know. You might talk to your animal because you were always with it. People on the trade route came and went, but you would be with your animal.

There were many little remarks made to the animal, and sometimes they would treat the animal better, because it would be a curiosity to them that these people from so far away would treat the animals with so much respect and honoring. Not that they did not treat their animals well, but not that well. They would ask and the people would say,

"What you call animals on this planet look very similar to beings we have seen on other planets, and there they are not called animals but just the people of the planets. So we treat them like we treat those people." Of course, the people would reply, "Tell us about those planets," and so on. It would be lots of fun. On your trade route you could conceivably visit these people five or ten times in a lifetime, for instance, maybe more, yet never hear the same story twice. So you would very much look forward to seeing them again.

We don't hear anything about this in anyone's stories or writings. You would think it would be so unusual that it would be passed on from Earth people to Earth children.

Think about it. Even today when you have symbolic writing for books, there is a great deal of disbelief about people from the stars. In those times it was not much different. There was some understanding that this was real, but people wanted to preserve their own culture and their own stories, and they did not feel the need to replace their culture and stories with the stories of others.

It makes complete sense when you think about it. Look at the history of the United States. The United States still treasures its original documents, because these documents come as close to establishing a foundation of culture for the people of your country as anything else, and also because the people are so different from all different cultures. This is the one thing you can share, a belief in these documents; but you do not expect to throw these documents away and replace them with somebody else's documents.

A good thought.

We are probably going to cover only one culture a night now that we are coming into historical times. Before, we moved along quickly because it was less important to be detailed with those civilizations, but it will be more detailed now.

Did the Sumerians build temples?

If they built temples, they were always considered works of art, and they were hoping to influence the people who passed by. The funny thing is, if they had chosen to land in Europe, these temples would have influenced the people. It would not have been much later in history when castles were built. Look at the civilizations of the earlier time and place; castles were not being built because they did not have the raw materials, much less the interest.

These were works of art that they hoped might influence people, but they did not build in a geographic location where they might have had the most influence. They did not want, as I said, to convert people to their own thoughts, but they felt that anything produced artistically would be an acceptable influence.

That brings up a question: Why did they choose that particular area?

They chose it because they felt that the people in that area at that time were the most open to visitors from afar and that there would be quite a few people coming and going there because of the trade routes. They could have gone to China, where a culture was well established, really quite entrenched. They could have gone to other places, but they chose this place because, as one might expect with artists, it *felt* the best.

When they were there, the rivers went right by their front door?

That's right. Of course one would tend to settle someplace where there was fresh water.

I think the remains of the city are now ten miles or so from the water.

Well, it is typical of water to go where it is welcome. Sometimes it feels welcome in other places. Even in your time rivers change their courses.

When we find tablets that talk about the king list, these refer to the teachers back on the home planet on Sirius?

Yes.

Did they leave myths and legends that we can trace directly to them?

I think that the only thing you might trace—not exclusively to them, since this might also have started in other places and cultures on Earth— the thing that would stand out to me would be the idea of <u>an animal as your great friend</u>. This was supported in other cultures, in other places; they would tell stories about that. They would often point to the animal and say, "Oh, we knew someone like this from another planet who talked about this and sang about that and danced this way." So the idea of having an animal as an equal was promoted by them, but it might have eventually become incorporated into the idea of pets.

Do you want to continue with the beings who carried this forward to modern times? There were several other groups who evidently lived in that same city.

I don't think so. We cannot realistically cover every civilization. You will need to pick the ones that appeal to you or that you think the readers would be interested in.

Here are two pictures of standing animals. Does that relate to them?

Yes, that is the perfect example. You can see the animals as equals and the animals indicated are intended to be Earth animals. The idea is shown here that on other planets, these (what you call animals) are people of those planets. That is the artistic message.

Fig. 29. Standing animals.

Here is a photo of a solid silver cup and a gold straw [Fig. 30].

The silver cup is not theirs. The gold straw, I think, might be theirs. This would be considered a whimsical item, like a toy.

Here are animals that have birdlike heads. They are crude, so that's from a later time, right?

This is from a later time.

We have many examples, then. Is there any significance to this man with the strange spiral [Fig. 32]? Does it represent something he's wearing?

The spiral goes down the body and continues into the garment. I think this is meant to symbolize the spiral of life. Later on one might find this symbol pictured in a different way. If one were to see the back of that garment, one would see that pattern continuing as such. This is, I believe, demonstrating the spiral of life.

Comment on this standing animal [Fig. 33], which is in all the archaeological books. Is that one of theirs?

I'll have to use the spectacles. [Looks closely.] This is theirs, yes. You can tell by the fine detail. Here we have a being standing up. This would demonstrate almost exactly a being from another planet whom they had met. This is an attempt to demonstrate that what are considered animals on this planet are in fact simply people on other planets.

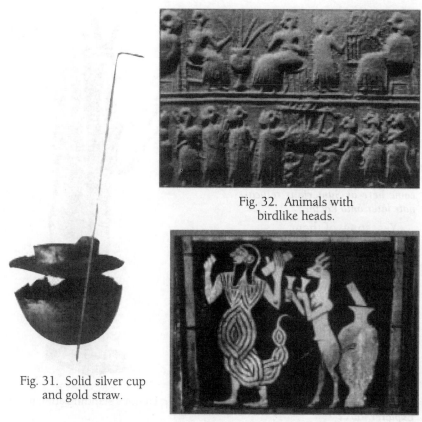

Fig. 32. Animals with birdlike heads.

Fig. 31. Solid silver cup and gold straw.

Fig. 33. Man with a strange spiral.

I might encourage your artists of today who have continued this tradition to keep it up.

It is especially important that children are shown such images, because it is in a child's nature to dream of animals who walk about this way, since children might have memories of such planets. It is most important to remember that just because one sees someone walking on four legs does not mean that they do not have great wisdom, even if they cannot speak your language.

You will meet many people in life who do not speak your language. If it is a four-legged being, it is just like any person who does not speak your language. But look at their eyes—they will demonstrate the same feelings you do.

Ah, here's one more [Fig. 35]. I haven't shown you this one, but I know it is the same thing. They are standing up, and they have personalities.

Here is another on the bottom, with the animals standing [Fig. 36].

The bottom [Fig. 36] is their work, yes. The top one [Fig. 35] is not their work. This was added to it, perhaps; the bottom is their work, but not the top. One can tell by the delicacy, the fine work rather than the coarse work.

Reincarnation on Earth

Did any of the souls who decided to come here as Sumerians reincarnate later onto Earth?

Yes, some of them.

Are those the archaeologists who found this site?

No. Some of the souls were very interested in Earth life and have really joined the Earth's reincarnational cycle. Some of them have had five lives on Earth since then, which is a lot for their people.

Would they then become part of the Explorer Race?

No. They would enjoy Earth life, they would become an Earth person, but they would not be

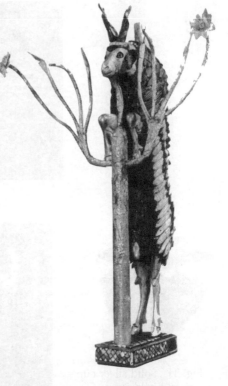

Fig. 34. Famous standing animal.

Fig. 35. More standing animals.

part of the Explorer Race. They would maintain a connection to their culture.

They were conscious of this?

No, they would not be conscious of this. At the end of their natural cycle, they would return to their home planet and have their ceremony there, but they would not be a portion of the <u>Explorer Race</u>. <u>These are Earth people</u>, yet they are only visiting. I do not think you have an instrument that can discern these people, though.

Fig. 36. Authentic standing animals.

Did any of them do anything that got into our history books?

No, which isn't surprising. If you are just visiting, you don't want to make waves. Even if you are not conscious of just visiting, you are going to be driven somewhat by a soul that wishes you to be one of the crowd. If you are tethered, connected to Sirius even unconsciously and if you were a leader on Earth, you might turn the civilization in some way it wouldn't otherwise have turned. So you are going to be very careful to be anonymous.

11

Nazca Lines Radiate Enthusiasm for Life

Speaks of Many Truths and Zoosh
August 24, 1998

All right. This is Speaks of Many Truths. Greetings.

Good evening. Tonight it is Nazca lines in Peru.

A Visitation from the Pleiades

The people responsible for these lines are Earth people and those they would have called space brothers and sisters. There was a visitation. The people landed from the Pleiades, found a small group of people and had a long talk. They told them that they would appreciate permission to decorate the landscape with some pictures that were intended for the children.

So of course the people, being native to the area, said, "Our children or your children?" They said, "Both," and that the future of the Earth depended on the capacity of human beings to remember things they would not learn in their own lifetimes. And since the people who the Pleiadians were speaking to were mystical people, no explanation was necessary.

Within the genetic code of all individuals and also within their capacity to function clearly, there are keys that allow the spiritual self, the physical self and the feeling self to unlock such symbols by a prompt (as they would say in school) that is not mental. To the degree that modern man and woman have been unable to understand the Nazca lines, the fault lies entirely in the mental body of modern people.

Most people who do not focus on thought as their number-one mechanism of communication have no trouble at all interpreting the Nazca lines. The lines are not so much a mystery as that they are not intended to be interpreted mentally; they are intended to have a feeling and physical response. If you show a child a bird flying in the sky, the

child will jump up and down and often flap her arms or stick her arms out or do something birdlike. The child is not unsophisticated, but is doing what is intended by that physical prompt.

The Nazca lines are intended to have that effect on people. The lines I am referring to here have to do with pictures, in some cases mystical pictures of birds and other flying creatures. In other cases, lines are drawn to connect different pictures with one another so that future mankind would understand that there was nothing random.

Fig. 37. Grandmother Spider.

If one simply draws a picture on the ground, then another picture somewhere nearby and so on, modern man has a series of massive pictographs. But if you superimpose lines that connect or go through these pictures, regardless of what time one or the other was made, you necessarily make the connection. These lines drawn through the picture (diagrams) are intended to grab your mind's attention so it will understand that there is a connection.

This was done because it was understood that in your time the mind would discount the pictures alone, because the pictures would seem very much like what is found in caves. The Pleiadians thought, "How will we intrigue modern man?" So they flew into the past, which they can do. (Anytime a ship can travel in time to cover distance, it can also travel in time.) So they went back into the past, encountered these people and asked them, very much the way you would ask anyone if they would mind your doing something in their backyard. The Pleiadians, like most natural spiritual beings, are polite. Most beings on this planet are also that way, though not necessarily most human beings.

The Message of the Nazca Lines

What we have here is a message meant for today. If you want to know how to interpret the message, it is to be interpreted in the same way the child would interpret the bird and the other designs, some of which are understandable. All are intended to be interpreted in just the way a child would do.

Think about it. When a child does that imitation of a bird, it is not just an imitation, a mockery; rather, it is a celebration of the bird. The child *is* the bird in that moment, with the same joy and happiness the bird has when it flies, and the child is united with it. You have all done these things. When the adult is conditioned by society, the adult most often feels foolish, having cut himself off from his feelings, and can no longer capture that moment of exultancy that the child feels.

The ultimate message is the feeling, recapturing the feeling of the child who imitates the bird or animal. In your time you have a condi-

Fig. 38. Bird.

Fig. 39. Flower.

Fig. 40. A fish, possibly a whale.

tioning of all societies, where only certain feelings are allowed, and then only under certain circumstances. If these feelings come up at other times, they are ignored, discounted or put down by yourself or others. Yet in the natural life, meaning one that is not restricted but responds entirely to natural impulses (and those natural impulses have everything to do with the physical makeup of your body and Mother Earth), you

Fig. 41. View of a bird located at the end of a large slope.

will almost always do exactly what is right for you in that moment, at the same time honoring what is right for others in their moments. It does not give you the right or authority to hurt, but rather it gives you the ability to know what works, and you do not even have to know what doesn't work.

If you know what works and you do that, you won't even have to consider, analyze or otherwise examine what doesn't work and why. Herein we have the complete equation. The final equation is that humankind now, in your time, is caught up in "why." This word, why, simply means "justify that to me." I grant that "why" can often be fun and adventurous, exciting and interesting, but it is also "prove it." "Why" does not accept anything at face value. Nature accepts everything at face value. You are all losing your capacity for "why."

You are losing your linear capacity and the part of your language that is based and rooted in linear time. You will not lose the language that is rooted in feelings and in the present. That will be retained, but justification and "why" are rooted in the past or the future.

If you are a deer and you need water, you can perhaps smell it, but if water is so far off that you can't smell it, you will respond to your instinct. What is the instinct? It is simply the knowing based on feelings responded to by the physical self. So here's an assignment for you out there who want to be and who are shamans; if you already are a shaman, feel free to give this as homework.

Training Your Instinct

Go out somewhere on the land where you are not going to have to worry about where you put your feet—no big anthills, no rubber hoses and no bears to worry about. Do not go on the pavement if you can help it. If you live in the city, try to find a park or an empty lot or a big yard, one with the buildings far away from each other.

Then focus into your feelings, not your thoughts, and just allow your body to walk in the directions it wishes to. You will find that you will turn left or right unexpectedly. Pay attention to where you are going. You don't have to bump into things or people. You can stop and turn around and walk in other directions. This is training for the instinct. I will give more on that some day but that's the beginning.

These Pleiadians were not just average citizens—although, even the average Pleiadian is a noble being. They were all philosophers and students of Earth religion as it has developed in your past ten thousand years. This is another reason they knew that messages have to be left in the past and that they have to be in remote places, where people are

Fig. 42. Aerial photo showing a large quantity and complexity of marks.

exposed to and tend to honor the mystical. They knew they would have to catch the eye of scientists and explorers, so they would have to be unusual and have special qualities. That is why the lines can only be seen clearly from the air.

These people are most profoundly interested in the way you manage to work things out. They know that the ultimate battle of wills is not between good and evil, because good and evil are words that are interpreted from culture to culture. Rather, the final battle has to do with religion.

Fig. 43. Animal feet.

The Benevolence of Your Religions

Religion was created by many different individuals to support, control and otherwise maintain some level of a predictable and potentially (if not always) benevolent society for a given group. Yet since religions tend to be structured in your time on abstract ideas and not on nature and its natural ways of being, you are destined to have clashes.

Right now, you in this part of the world are conscious of a concern over the clash between Islam and Christianity. I'm not going to include Judaism, because I want to focus on religions in this part of the world where there are many, many people. Judaism is a worthwhile religion and definitely related more to Islam than to Christianity, yet the great challenge for you all now is that even though the ideals of these religions are very similar, what men (not women) have written about these ideals is not alike.

For those who are religious scholars, take the essence of each religion and compare it to the others. The essence of each religion will have to do with God or Allah or Jehovah or Jesus. It will have to do

Fig. 44. Destructive process at Nazca figures. The white lines
running horizontally above the whale are truck tracks.

with the basic philosophy. God is not an authority. This is a false ideal
of your time, based almost exclusively on the masculine fear of being
controlled by outside forces. God is love, nurturance, acceptance,
allowance, which is expressed most easily through warm physical feelings, the foundation of the instinctual work I and Zoosh and Isis have
shared with you.

I repeat what has been said by me in the hopes that you will do the
same. What will get you through these times is to practice the benevolence of your religions and to accept, even with nervousness, how vastly
different your peoples are.

The difference is representative of cultures from different planets,
but the only unshakeable rule I know is that love binds together in the
most benevolent, gentle, nurturing way that which wishes to be together.
That is why ancient stone structures do not require much repair if the
stones desire to be together. That is why houses and other things that
do not desire to be together don't last.

It is not because of what they or you think. It is because of what they
or you *feel*. This is the message of these ancient Pleiadians. The Nazca
lines are their creation, which they have managed with their technology
from a distance away from Earth, in concert with the people who lived
near there at that time. The people came on the ship with them to make
suggestions as to how the pictures ought to look, what would prompt

people in all times to be excited and happy—and, most importantly, what would intrigue and stimulate the children. Children, especially little children, are the same in all times.

Well, the children aren't going to see them. Is that to appeal to the childish part of the human?

Why do you say that the children aren't going to see them?

They might see them in books, but they're probably not apt to fly over the area.

They will see them in books then, and children see birds fly overhead, so they don't have to see the lines. The message is really to the adult. I have said this about the children because you have all been children. Some of you can remember it, and many of you cannot. But you have all had that wonderful excitement and happiness about something and tried to imitate animals, plants, even adults, and your body will remember that feeling. When you can find it by what you do physically as an adult, you will feel it as a much greater exultancy of feeling than what you are doing as an adult would prompt you to feel. In other words, it will be bigger than the moment because you are uniting with your past as a child.

The Nazca Symbols

That's beautiful. I have a page of all the different combinations [Fig. 45]. Let me show you this one. Is there anything you can add to the significance of any of the others?

This one is obviously the monkey; this one is the phoenix; this one is the cat; this one is the bird, but the bird has its head underground.

This one is probably a lizard.

This one is the alligator, this one is Grandmother Spider and this one is the butterfly.

This one is a message to man of today. Animal feet, yes? The maze—technology, but it is like a scissors, yes? Humankind must struggle out of the maze to find his roots, the animal's legs, in eternity, the triangle.

This one here represents the heart of the human being.

This is like a synopsis of the whole thing. Did the Pleiadians come in our now time, then go back, or did they come in the past and become part of the past?

They came to your Now time. These particular Pleiadians have been studying your religions for the past ten thousand years. Then they went back in time and did these things with the people in the area . . . A moment . . . There is some interference.

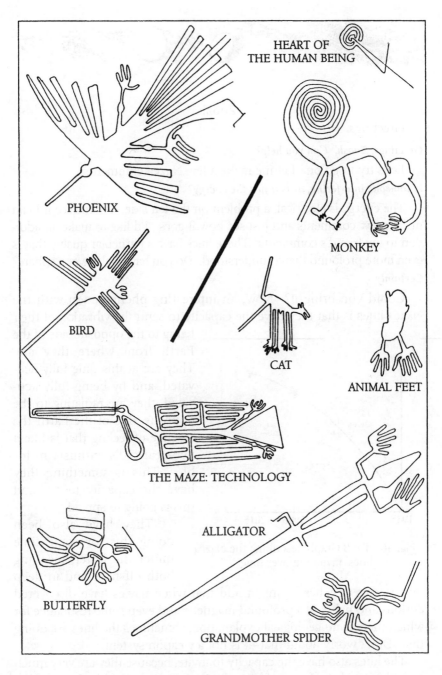

Fig. 45. Various figures.

Zoosh

Greetings.

Greetings, Zoosh. Can you help?

Let's try to go on. Let me make a few Nazca comments.

Is someone interfering, or is it just the energy?

The energy is electrical, a problem on the left side. Let me see if I can make a few comments and just see how it goes. I'd like to make an addition to my friend's comments. These lines have a particular quality that is even more profound than is understood. Do you have a globe or a sphere?

Certainly.

Could you bring it? Now, an interesting phenomenon with the Nazca lines is that they have the capacity to send the vibration of their being to the opposite side of the Earth from where they are. They are at this time fully activated, and by being fully activated, they are radiating to the opposite side of the Earth the essence of feeling that is like a two-year-old's enthusiasm for life. This is something they have the capacity to do, and this is going to spread.

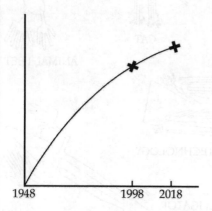

Fig. 46. 1998 Graph describing the Nazca lines' invitation over time.

They have also been doing this for some time under the water, meaning both offshore and in deep underwater trenches. I might add that when navies have discovered curious anomalies of a profound magnetic and even sonic resonance for which there is no geological explanation, sometimes the lines are doing this. Don't worry about that—it is not a weapon system.

The lines also have the capacity to invite, because they are very much geared toward the joyous feeling level of a two-year-old who is at the time just starting to explore his world, walking about long enough so he

is not falling down every five seconds. The lines have been inviting profoundly spiritual and insightful souls to come to Earth to be born. They
have been doing this for about the past fifty years, although the zenith
has not yet been reached.

This is our graph [draws], the invitation and the strength of the invitation. Here's the location on the chart. It started . . . this represents a time
fifty years ago.

1948?

Yes. This is the strength of the broadcast. It hasn't peaked. The peak
will occur . . . you really need a moving picture for this, but it started out
like this and it's picked up the pace and it's continuing to accelerate.
This mark will be reached in about twenty years.

2018.

Yes, 2018. This is ongoing. We have, then, these lines that are performing a function as well as the subtle function that Speaks of Many
Truths mentioned, which is, of course, their primary intention. I
wanted to mention that as well. It is a hopeful sign, and I feel that
fully. Now let me give you a percentage. As of today, fully 40 percent
of the world's babies born now have this capacity that the lines are
attempting to encourage. In twenty years, 100 percent of the babies
will have it.

Breaking this down into male and female, of that 40 percent of the
babies who have it now, fully 75 percent are girls. In the beginning it
was 100 percent, but it has reduced itself now to 75 percent. Of course,
conversely, the masculine ratio has risen to 25 percent, and twenty years
hence it will be 100 percent of all babies, both boys and girls. This is
why we have been seeing, especially for the past 50 years, a profound
increase of spiritual things by women.

What caused the lines to be activated?

We know that 1948 was just a few years after World War II, and
tensions were rising again for what would soon be the Korean War,
to say nothing of other skirmishes around the world. There was some
concern then that World War III could come up and be devastating.
That's when the lines were activated by Pleiadians in the sky over
Peru.

It was done because there was a serious concern that the coming
generations would be blinded by propaganda. This propaganda did
not come from the warriors themselves, who know what war is about,
but from those who glorify war and sometimes even the civilians back
home who are not told the real truth about what war is really about.

How are the Nazca lines created? They are basically dark rocks moved off of the white soil underneath?

There was some indentation in the land, at least initially. The mechanics have almost nothing to do with the actual appearance of the lines, but with the polarization of the matter in and around the lines. Even ten feet to either side of a line, the material is polarized, though to a lesser degree than the center of the line.

Would you feel anything if you walked on it?

Yes. Even today, after all these years, a sensitive person or any spiritual person can feel it. If you walked near those lines, you would feel something.

And that would activate something in you, then?

Not necessarily. Proximity is not the activator. You don't have to go to Peru to have the experience. However, I will say that the civilization of Peru, with its geography and, to some extent, its geomancy, has long been a favorite place for the Pleiadians. Some of the more isolated civilizations have for many years, including up to relatively modern times, managed to maintain a strong and firm association with the Pleiadians, so there has been a supportive energy on Earth for the Pleiadians' good works.

We have to stop now. Good night.

Good night. Thank you.

12

Easter Island Statues: A Gift for the Future

Speaks of Many Truths
August 26, 1998

I cannot give you a possible timetable for the statues on Easter Island. They were not placed there for human beings, but for those beings who are inheriting third-dimensional Earth. If you were to look at those beings the way they looked on that former planet of Sirius, you would see that they looked very much like those statues on Easter Island.

Although they will not look exactly that way on third-dimensional Earth, they will remember that appearance, and they will be making those shapes. They will carve them out of wood

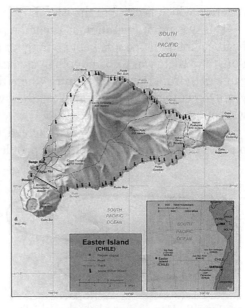

Fig. 47. Map showing how the vehicle came to Earth.

and stone. They will do what artists have done over the years, and when they begin exploring the Earth (which will not be for a long time yet), someday they'll discover that island and those statues, and they will have a great revelation. That island isn't for you; the statues on the island mark the planet for them.

The statues themselves function as a navigating device so that those beings who came from the negative planet of Sirius could find their way to this planet, originally from Sirius. Those who placed them there and who revealed these statues to islanders who used to live there told the islanders that it would someday be a beacon that would attract long-suffering people so that they could come to this planet, survive and, after a time, prosper.

They were also told that it would be a way to prepare the planet to serve more easily the needs of all people from Sirius, including the so-called animals who originate from Sirius—dolphins and so on. The project was set about in this way.

The Migration to Easter Island

The island people had come originally from many different places. They felt pulled to go there in primitive boats. Some of them hitched a ride, as you say, on ships from other planets that dropped them off there. But they found the place. Some of them were attracted from South America, which is close to the island.

This was not a migration as nomadic peoples do; it was a calling, a heart calling. The people kept coming for a time from different civilizations, and there was a cosmopolitan civilization there for a time. People came even from the north country where there was snow, taking fifteen years to get there, gradually making their way and finding the place. It was an odyssey in itself.

When they all got there, they all agreed, with their mystical traditions, on one thing: The island and the people there were not the reasons they'd come. There was something they needed to do. They had to stay alive and thrive and learn how to get along together, to find their common ground and do different work together so they would be prepared for what they were going to do. But they didn't know what that was.

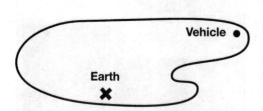

Fig. 48. Map showing how the vehicle came to Earth.

They worked on this once the population stabilized on the island. They had about thirty-five years of stability, so a generation turned over. Then a vehicle came from a great distance. It did not originate in Sirius, but it had stopped there. This vehicle came again, in a shape of the time.

[Draws.] You are here, of course (the X is larger than necessary). The vehicle originated here [marks again]. This is where you are—X marks the spot. You know where Sirius is; you can look it up on a star map.

The vehicle came because the people on their planet were told that a calamity would befall the universe that could destroy it unless they made the commitment to fly across the universe and work with people who had been invited energetically to an island in the middle of an ocean to prepare that island to welcome guests who would visit it thousands of years in the future.

These people said they would do it. Then the teachers and guides said, "And while you're on the way, since it will take a while" (even traveling in time to go that distance takes a while), "we will tell you about it." So they told them about the negative planet on Sirius. They said that the souls (on the planet that would destroy itself or blow up) could not simply move on into the light and be reincarnated. They would have been permeated with negative energy beyond that which a soul can tolerate (the negative energy was beyond 60 percent on that planet, and a soul really cannot tolerate that), but they could not escape. If the souls from that destroyed planet were not immediately transferred and welcomed to a planet that had some negative energy and was used to dealing with it, the universe could not accommodate these souls.

Universes must be able to accommodate everything that is created within them. If an anomaly like this occurs and the universe cannot accommodate something of its own creation, it gradually self-destructs, similar to the way cancer goes through a healthy body. In about the time it would take for virulent unchecked cancer to go through a healthy body (maybe five, eight or ten years), the universe would be destroyed.

The people said that they'd do it, they'd do anything. These were people on their planet who are entirely reactive to the needs of others. They lived for service.

Which is why they were chosen?

Yes, exactly. They were happy to do it. It was a great cause. They were the ones, after the thirty-five years of stability on Easter Island, who came to visit the people there. The people of the island had come from all over on the Earth; some were dark-skinned, some were lighter-skinned, some were tall, some were short and some were stocky—they looked all different ways. Some had come from as far away as Africa and some from the northern parts of Canada. There were even a couple of representatives from Greenland. All of them were getting used to living in the South Pacific–a big shift for the ice-country people.

They had developed a civilization. They had brought their seeds with them to plant crops and had more than enough food. They had the knowledge to fish and some of them, the truly mystical people, did not need to go out in boats and spear fish or fish in other ways. They could go to the shore and ask the fish to offer themselves, the ones who were ready to be consumed by the people. They would then honor the fish in that way. They were very advanced spiritual people, all of them.

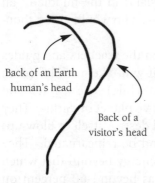

Back of an Earth human's head

Back of a visitor's head

Fig. 49 . Back of Earth human's head compared to back of visitor's head.

The Arrival of the Sirian Ship

The ship landed and everybody on the island said, "This is it. This is why we are here." The people got out of the ship, and they looked almost exactly like Earth people, only a little different. Let me show you the head shape. Pardon my poor sketch [draws].

This is the back of an Earth human's head, but this shape was the back of the visitors' heads. It comes out like that. Inside was a huge bundle of nerves that created an expanded nervous system and added to their intellect as well as their instinctual capacities and abilities of knowing and insightfulness–all these things. It was something that stuck out. Other than that they looked pretty much like human beings. Their skin was very light, almost like the color white. The color was closer to . . .

Like albinos?

No, just a little darker than that, but they had a special covering so they would not get burned from the Sun. It was not exactly a helmet like your space explorers wear, but more like a transparent membrane that protected them from infrared and ultraviolet rays and from any foreign substances and germs they weren't used to.

So all the people came and waited. The visitors landed, you see, and waited until everybody had gathered around the ship. The ship was glowing, so of course the people thought it was hot. They stood back at quite a distance, but then they nominated one of their number. The person walked up and got close to the ship, but there was no radiated heat and so he very carefully reached out and touched one of the landing feet that had come down. It just glowed light, but it wasn't hot.

Then he went back to where the people could see him and motioned for the people to come closer, that it was safe. All the people came very close to the ship then, and the ship simply glowed for a few hours. Then, when the Sun came up (they waited for the Sun to come up), a door opened and a ramp was lowered. The people backed away but were not frightened, because they knew that this was why they were there, at last.

People then came out of the ship. Maybe twelve people came out onto the land, and they could speak every language that existed in the universe and understand it, too—including emanated feelings without the spoken word. They could converse with the animals and plants and with the conscious minds of the people there. They could also converse with the people's unconscious minds, their souls and their feelings—everything. They could create total communion between everybody there, and they came out and did this [gestures].

Arms in the air like a V, palms forward.

This is not really meant to be a V; it's like a group greeting. When you open your hands like this, it has come to mean over the years (it didn't used to) coming in peace. "See, there is nothing in my hands, no weapons. I come in peace." It has come to mean this. Now when you see people do this, you know that's where it originally came from.

They came off the ship and waved like that. It did not mean victory or peace, just that they came in peace. So they got out and formed a complete circle, facing outward. All the people gathered around them in a circle, and they began to communicate to the people in the language they had developed as a common language, and simultaneously in the native tongue for those older ones who remembered it, and also to their hearts, their feelings, their souls, everything.

They all sat down and talked about who they were and where they were from, where they had been and why they were here. This took two or three hours. Then afterward, even though they knew the people were from this distant planet, the people all came up and said who they were and where they were from and why they were there. All the while people brought food and drink so that everyone was comforted.

The flight crew (not serving members of the instructional party) came out bringing special food, so everybody had things to eat and drink while all this was going on. These talks went on for about eighteen hours. People went to sleep and woke up and finished talking. Everybody knew everybody else at the end.

A Cooperative Effort: Carving the Statues for the Negative Sirians

This is a summation of what they said: "We need your help because we cannot do this ourselves. If we build something here on this island, future generations will feel it to be foreign and strange, but if you make it, you are people of the Earth. Future generations will just consider it to be an enigma, an oddity, and enigmas are good for generations on Earth, human beings. Human beings will need enigmas," they said, "unexplained mysteries, because human beings will develop in the future" (meaning you now) "the use of the mind and forget the use of their senses.

"The mind must have things it cannot solve for certain, meaning things that the mind cannot be sure it has solved. If the mind can understand everything, then the people will get bored and destroy themselves. The mind can only remain excited and interested if there are mysteries. That is why these people" (they were talking about you) "must have mysteries. So it will serve them in that way, but it is not meant for them. It is meant for these other people who will come from Sirius."

They said to them, "There is much rock on this island" (there used to be a lot of rock) "and we need to have you carve this exact appearance." Then they brought out very beautiful stones, many of them. They brought out twelve examples of beautifully carved stone that looked like the beings who are on Easter Island.

They had carved them before they got to Earth. The material looked like a cross between ivory and white marble, but it was very light. At the top it had a little loop and a little cord made of a material like silk. They said, "We would like everybody, if you want, to wear these things, but we have only twelve of them, so you can all take turns." The people agreed, and then the visitors said that they needed to have the islanders carve these things themselves.

"We will help you in any way we can, but if we carve them, the figures will feel foreign. So we will support you. It will take many years, perhaps as much as a generation and a half, but when you are done, some of the things will need to be buried and some will need to be exposed. When you are done, you can all go back to where you came from or go live on another island somewhere. But it would be good if you would then leave. We will help you go wherever you need to. We will stay with you and support you this whole time, and if you are working hard, we will help you with shelter. If you need anything done, we will do it for you."

So the people said, "We are happy for your help, but we can take care of ourselves. Even so, we are happy for your help and your company." So they set about doing it, and it took about forty-five years for the people to carve these things. They didn't have to move the stone. The people from the long way off could move things, float them around and so on. They could ask which stone wanted to do what; then they would remove pieces of stone and people would carve it.

The visitors removed the stone and prepared the block to be carved. Then the people of the Earth had to carve it. They would move it and plant it in the Earth, lay it on the surface or stand it up. Originally, some of them stood up, but in time they fell over. That's how it got to be that way. When this was complete, the visitors asked the people if they were going to go home, or did they all want to move to another island. The people said, "Some of us want to go home. Will you take us there?"

The visitors said, "Yes, we will take you back to your native lands." The people said, "Some of us want to move to another island," and the visitors replied, "We will be happy to take you there." Others said that they would like to stay there and live out the rest of their days. The ones who wanted to stay there were old people who didn't have any family left. The visitors said, "We would be happy to stay with you if you like and provide for your needs." The old ones said, "We would like that very much."

Before the visitors left, they had a big ceremony and went around and blessed all the statues, touching them with the little white carved ones they had brought. Everybody who returned to different places got one of these little carvings, but they were not made of a material that would last forever. The material did not come from this planet, and when it fell apart, it would just turn back into light. They didn't want to impregnate the soil with anything foreign, so as it was handled over the years, it would turn back into light. After about a thousand years it was all gone, including the cord that held it around people's necks—no evidence, you understand. After they had taken all the people to where they'd wanted to go, the ship came back and stayed with the old ones and kept them company until they had all passed over. Then they checked the island to see if everything was okay and went home.

Were they immortal or just long-lived?

They were long-lived beings. I think their life span (in terms of Earth years, by your measurement now), depending on their job, was maybe thirty-five hundred to seven thousand years. They are philosophers and teachers; they live longer. As you know, philosophers or teachers might think something when they are children, but when they are middle-aged or old, they think something else entirely. So the longer life for philosophers and teachers gives them more time to pass on their knowledge.

Some people believe that Easter Island was one of the high places of Lemuria before it sank. Is that true?

No. Sorry, this is not my understanding. I recognize that there is a special energy there and many people feel it, but that energy has to do with what was done there. I know that some people say there is an ET base there. There was one for a while, but it is no longer active. It has been inactive for about twelve hundred years, but it is well underground, offshore a little ways.

Did they know that the planet in Sirius was going to blow up that long ago, or did somebody go back from our present time to those people?

The teachers of those people on the other side of the universe told them. They said that this would happen. These people who came were not Explorer Race people, you understand, but they had their knowledge and they had their mission. Things are told in a sequence to different people according to what their knowledge and their mission is.

No one went to the future to see what was going to happen. It's just that they were told, according to their timing and service, what they needed to do.

Who told their teachers?

Whoever tells teachers. Who tells the teachers of the teachers? Et cetera, back, back, back, back . . .

Yes, who?

When you find out, you will no longer have curiosity. Think about that for a moment. Can you imagine having no curiosity?

Would I get out of bed?

What you said was very profound. Why get out of bed if there is nothing to find out? This is why you are not told how far back it goes and who tells you. This is why even the most advanced beings—and I have seen them and met them and interacted with them from a distance—even they do not want to know where it originates, because they feel that if they know that, life will lose some of its meaning.

I've discovered that the more advanced beings become, the more stable they are in terms of their connection to curiosity and the adventures of the mind and heart, and the more reluctant they are to understand at all.

Well, that helps. Thank you. So within the past thousand years or so, various islanders have lived on Easter Island. They have cut the trees down. Those were other people who came to the island, right?

That's right. People came and saw what an amazing place this is. They felt the energy, that this must be a place of the gods, and

Fig. 50. Birdman carved on the rocks.

decided to live there for a time. But usually no one could stay there very long, because the place is meant for these other people. Therefore, no matter how long the people wanted to stay there, they would feel uncomfortable after a while, and they'd know it was time to move on.

It wasn't compatible. Let me show you some other pictures related to Easter Island.

Sometimes the people who cut down the trees weren't even the islanders. They'd come by on water-going ships and cut down the trees for this or that reason.

These bird men were carved in the cliffs [Fig. 50]. Was that done at another time?

Yes.

And the language on what are called the Rongo tablets [Fig. 51]? Was that from the original people or people who came later?

I cannot see this, but I'm pretty sure that this has come from Africa. I'm pretty sure that this has a Tahitian connection.

Which would be people who came later and tried to live there?

Yes.

What were the red hats put on top of the statues [Fig. 52]?

Fig. 51. A Rongo tablet.

Fig. 52. Easter Island statue with red hat.

Fig. 53. A 1786 drawing of Easter Island statues with hats.

Red hats? Show me.

Well, this one isn't in color, but it looks like that.

This is meant for people of South America. It was understood that they would be the first to discover the place, for obvious reasons—it is close. This was to honor them. It was understood that such a hat would come to be part of the garb, the clothing, in that southern part, so they thought, "We will honor them." But they are not on all of them. They were not on all of the statues, were they?

Oh, here's one [Fig. 53]. Here's one on top in 1786. Someone went there and drew a picture of one of these. This is when they were still standing.

This is not a picture of the way they looked; the picture is highly stylized. Only a few of those hats were on them originally. It's not really that important.

The Negative Sirians on 3.0 Earth

Let's talk about the negative Sirians. They are at 3.0 dimension. Where are we now—3.48 or so?

Right now you are at 3.479.

Almost back to 3.48. They couldn't see us now even though we are in the same location. The vibrational distance is that far?

Sensitive people can see them a little bit at night. They are not very sensitive yet, so they can't see you. You Earth humans are more sensitive than they are. You would have to be about 3.04 or 3.05 at the most (an extreme) for them to see you, but you can still catch them a little. Sensitive people usually do not see them in their entirety at night. Sometimes you might have a dream, but I am talking about seeing with your eyes. When you see with your eyes, you might see a portion of them that looks like a piece of a shadow at night. It makes no sense and you would normally dismiss it, but it is enough to catch your eye.

Please explain how we can be at 3.479 dimension and the Sirians are at 3.0 on the same Earth.

Picture a thermometer or a carpenter's ruler. The ruler of a machinist has very tiny lines that divide an inch.

Like into thousandths?

Thousandths, that's right; dimensions go past the scale of inches. Let's just say the first ten dimensions . . . every single increment along the way is a dimension. There is 3.01, 3.02, every one of these things; Earth is there. Dimensions are thought to be third dimension, then fourth dimension and so on, but there are dimensions between them. If there weren't, a being who can travel between dimensions would have no way of doing so. You cannot just travel in a light tunnel or step through a membrane.

Let's say you're traveling from one place on Earth to another. If there is no portion of Earth in that place, you would step out into space somewhere. You would be somewhere, but you wouldn't know where. Earth is in all those places and exists in minute dimensions, which means that you can go out to 3.0001. There's a dimension there and even further than that. I gave you that as an example.

So the Easter Island that we can see and travel to is at 3.479 dimension then, as we are?

That's what you see, that's right. Years ago people saw Easter Island at 3.0 because that's where you were. Now you're almost at 3.48 and you see Easter Island as it appears to you from there. There are some beings now from the negative planet Sirius on Earth. They might be close to some Explorer Race beings, but you don't see them. You might trip over one another if you were in the same dimension, but since you are not, you just go right past one another without seeing one another.

So they are all over the planet, not in one isolated place?

That's right. They are all over the planet. Some of them are living in colder places because they like the cold. Some of them are in warmer places, who like that. They were allowed to go to places where they would feel most comfortable and compatible.

So even when we are at 4.0 and the Sirians move up to wherever they are going and then we go to 5.0, Earth will maintain this multitude of dimensional bodies?

Yes, because different people have to experience different things. Even when the so-called negative Sirians are done with Earth, there will be other beings who will come, for their own reasons, to do their thing. Maybe they won't be negative at all. Maybe they will just be exploring the different dimensions.

Maybe they will try to restore Earth. You look around your planet today and say, "Oh my, so much pollution. Earth is so wounded," and "This is terrible! How are people at 3.0 dimension of Earth going to survive?" Well, they are used to a certain amount of suffering, and if you throw them into something that is all positive, they can't deal with that. That's been covered in previous books [*Shining the Light* series, books 1-6, Light Technology Publishing].

But here you have a situation. Earth right now is very polluted at, say, 3.48, and at some point you, the Explorer Race, are not going to be here anymore. Then that part of Earth, 3.48, gets to rest. Maybe it rests for a million years and nobody lives in 3.48 for that time while it rebuilds itself. Perhaps people come and live at 3.15; maybe they live in 3.17. But nobody lives at 3.48 or anyplace where it is polluted or destroyed or where Earth needs to repair itself. If there are fractions of a dimension that are fine, then the people will live there.

Anyone can go back and reincarnate at any time period, right?

Yes, you can reincarnate in time if you wish—people do it all the time. If you want certain conditions and you need to learn certain lessons . . . maybe you need to learn about horses. You would have to come to a certain time period because by the year 2500, there aren't going to be many horses on this planet, at least not as you know them. No horses pulling plows, none of that. Horses will be wild, so you won't know horses as a beast of burden. They will just be like grasshoppers; you wouldn't think of putting them to work. They are who they are and you are happy to see them, then you go on about your business. It will be like that.

They don't ride them the way we ride horses now?

No, you would not do that. When was the last time you heard of a wild horse that galloped in from the prairie, nudged a person and wanted him to get on its back? Horses do not choose this. Humans choose this. A horse runs its own life. It does not want to be ridden, but it might choose a human being as a friend.

There have been some great friendships with horses who were ridden, though.

Yes, but it was a top-down friendship, meaning hierarchical—humankind in charge and the horse as the humble servant, which is not an equal relationship. In an equal relationship you look at a horse or a grasshopper and say, "Beautiful being." You don't say, "Beast of burden."

How many years from now will the 3.0 beings discover Easter Island?

They are on a different timeline, not years. Their years would be close to being measured on the lunar calendar, not months as you know them. The lunar calendar is, by the way, the normal calendar. It is the most accurate. The calendar you are using now is not very accurate.

Fig. 54. Easter Island statue.

Based on the lunar calendar, how long?

Based on the lunar calendar, the beings would discover Easter Island in about twelve hundred or fifteen hundred lunar-calendar years. Right now they are not exploring. They are just settling and discovering and surviving and trying to re-create their civilization in a more benevolent way. Yes, some of them are still breathing a sigh of relief, "We're out of that place, thank heavens." They don't say "thank heavens," but something like that.

Did they look like this statue [Fig. 53]?

Yes, they looked very much like that, but the jaw line is not quite as exaggerated. It was a little more round. A certain amount of artistic license has gone into this, but basically they are short and kind of squatty-looking.

This is something done by somebody else?

This is different, but it is very beautiful. It is an actual picture of someone.

But a later being, not one we're concerned with?

Not having to do with these beings.

What about the people who carved the statues?

This, I think, was brought from some other place.

By one of those beings?

I believe it came from Africa. Lots of sophisticated, intelligent, educated people were in Africa years ago. As a place in general, Africa stands for higher wisdom.

And soon it will be allowed to be that again?

Yes. It must be allowed that the people redevelop their own wisdom. We'll see.

That's pretty much it for Easter Island, then. It's very simple; it's not an enigma at all when you know what it is, right?

No, it's not so enigmatic. It's still beautiful, though, and it has been very influential in the arts.

13

Shamanic Exercise to Release Anger

Speaks of Many Truths
August 29, 1998

The *Explorer Race* books are intriguing the interest of many. Many people will write stories; some will be loosely based on this and some will be in entertainments you see and hear about. Other beings who act in such a way as this [channeling] will perhaps be inspired to channel further details. With all these books, we are attempting to place a cornerstone of a structure—not just another foundation block, but an actual cornerstone—upon which other foundation blocks will be laid, not all of which come from what we do together. They might come from other people, and that is actually desirable. In this way it is more likely that the wisdom will be added to the general pool of knowledge available to all people.

When we weren't taping you mentioned the way you lived in your society and how you dealt with releasing a disagreeable conversation. Can you explain that again?

Yes, thank you. In my time, should there be an exchange of anger between individuals—especially for people such as myself, the mystical people of the time (or even a medicine person, but I think of myself as a mystical person because I do not have all the wisdom of all the plants in terms of how they can be used for the people, and medicine people are almost always women)—or a disagreement or an argument, when both parties are done they must step off onto the land, creating some distance between each other, and find a spot on the land where they feel welcome even though they would feel somewhat wounded because of the harsh words.

Then you touch the part of your body where you feel discomfort. Many people will feel tightness or discomfort in the chest or the stomach area. What do you call this?

Everything across the midsection.

Yes. Others would feel a tension in the head and so on. You would put your hand, or both hands if necessary, in the area where you feel the discomfort. You would ask benevolent beings or beings of the golden white light to come and take these discomforts to places where they need to be, where they can be resolved, and remove them from your body. You would stand or, if you are infirm at least for the moment, you would sit or lie down if necessary, and the beings would come. I have never known them not to come.

Let's say you do nothing. These discomforts—even just one argument and certainly many—would lead to premature death. In my time, discomforts that are ignored get more and more uncomfortable. One cannot go down to the medical clinic and see the friendly doctor or the person who dispenses pills or liquids in bottles at your friendly store. You must maintain your sacred connection to all beings, so if something within you is uncomfortable (the anger of the other person), then you must release it.

You do not pull it out of your body and send it back to the other person. That is an attack. You, regardless of how wise a being you are, may not have the wisdom or the heart in that moment for that person, so you ask other beings who have no conflict. They will come and take these pieces to where they need to go, giving you love and support and helping you return to balance.

Then you can go on. Both parties do this. You could say, "What about wars?" When wars came to the plains or the mountains or the valleys in my time, people like myself would, if necessary, move into a different energy. We would not participate in the war, but we would ask for different energies to come. I am being vague now because I do not wish to give or put weapons in the hands of those who would use them. I might talk to you about that someday when war is no longer an option.

So you learned this as a child. One of the things you are taught as you are growing up is how to release discomforting energy.

Yes, it is part of being taught balance. It is one of the first things a youngster is taught. It is essential, because even though youngsters who survive are, of course, strong and young and full of energy, you might not always be that way. A certain amount of conflict between youngsters even in my time is natural, if not desirable, and so they must know. Mother or father or grandmother or grandfather or brother and sister might not always be around. So even as a youngster you must know not only how to do this, but you must be encouraged to do it. So youngsters are often told that it is not only their duty to themselves and the person with whom they have been arguing, but to the land, the animals and our total way of life.

As you get older, you hear other things, other stories, and you mature, as you say. You understand your responsibilities, but when you are young, you need to be told something simple that is also true.

As a mystical person, could you see the auras of the people? As you walked through the village, could you see someone who neglected to do that and would remind them?

Yes, but I can remember only one time when I saw someone like that, and the being was not one of our people. He was a visitor and he wanted to know. He did not ask me, but he asked another one of our people, "How come the people don't come close to me? Why do they stay away?" The person who was asked said, "It would be good for you to see our medicine person, because you have some discomfort that you don't know about, and she can help you. Would you like that?" And the person said, "Oh yes, please."

So the medicine person helped the visitor come to balance and then spoke to him about our knowledge of this balance. I cannot say that everybody in our time knew this. This person was from far away, not from the peoples in my general area, but from far away, a traveler—I think maybe even from another country. He did not know of these things, so we explained. The medicine woman helped him. It took about fifteen days, and then he felt fine.

He told her afterward and he thanked her, because a backache that he'd always had went away. At the beginning of his journey he had been able to walk many, many miles, but by the time we saw him he was just traveling a few miles a day because he was in such pain. She helped him and gave him some things to do. She suggested that he do certain dances, saying, "We have people who would show you how to do things like that." When he was purified, the men took him out and showed him the dance. He did it; then he had something to do in the future to take care of such discomforts when the medicine woman was not going to be there—which, of course, she would not be.

The dance would keep him in balance. Someone explained our philosophy, then we heard his stories. After another week or two he moved on. But he was the only person I ever saw with such energy of a dark color. Usually the first color that comes is red. The second color, when the first is ignored, becomes like black. If you were to examine the color, it is really more of a dense blue, but it looks black because the colors have to be the colors that make up the normal existence of Earth. The night sky seems to be black, but it is not quite that color because there are stars, you see. So this dark color is a dense blue.

This being had a bad back because he had this energy of conflict that hadn't been released, right? That's what started it?

Yes. He had arguments and battles, and apparently during his travels, he had more and more of this with people as he went along. These discomforts tend to make an impact on your personality, and although you were once cheerful and happy and so on, you later become unhappy and begin to see everything in the worst possible way. You hear about something, and you think the worst of it rather than believing it could get better.

14

Lucy and Her Laetoli Footprints

Speaks of Many Truths
August 29, 1998

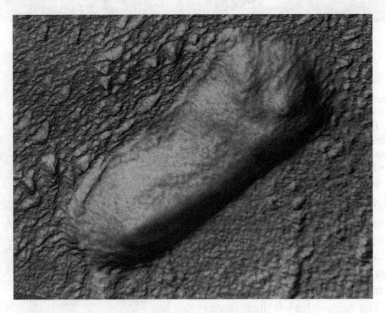

Fig. 55. Laetoli footprints.

Footprints in Africa

These are called the Laetoli footprints. They were supposedly made three and a half million years ago in Africa. [See Scientific American, *September 1998: Cover and p. 44–55]*

They are in tuff, which is a slab of rock. I'll show you a couple more on the inside. They coexist. People have created a picture in this magazine article of what they imagine could have happened.

Fig. 56. Two views of the Laetoli footprint, 1979 and 1998.

We can overlook that. Let's just look at the footprints.

What is so interesting is that there's just that one set of human footprints, but there are footprints of fifty animals, all kinds of animals. There were an amazing number of animals in the same area. This is close to where Mary Leakey was working.

When seeing such footprints, one might ask, "What could have happened to the being to make such a footprint in such a material? Was the being harmed?" (One might assume that she was harmed.) "Were there things left over?"

The being who left these footprints was not from Earth, but while that being had the capacity to withstand much heat, she was injured by exposure to this great heated material. The being herself did not get back to the ship, but she was able to assemble her children who were with her (she had about thirteen or fourteen little ones

Fig. 57. The reexcavated Laetoli trackway.

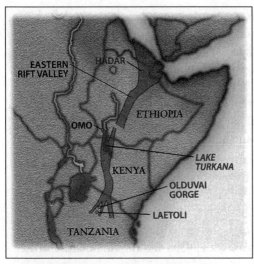

Fig. 58. Laetoli area in northern Tanzania.

with her), and all but three of them were able to get back to the ship.

The ship was not captained by a person but it was run by a machine. Therefore, she had to give the eldest child something that came from her body, which was very painful for her. She took it out of her body and inserted it into his body. Even though he was too young to receive it, it was all she could do.

Do you mean like take some skin off her hand?

No, it would look like a rod that she took out of her arm, right here [Fig. 59a]. The mark on the surface of her hand was very small, but the object itself, as it went inside her arm, was quite a bit bigger.

The tiny mark of the object was right here and the length of it ran up to about here [Fig. 59b]. She had to take it out of her body. She was in so much pain from her injuries, but still it was very difficult. The three children who were also somewhat injured helped her with the pain. She was very brave. She inserted it into her eldest, and it was painful for him too, because it is normally inserted in more benevolent circumstances—gently, with a sacred process and ceremony. Then there is no pain. But

Fig. 59a.

Fig. 59b.

it was an emergency and it had to be done, or all the children would have been stranded. The ship was run by the interactions of this device with one of their people.

So she took it out and the children made it back to the ship. Then they brought the ship over and hovered over her. Using the mechanism of the vehicle, they were able to get the other three children up into the ship where they could be treated, but her injuries were so extensive that she died. The children were terribly sad, as any children would be. The mother had taken the children to explore because their father had died. So here they were without mother or father, and they grieved for a long time.

They decided, after about three days of grieving, that they would leave their mother where she was. She had wanted to come to this planet because it was so unusual and because others of her kind had been here before. She had wanted to share it with her children. So they performed a ceremony and left her here. That's how the footprints came to be, and I believe that's also the part of the famous skull that was found.

The one called Lucy?

Yes, I believe. This is what I am being shown. She was a wonderful, brave person, and her children lived their normal life cycle of about twenty-five hundred years. They were adopted by other adults, and every year at the time of her death they would sing a song to her great courage. In time, that day became a special holiday for people of her whole culture.

Where was that? What planet?

The planet sounds like a clicking sound. It sounds like Cabongaday, suggesting that it must have been in the star system Sirius, where many of the darker-skinned people even in your time have their origin in their physical makeup, if not in their ultimate soul. I think there are remnants of this language in existence today that are being studied by some of your scholars.

When they arrived they must have been barefoot.

As you would see it, they would not be clothed, but their bodies were very sturdy. They have a hard material, like an exoskeleton; they are a human-type being, but have this very firm material—not exactly an exoskeleton on the surface, but it's a very hard material, especially on the bottoms of the feet. Very durable.

Why did they get out of the spaceship? Was the volcano erupting at that time?

You have to remember that even though they are from Sirius and they are spiritual people, they do not know everything. They do not always understand what they see.

They did not realize that it was lava?

They did not realize that it was dangerous because they had flown through and around so much of it, and it had been firm and safe to walk on. I think that she did not realize the level of danger.

15

Underground Origins of China, Japan and Egypt

Speaks of Many Truths
August 29, 1998

Origins of Asian and Other Civilizations

So this one is pretty late in time, but the people are so unusual. Angkor Wat—was that built by people who were already on the planet?

I think yes, but let me look. This is a more modern civilization. This does not have great mystery associated with it.

But the people are so unusual and they came out of nowhere. Are they related to somebody?

What is the country called today?

Cambodia.

Yes, near Thailand, is it not? I think the people originated in what is now called Thailand. They wished to speak directly to God and they utilized physical form. Not only did they make such beautiful artworks that are monuments, but also living prayers, in structure and form, to the great beings they believed in. They also developed and expanded on dances of the region. Sometimes their people would stand or take a certain pose that they believed was associated with godlike beings. They would stand in that pose not only to honor that being, but the feelings they would have in their hearts were intended to be felt by the godlike being. If that being was satisfied with the beauty and the demonstration of devotion by the person standing in a certain way, the people's needs would be served. This is what I'm being told.

What about the Eskimos? Did they come from somewhere else?

Yes, as a people. In their original migrations they came from what is now called Siberia, so their culture relates to the Siberian culture. Then there was some connection with other beings. That is why the Siberian people and the Inuit people do not look exactly the same. But I think this is known, so there is no great mystery here.

What about the Chinese? Supposedly their civilization was started by sixteen immortals from within the Earth.

This story is not a casual story. Most of the Asian civilizations began as a result of beings living inside the Earth in ancient civilizations communicating with surface dwellers who were not human beings. The beings would come up from inside the Earth and talk to plants or animals or parts of Mother Earth's body—on the surface, but not deep down below, in the hollow areas or cave areas. The surface civilization was created as a response to a need of the plants and animals to be in reaction and to assist or perhaps respond to, let's say, a growing society.

Plants do not need to teach one another. They do, but they do not have a need for it. Animals do not need to teach one another, although they do. But they all know that human beings have a need to learn. So the plants and animals said, "Do you have people who could come to the surface whom we could teach, whether it is by what they learn from us or by consuming us, in which case our knowledge will turn into their bodies and they will dream our knowledge?"

So the Inner Earth dwellers said, "Let us consider this for a time." They went down below Earth, and after a while they asked other underground civilizations, "Would you care to have anybody live on the surface?" There was a civilization under the surface where the people were from a star system (known as Ganymede in your time). They were like human beings, but they were much stronger and more durable. They said that some of their number would be happy to start a civilization on the Earth's surface.

Then the wise one said they would have to make a sacrifice to do this. The people said, "What is that?" The wise one said, "You cannot be quite so strong to live on the surface, because the lessons of the human beings to follow—not your own lessons—will have to do with requiring the assistance of all beings because those human beings will not be sturdy enough and strong enough to resist all discomfort."

So the people from Ganymede thought about that for a time. They again asked their people, who would be prepared to do this. They had about forty-five volunteers, all of them young, of course. (The young are always more adventurous.) The parents said, "Well, we are prepared to let them go to the surface, but you must let us visit them so that it is not such a terrible loss for us."

And the wise ones said, "Yes, in their lifetime and in their next generation's lifetime, you are allowed to visit, but when the third generation comes along, you must let them go their own way."

The people went to the surface, and they looked very much like the Chinese people of today. That's how that started. That is not just myth, because myth is a word used in your time that means the wisdom of others that is questionable to us. So I don't like to use that term, "myth." Also, it is a way of dishonoring the wisdom of others. I wanted to put that in the text, because it is very important that the words the intellectual community uses (sometimes unintentionally on their part) are very insulting to other cultures. Anyone who has studied other cultures as an intellectual or an anthropologist, for instance, knows that if you are dealing with people who are insulted by the way you act with them, you won't find out much about them, will you?

No. All right, where is Ganymede?

It is a star system. You can find it.

Why were they under the Earth?

As an outpost. Very often, on Ganymede and other places, the surface of planets was never lived on. In this way they honor the surface of the planet, saying, "Whoever lives on the surface has learned how to live in complete harmony with all other surface life." The people from Ganymede could not live in complete harmony. They would create some matter that came out of their bodies. They would consume matter, and the matter that came out of their bodies would change the surface of the Earth—whereas the matter that comes from the bodies of the plants and animals is in complete harmony with all other beings.

So they do not live on the surface. This is typical, I might add. It is not always the way, but it is very typical to many planets. Many civilizations do not have surface places of residence, although they may have some buildings that are placed in areas where they do no damage. Those buildings are only for schools or government functions—greeting and visiting with people from other planets and so on. But the people live underground and process all the matter that comes from their bodies into something that does not harm the planet underground. It is all done with honor and respect. That's why they live underground.

All right, so one group from Ganymede is the progenitor of the Chinese people, then.

Well, with the assistance of the wise ones, of course.

Who were the wise ones?

The wise ones were another underground civilization that could go to the center of the Earth and up to the surface. I think they are sometimes called the Founders. They do not come to the surface, but sometimes they will allow pictures that represent who and what the individual beings most care about: This one cares about love, and this one cares about truth. They will allow the people to draw a picture of what they look like, but they don't really look like that.

It is better not to draw a picture of what they really look like, because then you will be attached to that image of that being as being the best example of the quality or characteristic you are trying to emulate or be like. You want those qualities and characteristics to be pictured with beings who look like you so that you can believe you can have those qualities and characteristics. But if the people look completely different, you would say, "I can never achieve love, so why even try?" or "I don't look like that person."

That's why people of such wisdom encourage people to make pictures that represent what each individual cared most about, not what they were in charge of but what they cared most about. They would nurture and support truth or wisdom in other beings and would encourage them to draw a picture of someone who looked like them. Then they could add other symbols. That's how they would do it. If they were concerned that a civilization such as a surface civilization would draw pictures of them as they actually looked, then they would appear to those people either looking something like them or, more often, looking just like a ball of light. That way the people would feel free to describe them in the way that was most acceptable in their culture, such as in your Bible: "In the beginning there was the light and only the light." Well, they weren't talking about the daylight.

What were they talking about?

A being. They were talking about someone in that book. In that book they were talking about, from their point of view, the Creator. That's what that means.

So the Founders encouraged the ones from Ganymede to start the Chinese culture.

Then they asked other volunteers to start the Japanese culture. The Japanese culture is a little different. The people look a little different—

not a lot, but there is a difference.

I thought there was a connection to the Zetas.

Well, this is what I am being told and it's how I am telling you. There may be a soul connection to the Zetas, but needless to say, the Japanese people do not look like the Zetas. The connection with the Zetas, if there is one, would be along the soul line and not physical. Now, what was your question?

Another underground civilization was encouraged by the Founders to start the Japanese people?

Yes, the Japanese people were founded by another group of beings from Ganymede who looked a little different. Sometimes it is hard for Western people to tell the difference, but it is very easy for the Japanese or the Chinese people.

So there is historically a connection between their origins?

Yes, the origin is from the same underground civilization from Ganymede.

There's a moon of Jupiter called Ganymede.

I do not know about that. There is a galaxy named Ganymede. That's where they are from, not from a small body.

Somehow that word got into our language.

The Origin of the Egyptian People

The people of Egypt also started from the underground wise ones. The Egyptian people, as they began, had a slightly different brain. They were intended to have a special capacity in the beginning, and I think that some of this has survived. I move my finger.

Finger on forehead between eyebrows two-thirds up to the top of the hair.

This is a special place for Egyptian people. It allows them on certain occasions (especially when you begin to move past 3.50) to take over the navigational task that third-dimensional Earth will not be able to perform at 3.50 because that is the midpoint. At the midpoint, third-dimensional Earth is taking care of only 3 to 3.49, and fourth-dimensional Earth from 3.51 to 4.0. But 3.50 is one of your challenges as creators in training.

There are human beings who must be able to take over and navigate Earth, not only dimensionally, but also take care of Earth's spin and her relationship or orbit to other planets. They do not have to think it, but they need to have the capacity to think and do this. They will have to do it for the whole planet both while they are asleep and while they are awake.

That time, when you come to it, is why the Egyptian people are very important. So make sure you encourage them, make sure they are happy, because you can't make it into the fourth dimension without them. That time is when the activation of this part of their brains will start, all those who have at least 30 percent Egyptian blood. Don't try to figure out how to do this if you are not responsible for it. You will get sleepy at your normal times, but those's who are responsible will probably sleep longer and need naps. (If you work at the university, you will have to take a nap, so make sure everybody knows so that you don't fall asleep on your computer.)

This is the arrangement: Their minds will go into an altered state. They will be able to do what they do on a daily basis and the average person will see no difference, but those who are very sensitive will be able to tell that there is a temporary third hemisphere of the brain of the Egyptian people that comes forward but doesn't go from side to side. This temporary hemisphere would be seen as light or, to the very sensitive person, look like another brain lobe coming forward, but it will be in light only. It will not leave a permanent mark on their bodies. At 3.50, it will take over the duties of Mother Earth, and the people in Egypt have been prepared for this great responsibility that is vital to your survival.

Do they know it consciously?

Some of them might, but I reveal it to the world at this time so that you will know their great importance and honor them.

Is that the only civilization to do this, or are they in cooperation with others?

They are the ones. Other civilizations may have other responsibilities, that is possible, but this responsibility is only for the Egyptian people. Their brains have been altered in such a way as to accommodate this capacity without interfering in their day-to-day lives.

How long will this last?

As long as you are in 3.50, whether it is a day, a week, a year, a hundred years.

There's no fixed time?

There has never been a fixed time or any digital way to measure it. It is as long as it is.

Go back to the beginning. The Egyptians came from an underground civilization.

Not unlike the Chinese people, the wise ones came to the surface, but they were not uninvited by the plants and the animals. They came to the surface and looked around for volunteers, but there weren't many people on the surface then, so they went back down and asked for volunteers. There were a few—not many, but enough.

Some of them were from this group and some from that, not all from the same group. The different groups got together and put together about sixty people, who made a symbol. Please understand, this symbol is supposed to be an equilateral triangle [draws]; it's pretty close. This is supposed to be the crescent moon [draws]. This is their symbol, then.

The triangle and the crescent.

Now the symbol has come to be more. In your time this has been added [draws], the circle above the apex of the triangle. In the past hundred years it has become their symbol.

The people who volunteered went to the surface with admonitions similar to those given to the Ganymede people who went on to form the basis of the now Chinese culture, and when the Egyptian people went to the surface, they were given a great many teachings. They were given this teaching because they were intended to do something important.

Fig. 60. The triangle and crescent symbol created by the volunteer group from the underground who went on to form the basis of Egyptian culture.

When they died in their natural cycle, their bodies were intended to naturally decompose and become part of the soil. It was intended that after death their bodies be placed on a pier—not a pyre, as they call it in India, but something higher than that, not dissimilar from what some native peoples did in this country, about five feet high. The body would be placed there, perhaps with special objects from the life of the person; then it would decompose gradually. A ceremonial circle would then be walked around—one way three circles, then the other way three circles. Then the animals would not come to eat the body, and the body would gradually decompose into the soil. These original sixty were told to do this. All the teachings given to them would in this way go into the soil and be there in the land for the day that would come when the Egyptian people would once again have this wisdom and be able to freely give it to all the peoples of this universe.

The Egyptian people were intended to have a great responsibility, which is why even to this day, the Egyptian people sometimes feel overwhelmed more than other people—not because they do not have the capacity, but because so much wisdom has been placed in storage for their culture and so much is needed from them. Because of this extra brain-lobe activity stored to be ready when it is needed, they have some capacities that are more easily overwhelmed. That is why they need to be supported, nurtured and helped if they ask for it from other cultures, so they do not have to overstress themselves.

They have something else to do besides steering the planet during the 3.50?

Yes. In time all the knowledge and wisdom that the Founders contain, with a few exceptions only, will be shared by them with the universe from that place now known as Egypt. That will be the place on the planet where people will come to share knowledge and wisdom and receive that knowledge and wisdom all over the universe. They will be responsible for the broadcast from Earth of that knowledge and wisdom from the Founders to everywhere in this universe.

Many of them will do this in great universities, utilizing ceremonies and special prayers. Others (the average citizen) will do it in their sleep or at times when they are resting (you don't have to be sleeping). You can see that this culture is not only vital to your survival on Earth, but will offer a great deal to the universe at large.

Is that quite a ways off in the future?

It is a ways off, at least the sharing of the wisdom. The universe is a ways off, but not so terribly far.

But the 3.50 is very close?

Close perhaps.

What other civilizations contributed to the Egyptians?

To the Egyptians? Let me ask. There is a civilization that is pronounced "Hardé," with an accent over the "e." The Hardé people are, I think, related somehow to the Indian civilization. These people are very far away and are profound believers. All over the universe they encourage every aspect of thought, especially what you would call transcendental thought, which is thought that transforms in and of its own right as compared to the term "transcendental" as used recently by your culture. The connection on the soul level between Egypt and India is very strong.

So the first sixty beings in Egypt, because they were from another planet, were much stronger and had more capacities than the human?

Yes. Again, not unlike the Chinese or those who came to make up the Chinese culture, by the time the third generation came, they were not allowed to have contact with the underground civilizations so they could continue on and develop their own culture. The difference was that the great wisdom learned by the first generation was allowed to be passed on to the second generation, but the second generation was told that some of the wisdom was a secret and that they must take it to their grave. The third generation was told the same thing, so by the time the tenth generation came along, none of that wisdom was available anymore. But by that time they had integrated it into their own culture.

They do not interfere with generations of your time, but they were able to place this wisdom into the ground because the people's bodies would become the ground when they finished their natural cycle.

And into what they call the akashic record, which is another way it can be contacted, right?

Not by the average citizen, except in your sleep. But I feel that it is much more important that the soil contain it, because any person, whether he or she be a wise, spiritual being or a simple schoolchild, can walk on the Earth with bare feet or touch the land. Anyone can do that, so I feel that it is much more important for the soil to have it.

Where were the first sixty buried?

You mean put on those piers?

The information in the soil.

Oh, it was intended that it blow all over the area. But I can show you roughly if you have a map. If you can draw an outline of the map of Egypt, I will show you where it was originally and where it has somewhat drifted to.

It needs to be about this big. Your sketch is for context. I can make a dot and a circle, but it means nothing without your sketch. A perfect illustration is not required; general proportions are sufficient.

Here's the Nile and this is the Suez, the part that sticks out; and this is water. This is Africa and this is Egypt.

This is the north?

Yes.

This is the south? [Draws.]

Oh, it started way down in the center.

It started right here where I put a big dot.

To the left of the Nile?

It started right there and then drifted out with the winds and so on,

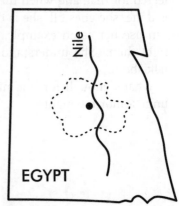

Fig. 61. Area where the first sixty Egyptians were buried.

to about there. Of course, some flowed into the river.

You don't like time references, but is there any way that we could put this in time?

If you asked me that question forty years ago, I would have said that this happened about nine thousand years ago, but you are asking me today, and I'd say that it happened about a million and a half years ago. That's why I don't answer that question too much. <u>Time has changed so much that it is almost irrelevant.</u>

But there has been a lineage of Egyptians for that long?

How long? Nine thousand or a million and a half? You can use that if you want, because it gives you some evidence to know how much time has changed. See this citizen [Moana, the cat] in front of me. She represents much of the change.

Forty years ago, this cat was alive but in another body. Forty years ago, she would trace her lineage back to great regal beings of her type of being. Now, because time has changed completely, she has been relieved of such responsibilities as those of royal blood have. Now she is more connected to the times of this side or that side, meaning other universes. (I tell your story, honey, if that's all right.) Now she is more connected to her future incarnations, so she can have more fun and doesn't have to have so much responsibility.

That's why she knows how to do spiritual things but likes to have fun, because she has mastered the spiritual and is still learning about fun—aren't you my friend?

We're going to put a picture of the cats in the book.

Please put a picture of my friend in here. She volunteers. She came over and volunteered for that, and when the story about her is done, she goes off, she is done. She says I can use her as an example. She came over right then. She understands everything we talk about.

That's enough for one night. Let's continue tomorrow night.

Fig. 62. Moana.

16

Egypt and Cats as Teachers of Humans

Speaks of Many Truths
August 30, 1998

Greetings, my friend.

The Building of the Sphinx

Now we're going to continue our talk about the Egyptians, especially the Sphinx, since my associate [Moana, the cat] is here to assist us. I would speak of why the Sphinx was built as well as who built it.

This great edifice was built to honor the teachers of man. We know that the world around us teaches us with constant physical demonstrations, and our feelings react to these things. They urge us to respond in some way.

A long time ago, when the original Egyptian people were being trained (as we discussed last night), a message was given to those people that they were to indicate in a way that could not be ignored humankind's great and available teacher, which is the cat. The dog is humankind's companion. The cat is humankind's teacher, although sometimes the cat chooses to be the companion as well.

Those original people, working with the magic they were taught and with their special abilities, left a work in progress for succeeding generations. They moved a huge block of stone to where the Sphinx now sits and began the work of carving out the cat. They purposely did not complete it, because they wanted succeeding generations to continue with their work.

Over the years and generations the cat was created. Although today you see the face of a man, it was originally the face of a cat. So ten generations were left a message, which was done magically in this way. There was a place very close to the Sphinx (as it is now called), which in the ancient language means "the mystery." I do not have the word for its explanation or translation today, but in the ancient language it means the mystery. If you were to walk one hundred human-sized paces from the front of the Sphinx with your back toward the cat's head directly away from the Sphinx, there was once a place there where a three-dimensional picture of a cat would appear—not quite the same size as the Sphinx, but it was big.

Like a hologram?

Like that, only with more colors than you have in today's technology. First it would become a bright light—that was by way of calling the people. That light would begin at night, and in that way the people's attention would be called. It would get very bright, but not so bright that people couldn't look at it if they shielded their eyes.

Then the following day the light would gradually form into the shape of the cat. This was intended, so that the cat would be thought of as a teacher—although, of course, it was assumed to be a deity. This was considered a mistake that could be tolerated. At the very least, the people would be inspired to continue the sculpture. Over ten generations, then, the sculpture was completed. Once complete, the picture of the cat in that spot no longer appeared.

So it was a model of what they were supposed to carve?

It was, and it was also to attract their attention in a magical way so that the people would *want* to carve it. There is more. A moment . . .

There was another place where sitting cats were shown (one was just sitting here a moment ago, an associate) in a posture that we all know. In a place I am seeing, perhaps a tomb, there are two figures sitting upright, one on one side and one on the other. They now look like people, but originally they looked like cats. It is now a tomb, but originally it was a temple where people could go and learn how to speak to cats and, just as important, learn how to understand what cats had to say.

Cats, like all life, have the capacity to communicate in a language that is instantly translated to your own language. You sometimes call this telepathy, but there are some people who do not speak a language, so we cannot call it that only. Calling it telepathy limits it. For those who do not speak a language, they would be hearing (if you can accept that word) the teaching in feelings or be inspired to act out certain motions, as in dances or whatever way the people communicated, so language was not necessary.

These sculptures were made, I believe, at a later date. But I thought that I would mention this because it was done in concordance with the Sphinx. The Sphinx, then, was to call the people's attention to "look and see" this mystery, and the temple would be the place to visit in order to learn.

What were the cats supposed to teach them?

No different than what they teach you today—how to understand and communicate with all life. Cats have been associated with what you do to communicate with people who do not understand you—making gestures with your eyes or your hands or your bodies. Some things are understood in this way.

My Teacher, the Mountain Lion

I will tell you a story, if I may, about a cat I knew in my life. I say "knew," because I have not seen this cat for a long time.

One day when I was walking between villages, I was camping near a river. I had built a fire and had eaten when I sensed a cat nearby (what you would call a mountain lion). The cat was not hunting me, so it made its presence known, not by making any sound or revealing any smell, but the same way the human being can make its presence known—by expanding its presence. You would say expanding the auric field—that is not quite it, but it will do.

I became aware of the cat. I wasn't sure what the cat wanted. All of a sudden I saw the cat. She came up to where I could see her eyes and then her face. I did not know what she wanted, but since she had called my attention, I knew that she was not trying to harm me.

She came within about twenty-five feet, you would say; then she looked at the fire and she looked at me. She did that one more time, making a gesture with her head. She wanted me to move the fire. Sometimes other beings do not understand that you can't just pick up the fire and move it.

What I did was take some burning logs, some sticks and so on, and I moved them over closer to the river near where I was camping. I let the rest of the fire go out and kicked some dust over it. When I had my other fire going, she got a little closer, and I could see something moving behind her. I realized that she had two kits.

I realized there was something she wanted to do. This is the place she would come at night to teach them, but I was camping there. She would teach them and play with them, and they would go to the water to drink. She tolerated my presence, which was very generous of her. I always built my fire closer to the river after that.

Well, a couple of years or so later, I was going through that area again and I built my fire right around there, in case she would come around, and she did. She was older, and she didn't have kits with her anymore. She came close and nodded to me. (They do that if they know you and respect you.) I asked her if I could do anything for her.

She looked at me and then lay down and looked up at the sky. I said, "Do you want me to tell you a story about where you come from?"

She didn't shake her head; they don't do that. Instead, she lay down again and looked up at the sky again, so I realized that she wanted me to tell her a story about where we came from, my people. I told her this story, and during this time she put her head on her front feet and listened to the story. When I was done she was very quiet, but I could tell that she wasn't sleeping because she was still sitting like that. I think maybe she was connecting to my people on the other planet.

Then I felt safe with her. She had made an effort to reach me. I went to sleep and woke up a little before dawn. She was gone, and I have not seen her since. I mention this because she was teaching me how to communicate with cats. You can expect certain gestures. All people gesture, but cats do not shake their heads, meaning no. They don't do that, but they will nod their heads, which is a greeting or an acknowledgment, something like that, but it doesn't mean yes.

Cats Teach Humans to Communicate

Now, the cat's job with human beings is to reveal new ways to communicate. This is why the cat has sworn an oath to be enigmatic. The cat will reveal to the human being things that the human being does not see. This is part of communication. Anybody who has lived with cats or been around a cat when it is visiting knows about cats suddenly looking at things. Dogs do this sometimes too, but cats do this all the time.

This tells human beings that there are other things to see, even though the human being may not see them, and this gives the human a great deal of permission to learn or at least know that such things exist. The cat is the only animal who lives with human beings who does this all the time. On the cat's home planet, they don't do this. They do this for people exclusively.

So the cat is here to help humans. That's why the cat is so important. There is also a special connection between the Egyptian people and the cat. The cat has the capacity to translate wisdom; if it cannot be heard by you (in your language), then it will act out or demonstrate something that in some way might communicate it to you. It will do something, and if you think about what it is doing, maybe it means something. So the cat communicates; that is its job.

This connection to all wisdom has very little to do with a cat's personal life, but many times in your personal life, since cats live with you (I speak to all people here), it will give you a message about your life. Other times, the cat will give you messages about everybody's life. There need to be so many cats because you need an intimate teacher, a teacher who lives with you all the time but is not one of your own kind.

You also need an intimate companion, a companion who lives with you and is not one of your own kind, such as a dog. Dog and cat do not feel comfortable with each other, though, because dog's message is always of the Earth, whereas cat's message is always about other dimensions and other planets. The cat's message is about more—the more you can be and the more you can know. The dog's message is always about now and what is. These two philosophies are still at odds with each other, even in your time. Look toward your religions and you will see, but it is not a bad thing.

When and why did the Egyptians change the face to a human?

This was done much later. I think that archaeologists have this pretty well pinned down. It was done later, when humankind became more, as you say, dense.

This density takes place when people allow themselves to be led by a religion in which they have no interaction, when there is a hierarchical religion in which the priests do it all for you. You might support the priests so they don't have to work like you do, and they can do their work for you. But when this takes place, it is easy for the people to forget their mystical roots.

Look toward your culture: Churches are torn down and other churches are built on top of them. In that way great and important messages from the past, such as the mystery known as the Sphinx, are altered in a way that damages them.

Did the first Egyptians, the first two or three generations, keep the bloodline pure and marry amongst themselves? How long was the bloodline pure?

The bloodline was pure for about forty-six generations. They were really careful at first, but coming into more modern times, you have people meeting people from other places and love blossoms, to say nothing of royalty intermarrying in order to create allies. So eventually things change.

Was it two thousand years ago or five thousand years ago?

No. I'll tell you why. Don't feel so bad. Can I explain why?

Past and Future Timelines

Right now, you are at about 3.47 dimensionally. This is a particularly precarious time because anywhere from 3.45-something to 3.52, the dimensional shift can be slowed down or speeded up according to the desires of the people. The desires, of course, have to do with your heart. In a polarized world it also has to do with the corruption of the heart, what others *want* you to desire.

If I were to name the year they show me, if I were to say that year, it roots what I am saying in a given time. But as you know, the time you are living in now is not rooted to that past. You've moved to a different timeline, and the timeline from the past—well, I can say this—goes to past dates, whereas the timeline you are on now goes to future dates. The present is not rooted in the past, but it must be rooted somewhere or it could not exist, and so it is rooted in the future. That is the timeline you are on now.

That's why I said that thing about a few thousand years or nine million years or whatever. I said numbers at random, because with a future-anchored timeline, this past timeline is like this [draws]: The past timeline is like that, a straight line. Yes?

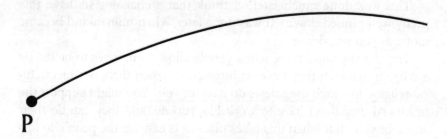

Fig. 63. The past timeline.

And that's anchored at the dot at the left.

Yes, just any past. Now, the future timeline is completely different [draws]. It is not anchored.

So we make the path as we walk?

All this jumble here, representing only about 10 percent of the actual jumble, represents choices and options that haven't been connected yet. So it is a dotted line coming to the present, and then there are all those choices, then it is solidly rooted in the future. This is why I think they are

being very firm about not
giving dates. If people
become attached to dates
from the past, they will
want to stay rooted to that
past, because people's
roots are and always have
been very important to
them. But here you are
moving through a cycle
that is usually experienced
by death—yet you are alive.

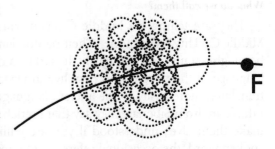

Fig. 64. The future timeline.

Speaking for the council here, we want to support your connection
to the future, which is more benevolent, whereas the connection or
the root to the past continues wars, hatreds, jealousies and so on.
This is why they would like you to dispose of any and all timelines in
any book you publish with this explanation, so that people can
understand why such things sound vague but are not really vague.

It is an encouragement, because as you feel a greater connection to
the future, each and every one of you, then you will not only engage that
future timeline more securely (because every time everyone is bound to
that it becomes more secure), but you will also let go of the old timeline,
which many people are still hanging on to because they need to feel
connected to their roots.

When you let go of the old timeline, many of the miseries and discomforts you have felt in your Now lives—plus lives that you've had
before on Earth where there was misery—will fall away from your soul
and from your Now personality. As you embrace the future timeline, the
gifts wait for you in future lives, and as this life progresses, they will be
more easily obtainable in this life.

Who is the council that is talking to you?

They sent the Founders to the Earth.

Have we ever talked to them before?

I don't think so. They say no.

Do they want to talk to us sometime?

They say, "Yes, after this book." They say, "Allowing for the details of
this book, what they have to say is not compatible at this time, but perhaps when you are done with this book, you might be able to reach
them." I will help. [See *Generating Safety*, published 2002, for a more
complete explanation of timeline.]

What do we call them?

They are telling me Middle C. You will have to refer to them as Middle C. This is their tone. Their natural language is sound, but it can be roughly translated to English. It is translated much more easily to the language of the people who now live in Uganda. I think that it is also translated more easily to the ancient language of the Inuit people, who I think are from Siberia. They say that French is also better, but they can make themselves understood if you are willing to accept, besides the spoken word, the occasional reference to a tone.

Absolutely.

It might be necessary to have the tones written out on a chart in big words that I (or Robert as the channel) can point to. They will be speaking, then they will point to different tones. The tones, you see, have to do with another level of communication and might in time be turned into some form of music by a creative person. Large printed letters like this—Middle C—on a big piece of paper. Then he can just point with a finger and so on. That's what they want to do.

The Hall of Cats

But, you know, cats really are the subject for tonight. We have not yet discussed the temple.

This was not a temple that was an exclusive temple. It was a temple for the regular people, and it mattered not what your station in life was. Just as today people in the Middle East will have their trip to Mecca, that most holy shrine, in those days people would have a trip to this temple, because this was long before that religion.

There weren't as many people then. Their station in life did not matter, and they would sometimes get there by regular transportation, but at other times, because it was far away, they would be supported in their transport. I will tell you how.

They would go to the Sphinx and sit down, one on one front foot and one on the other front foot, just two at a time, and they would be transported to the temple. If you were to look at them, you would say, "Two people sitting on the Sphinx's feet." If you were at the temple, you would see the same people there, conscious too—bilocation, in physical form.

The people would then go into the temple, always just one or two at a time. There would be several cats there, not only cats of smaller size, but big cats too, including ones with big teeth, the famous saber-toothed tigers. Every kind of cat who ever has existed on this planet would be represented there, and they would all be peaceful with one another. All different kinds, from the smallest to the largest. You would go in there and it would be like a hall of cats.

They would sometimes be sitting, sometimes standing and sometimes walking around. You would know you were safe because your body was sitting on the Sphinx's feet (to you, the cat's feet, because it was still a cat then). You would say, "But here I am," because the location gave you the feeling of total safety and comfort (that is the key to it, by the way). The humans would not be at all afraid of the cats, so you could be around them. You would not go over and pet them, but if one of them came up to you, you could. When a cat rubs against you, that's a cat petting you. The cat might come up and pet you or gently touch you. A big cat could not rub against you because you'd fall over. You'd be there just like in a social experience for a time. You would stay there at the temple for about ten days, maybe two weeks. All your needs would be taken care of. There would be food and a comfortable place to sleep.

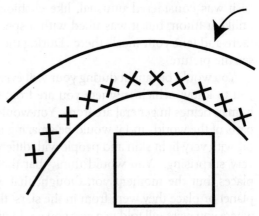

Fig. 65. Hall of cats.

Sometimes one or more cats might sleep with you or near you—not on top of you but near you. All the teaching the cats would do with you would take place in your dreamstate. When you were there, you would sleep maybe sixteen or eighteen hours a day; you would be very sleepy. The other six or eight hours a day, you would play with them. They'd go outside the temple and play gently with you, and they would sometimes show pictures of ancient civilizations of cat beings you could see on the wall. This is how it looked [draws].

The doorway was like the shape of any doorway, but wide enough for two people to walk through at once if they wanted to—that wide. You would walk in and it would look like this [draws]. This is supposed to be half a sphere. It was a gentle slope, more like that. These Xs all represent cats sitting there. Obviously, a cat can't sit on that. This thing here was the screen, but if you were to look at it, you would say it was just a flat wall that looked like some kind of shiny white stone. The shiny stone was what used to be on the Great Pyramid. It was the same kind of stone, a form of stone that is very compatible with communication of all sorts.

If cats wanted to show you something in picture while you were awake, it would sometimes show up in that space. Cats would sit on a ledge if they were not touching you—on the left side, where the ledge came to the wall of the temple, and on the right side; I think it was a very shallow shelf.

There was a flat area where you could sit or lie down to sleep at night. It was very comfortable, soft. Soft was not known then so much, so it was considered unusual, like cushioned would feel. It was not unlike a futon, but it was filled with a special sand. You would sleep there and take your meals there. During the day you might sit there and see the picture.

You would be taught during your visit everything about what cats want you to know, which is where you are from as an individual and where human beings in general are from. You would see human beings in other parts of the world, and it would be amazing to you as an individual—people with very light skin and people with different-shaped faces, which was very surprising. You would think that those people were from other places, but the moment you thought that, you would be shown what planet or place they were from in the stars, then that would be related to where you were—all told in a way you could understand. Then cats would teach you primary things—how to communicate with them while you are awake, because while you are asleep there is no problem; you communicate very easily with all life while you are asleep. That was your adventure.

At the end of the time, all the cats would be on their shelf, the place where they sat, and they would all nod to you at the same time. Then you would nod back, because that is the gesture of respect between beings, even today. Then you would back out of the temple while you were nodding and get out on the soil or the sand. Once you were about ten feet away from the door of the temple, it would disappear. You'd see only a rock wall. Then you would turn around, think of yourself back on the foot of the Sphinx, and then you would be there.

While your body was sitting on the Sphinx, your relatives or your clan or anybody who knew you would cover you up and shelter you—not that you particularly needed it, but it would be an acknowledgment of protecting your body.

They must have had a very small population then, because if only two people could go for two weeks, then that's like fifty a year.

After that, year after year it would add up. But as you say, there was a small population in the beginning, small enough to be comfortable for Mother Earth.

Is that building still standing?

The place, the temple? Yes. I can see it, but I cannot tell you where it is. They are not telling me.

Forgetting Immortality: The Time of the Mummies

For the first three generations, you said, the Egyptian people's wisdom was to go into the soil. You put a mark by the Nile River where that was [Fig. 61]. How did they get to the time of the mummies?

Much, much later.

Was that a distortion or corruption?

I wouldn't say that. It was just that as the generations got on and got further away from the mystical teachings and started following what the priest or the royalty or the people in charge would say, such things would become attractive. There were still great and wise medicine people in Egypt, and it was the Egyptian medicine people who developed these methods of preservation that are now what you call mummies. This is not something that was taught by . . .

By the Founders.

No. They had forgotten at that time that immortality of the soul is a fact, so they were trying to create immortality in their physical form, not unlike some people are trying to do today.

By freezing?

Yes, or other philosophical or spiritual means. They had forgotten that your soul does not like to look the same all the time. It would prefer to look different ways and have different things and do new exciting things. You exist immortally and you have your personality as you know yourself. You recognize your personality even beyond Earth. You know yourself. You're not something and don't remember Earth. You remember at least what is safe for you to remember. Then nothing is lost.

But when you are cut off from this knowledge, it is natural to try and live as long as you can, even after death. I understand the desire very well and I sympathize, but it is unnecessary. You die and go on and nothing stops. You don't disappear into some place of no feeling—only if you want to.

You remember what is safe for you. What does that mean?

You don't remember suffering.

In your soul body?

In your immortal personality. You don't remember that, but you do remember the wisdom. If you were to try to trace the wisdom as that self, however, you would not be able to trace it to pain because you cannot feel pain there. You might be able to see things, but you would not feel them. You are cut off from this and do not necessarily see all, because you are a feeling being and if you see terrible suffering, you will be uncomfortable—and being uncomfortable at that level will create confusions. Complications, they say.

Back to the Egyptians. What about the pharaohs? Was that part of the teaching of the first generation?

Pharaohs are much later.

They came at the same time as the mummies?

Pharaohs and mummies are pretty much the same sequence.

The Message of the Sphinx and the Wall of Mysteries Revealed

So we don't actually have a record of much of anything until the pharaohs and the mummies.

Yes, because when that happens and you have people who don't remember that they are immortal, they need to have a physical message. That's why the Sphinx is a mystery, because the huge physical message draws your attention. This must mean something, and the people who are cut off from the mystical knowledge will also, first thing, develop some kind of communication—language, numbers. It can be used to explain the mystery of life, and even if the explanation is not correct, it can represent symbolically that which is not known.

So any time we have a language, that equals separation and loss?

Not exactly equals. It is an effect of not remembering.

The Sumerians brought us a language and they remembered.

Yes, but those people may have brought the language to show you a way so that you are not miserable when you cannot explain existence.

Many ancient stone carvings go back, and a message was always left to command your attention. What is this? What does it mean? Of course, when the mystery [Sphinx] was changed to being the face of a man, a lot was lost for many years. Only in recent years have your scholars begun to say that maybe the face was a cat's, and maybe we don't have to worry so much about who the man was, but why was it a cat? Sometimes the question is more important than the answer.

I didn't realize that any archaeologists had even suspected that it had not been a human in the beginning.

Yes, there are some people advocating that there have been some changes, and show how the carving is different.

Okay then, we're not going to find any record other than the Sphinx and the bloodline. That's the only evidence we have then of the original beings?

Not quite, but it might be a time before you find it. There is a place (please excuse me if I am not saying where) near the Sphinx in Egypt. This place is where all mysteries are revealed, but the mysteries can only be revealed by people acting in concordance with a certain wall. First they form a semicircle around this spot on the wall, and then they touch the wall with their fingers. Each person—I count ten—steps away from the semicircle and touches the wall in a certain way that is connected to the . . . where is she? There she is, the cat [Moana].

You look at what cats do when they are exploring something. Yes, they smell, maybe even taste. But when they are making something their home, they touch it with their feet. This is also a way the spiders use. They touch with their feet. So people learn the ways cats touch, and they touch the wall in this way, each one in turn, going from left to right. I can tell you that because I am not revealing how the touching is or where.

After that, there is a block in the wall that slides out a little ways and reveals something. This block has a hole in the top and a hole in the bottom. Then people come over and again touch the block in cat ways. Then the block slides out a little farther and the hole is revealed. First it looks like a hole, but eventually the block slides out farther and it is like a long, rounded slot; a hole in a block, shaped like a slot but round on the ends. Then the people come over and put their hands in the block.

From the bottom.

From the bottom. Each person puts a hand (I'm not to say which hand) in the block and then steps back. Now a person appears in front of the block and teaches them everything.

First is taught the cat knowledge. The people will have some of this already. This will take time, and after the cat knowledge is taught, then people can ask about anything, anywhere—but not any *time*, only the timeline they are on so that they don't get rooted to the wrong timeline.

This is a physical place that exists in Egypt now?

Yes.

And it hasn't been used for this purpose since the time when they forgot?

Yes. After the people were trained in the temple with the cats (the Hall of Cats, as we say), this was the place they would come back to one lunar year after the training, and then they would do what I am describing, with nine other people. They would then have that knowledge available.

They already knew a lot of the cat wisdom because they had been at the temple the year before.

Yes, this is not something so terribly exclusive. Every cat has some of this knowledge. What you call spiritual cats will reveal their spirituality more than some other cats. They have much, much more and can access more.

Cat Volunteers to Teach at the Temple

Were all those representatives of the different cat species chosen? Did they volunteer? How long did they spend there?

Volunteers. They would arrive in that place and be there in the same way the other people got there, by means of bilocation. In this way their lives were not interfered with, yet they could be active in both places. Sometimes one or more of the cats might die in the other place, but the bilocated body would live on. When that cat's service was no longer needed, then the bilocated body would go through the veils as the other body did.

I'm assuming that these cats came from all over the planet. So they could bilocate from anywhere. They didn't have to go, like the humans did, to the feet on the Sphinx?

Oh no. They never went to the Sphinx. They could see it from the view of their vision, but they did not have to go there. These cats did not bilocate on their own. They were assisted and there were volunteers, a spirit source being of cats as cats existed on their home planet. They would come to the cat world and explain what was to be done. They would never take anyone. They would ask if anyone would like to come. One of each kind of cat was needed. Eventually, someone would volunteer and then this being would do the bilocation and transport. The physical cat would still remain to live out its life without being less in any way. It would live out its life as it had before, but the bilocated body would serve only a spiritual purpose.

So the cat might be there for years and years, then?

Possibly, unless other volunteers came forward or if cats with other personality traits were needed. Then the bilocated cat in the temple would be honored and would return to its physical self. If the physical self was no longer alive, then it would go on.

Does what you talked about last night—the Egyptians' protruding brain lobe in the forehead—trace back to the original first sixty beings?

The potential existed, but of course it was known that it would not be needed until modern times (your times). But only the potential was there, so previous generations did not utilize it.

Is it going to be only in the pure-blood Egyptians?

Nobody anymore is pure-blooded–almost nobody–but if you have at least 30 percent Egyptian pure blood, you will . . .

So it goes back to the original generation, then.

Other people might—if they are less than 30 percent and are still partly Egyptian—feel a little something. It won't be unpleasant; it will probably mean that you will sleep a little better, dream very pleasantly and just feel better about life. But you will not have to participate in what the 30 percent or greater bloodline people are doing.

The Great Pyramid

So almost everything we know, then—the temples, the tombs, the statues, all of that—is part of what you could call the later level of the Egyptians, the Egyptians who forgot?

Some of it, obviously. The Sphinx is part of the sacred peoples and the temple and the wall.

And the pyramids themselves? They came later?

The Great Pyramid is old.

Older than the Sphinx?

No, about the same time, but other pyramids came later.

And the Great Pyramid—we've been told it flew in like a ship. So it wasn't built by those . . .

There are lots of different stories about the Great Pyramid.

Tell me your story.

I also see it landing like a vehicle, but it seems that the pyramid beneath that one, the other diamond, was sort of grown into the Earth like a root.

From the vehicle?

Yes. It was part of rooting the object. I am not certain that the object that was landing was physical or whether it was a picture, like the cat picture that became the Sphinx. It's possible that it was this living picture, which was then built by people. They said it was built through the first seventeen generations.

The first few generations did the hard labor and moved the big stones, because they had the knowledge about how to move them and cut and form them without any great suffering. So the original and old story of slaves moving the blocks is not true.

Did the first generation come with the wisdom from their home planet but with spiritual technology? They didn't have machine technology, is that true?

Yes—and what is called natural technology. Natural technology invites the participation of anyone who wishes to participate, but no one participates without their permission. Big difference. But also everything is much, much easier then—and no big struggles.

Do you know that constellations communicate to this day with the top of the pyramid?

No. Talk about that.

Constellations themselves can communicate, like the thing that looks like the water ladle.

Oh, the Big Dipper?

Then the Seven Sisters.

That's the Pleiades.

Yes. Then the belt of the warrior.

Orion.

I think other ones, too. They communicate; the constellation itself communicates with the top of the pyramid, where some of that communication stone still exists. The constellation's apparent job is to reset the time you are on and to continue to reset it for that benevolent future-anchored time. If something happened to the Great Pyramid, they would utilize another place. That Great Pyramid is used because it closely represents, in its spiritual heart, the flexibility needed to reset all things without giving any support from the physical surroundings. All the support to reset the timeline in which you are now engaged comes from these constellations through the Great Pyramid. The Great Pyramid is like part of a navigation device, but navigating time rather than space.

Wonderful. Thank you.

17

Atox Brought Birds and the Joy of Flight

Speaks of Many Truths
August 31, 1998

All right. This is Speaks of Many Truths.

The Influence of the Race Who Flies

I'd like to talk about a civilization that was largely responsible for beings who fly on this planet. Some time ago, there was a rival of another planet. This is the name of the planet [draws]. I cannot pronounce it, but it's . . . the X is pronounced like an S, and so . . . Atoshksch.

Fig. 66. Drawing of the name of the planet Atoshksch.

They have a ship that is most unique. I have seen several, but never one like this. It looks a lot like a bird, in that it has what looks like wings and, not unlike a bird, the wings of the ship move up and down. But this motion apparently has nothing to do with the flight mechanism. It is more a way of announcing their presence, so it is, I suppose you would say, symbolic or ceremonial.

Is this planet in our galaxy or in our universe?

From your planet Earth toward the galaxy Arcturus, then about twice that distance beyond, along that line.

Still in this universe?

Yes. The ship gave off a great deal of light, but it was not a lightship per se, meaning that it was not made of light. When it landed, as I'm looking at it through my window in time, it appeared to be solid and metallic. They came here to this planet a long time ago, and the inhabitants of this ship got out. They have wings. They have feet, which do not look like bird feet, but they don't look like human feet, either. They look something like an elk hoof.

And their faces?

Very unusual. They have a long snout. But it does not appear to have the same function. A dog has a snout, but at the front of the snout is the nose. This is different. It is like an appendage of their face. It projects outward, but apparently it does not have anything to do with smell or taste.

They came out of the ship and started to fly everywhere. When they are in flight, they look not unlike big moths. They fly all over, and when they land (there are many of them), they seem to be taking measurements and are exploring the plants and meeting the animals.

This is their gesture. They have arms; the wings are not their arms. They have, not exactly fingers, but one digit that is like a finger.

Articulated.

Articulated, yes. And they have an opposing . . .

A thumb.

Like a thumb, but it is webbed. The other fingers, however many there are (three or four or maybe more), are joined in some way—heavily webbed, I believe. When they approach you or any creature, no matter what it is, this is what they

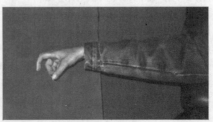

Fig. 67. Atoshksch gesture
of greeting.

Fig. 67a. Side view.

do. This is their gesture [Fig. 67, 67a].

They make this gesture to every creature they meet—large or small, it makes no difference; plants also. The gesture includes everything you would say in a greeting. It includes the logical responses to questions such as, "Where are you from?" or "What are you like?" It includes all these things, but it also includes something else. It includes in this greeting (which says all about them) the question, "Would you like to fly?"

These beings go all over the universe spreading flight, because they believe in its value. Of course, many of the forms of life say, "No, thank you," or "We are happy being what we are." But there are those beings who say that this is something they might like and ask how it can be done.

Then the beings say, "Since you might like this, we will show you how it can be done, either for you, which would be more difficult, or for your offspring or even for some of your offspring." Usually they would say, "Well, perhaps it would be as well for one or maybe two of my offspring, just to see."

This is really how birds got started. It's also how many of the flying little beings got started, the flying insects. It's also how butterflies and moths and other beautiful beings got started. They went all over the planet, and a lot of beings said, "No, thank you," or "Good to meet you," and "Let's talk again." About 3 percent of the beings were interested in this.

Of course, they brought some species with them, but before they released these species, they asked every being they met (they were very polite) . . . of course, they didn't have time to meet everybody, but they tried to ask at least one species of every kind of life that was here (they considered a rock and a river life), asking everything very politely . . . They asked all these life forms who were here not only if they would like to fly, but they would also say, "We have brought some flying beings. Would it be all right with you if we release them?" Then they would show them (not in person). They would say that this is what they look like and this is what they feel like in their feeling bodies and so on. Most gave their permission to release the flying beings, but because these beings were so diplomatic, if anyone objected to the release of any type of flying being, they would not release them. They wanted the beings they released to feel totally welcome, that's why. There was an objection to one of the beings, so they did not release that being. The being was not too disappointed; it was released somewhere else.

This is how flight got started. It was also how the inspiration toward flight got started. This was a very long time ago, and all those life forms were flying for all those years and being born and dying, putting the material energy of flight into the material of Mother Earth's body so

that by the time human beings came here and were born, so much of
the particles of Earth were permeated with the joy of flight that human
beings want to fly every time they see a bird, even if no one says anything to them.

It is not ordinarily natural for human beings to want to fly. It is natural because you are made up of Earth, and to a significantly lesser
degree because you fly in some spirit forms. The beings were here in
terms of experiential years, as Zoosh says, for about five hundred years.
In that time none of the team (as they would call themselves on the
ship) died and none were born.

As far as I am able to see, in terms of Earth years, they are practically
immortal from Earth's point of view. Their life span, according to Earth
time then, which is longer than Earth time now, was from twenty-five
thousand to thirty-five thousand years.

Can you date the arrival of these flying beings?

You know, I would prefer not saying, because when we put a time on
it, we limit it. They don't want me to say when. None of the civilizations
want me to say when. When I gave you the time before, it was because
you wanted it, but they don't want me to say when.

Was it before there were any human beings on the planet?

Yes.

And there were no birds? Weren't birds part of what was originally created?

Think about it for a moment. This is your home, but before you moved
in with your furniture and your personal possessions, it was a house.
Now it is a home. One thing follows the other. Earth was not created
in six days. One thing followed the other. Do you understand?

*Not exactly, but when we introduced animals I thought that some of them flew,
some of them crawled, some of them walked and some swam.*

No. "Animals" is a word that means lesser beings. That's what its
real meaning is, regardless of its dictionary meaning. "Animal" means
lesser being. Do you want an example? When a human being behaves
badly, sometimes they say that he's acting like an animal. What does
that tell you? So human beings, especially in the Western world,
although not in the places in the West where people are still living by
Earth ways, tend to create themselves at the top of some political pyramid. I say political because politics depends on where you stand. The
animals who surround you are your equals.

I would rather say that beings are asked or invited or simply welcomed to Earth, and these beings didn't all come at the same time.
Sometimes even later, when beings would visit from other galaxies, they

would bring their favorite beings because they thought it was a gift, that the planet would be gifted with these beings because these beings were so wonderful.

Think about human beings for a moment. Some human beings love dogs. Others love horses, cats, birds, what-have-you. The idea of giving a being as a gift is done with love: "Oh, here is a puppy." The idea of human beings bringing puppies to other planets would seem like you were gifting them. Other civilizations elsewhere are the same. Of course, a certain amount of carefulness is built in with them, but some of them are more spontaneous and do not always consider the consequences. Certainly the introduction of the flea and the mosquito . . . my best guess is that the consequences were not truly considered, but that's another story.

Well, we probably needed a catalyst, you know.

Well, there is an actual reason for them. When you are in total balance with your body, with all your physical and spiritual bodies and in complete harmony with the world around you . . .

They don't bother you.

That's right. So it is by way of a test.

Are you starting sort of at the beginning, then?

I'm starting at the beginning and then moving to the next point. I'll keep moving to the next point until we get up to the . . .

. . . civilizations that left some stones that are still relatively intact.

Yes. I'm talking about a civilization, and even though they were here for only five hundred years, they were an important civilization because of what they did. They would bring any species they found to their ship and ask them to come onboard. They wouldn't take them in a cage, they would ask them onboard. Some would ride with these beings and fly with them to the ship; others would want to be carried gently. Some were water beings, so the ship had to send a remote unit out to them. The vehicle was, in its own right, flight incarnate; just being on this ship would tend to support flight. They would put them inside something shaped like a pyramid, but a pyramid that has equal sides. The smaller the being, the smaller the pyramid; he larger the being, the bigger the pyramid. They did not put little beings in a big pyramid because they felt it wouldn't be polite. So they each had their own size and they felt honored. They also spread diplomacy while they were here by these actions.

The pyramid simply intensified the attitude of the ship. There is a modern flight term called attitude and we know that there is a mood in people also called "attitude." They would use these terms interchangeably. I am now learning, as I say this to you, that the ship was alive. Being in the pyramid would intensify the life of the ship, and then the beings brought aboard the ship would either grow wings or some of their offspring would have wings. That's how birds and butterflies and so on got started.

They were here for five hundred years, and every day they would send out their numbers to sing about the beauties of flight. They actually created certain musical harmonies in the wind. A bird can fly at a certain altitude—you will sometimes see this done by birds with bigger wings, such as ravens and eagles—and at this altitude, there is a special sound, really a song, that only winged ones can hear. But if you were to ask pilots in your time about the music of flight, you might be surprised (if they felt safe to speak frankly) that perhaps one out of three would say they understood. There is a sound you can hear in the wind only if you love flight.

Some pilots will know what this means, and at other times it will be people [hang gliders] who like to fly through the air with these big wings strapped to their bodies. So these beings added that song, through constant repetition, to the wind's repertoire of sounds. Is that not beautiful?

They were here a short time (for them), and when they left there were many winged ones all over the planet. They had gone through many generations, so the wings were stabilized. They waited for generations until flight was stabilized, and they taught the philosophy of flight to all who cared to listen. It wasn't exactly like religion; from their point of view, it was more like a revelation of the secrets of the unknown.

They would say, for instance, that flight allows a being to see his or her world from a different perspective at any moment. Sometimes you are walking along, maybe up the side of a hill, and the ground looks one way. Then when you get to the top, you look down and sometimes get inspirations, because it has literally changed your point of view. One of the reasons people climb mountains is because they are often inspired when they get up high. That is part of their philosophy.

So these beings taught this. They were here for just that short time, then they spent about a year flying around the planet and saying good-bye. Even though everybody could have said good-bye in a week, they went around and said good-bye to everyone they had ever met, one by one. They are really special. When they left they did not go back to their planet but continued on. As far as I can see, to this day they are still traveling, although they have changed over generations.

Were they the whole of their species, the population that came to this planet?

No.

Many, many ships travel around?

Many ships, but not a huge amount. As far as I can see, maybe forty ships.

How many beings were in the ship that came to Earth?

I should think no more than eighty.

And the beings they released? Do they have names we would recognize now?

One is a bat. They said the bat was very good. Of course, they needed beings who would be food for bats, so they released other little winged ones. Some of the animals are no longer here. They were here but went away. There used to be something that looked like a pig, but it flew. It was about half the size of the wild pig. But it was different; it had long, silky hair. If you touched it, it would feel very smooth. They were very smart, but because they wanted to be where they could do other things, they kept asking to be taken to some other place. Eventually a ship came to take them away, so they are gone now. I don't think they left any bones behind. That's the only name that is forthcoming.

Did they ever come back, or is that the only time they were here?

That was it. I don't know if they will come back. I hope so. They are special.

There are pictures of bird people in various rock art and in tombs. Was it these beings they were drawing pictures of?

I don't think so. These beings did not look like human beings with wings. You would say that they looked like animals with wings, but bigger than human beings.

They stood upright?

They stood upright, but they didn't have to. They could also walk on four legs, but they didn't walk much. They could stand, not unlike the way a butterfly lands on the ground and sits on its many legs but doesn't walk much.

When they did stand, they had a head, two arms and two legs, but they didn't look humanoid?

Well, I'm saying arms, but someone else might say, "They don't look like arms to me." So I'm going to call them arms, but they are the same length as their legs.

Is there anything else they want to say about themselves?

I think they want to keep themselves a little secret, but I felt it was important to talk about them because of the significant impact of their visit.

Did we have dinosaurs at that time? There's this scientific flurry about birds hav-

ing come from dinosaurs.

I wanted to say that the winged creature they associate with the dinosaurs was started by them, but it wasn't, so I don't know about them. I asked, but they did not take credit for it.

One more thing: Did the planet look similar to the way it does now?

Well, the landmasses were much more green and lush.

Were the landmasses in the same position, or was all of the land in one area?

No. I've heard this business about the land moving, and I admit that the land does not look quite the same as it does now; it's possible that it was different.

Were the continents closer together?

I'm not sure about that, but it does appear to be different. It takes a long time for land to move about, but to the land it is nothing. It is a very short time.

A different perspective.

Well, we'll ask somebody else later if, when the planet first came here, there is any reality to the theory that all the land was together.

Robert's Comments About the Bird Beings

I remember seeing the hand of the being. It had a really thick webbing and it was a dark green color. It had one digit that moved. I had the impression that there were other digits.

Three or four, he said, heavily webbed.

I had the feeling that they didn't really move apart too much.

He said connected.

Connected. Yes, that was my impression.

What about the actual being? He called them arms, but they were the same length as the legs, and they could stand on all four legs.

I got a vague look at their faces. The face is longer, like a human face, but bigger. They have a bigger head than a human being, but it has something that looks like a snout. But it's not like a dog's or any kind of animal's who has a protruding jaw. It's just like a shape that comes out.

But it looks like a big snout.

It looks like a snout, but it also looks like a beak that doesn't open, though it's not pointed. It's rounded at the end, very unusual-looking. The hand is dark green, but once it gets above the wrist or so there is some kind of brown fur. The face is furred too. The whole body is furred except for the wings, which have colors that remind me of an owl's, except they are more brown and not that much white.

Do they look like feathery beings?

They look feathery to me. I'm not sure if it is feathers, but they look like it, meaning that there are some parts of the wing that look denser than other parts. It reminds me a bit of lace. The part that doesn't look dense is lighter, more like beige, and it looks like lace.

And if they stuck their arms out, how much farther beyond their arms would their wings go?

Quite a ways.

Twice as far?

Maybe half again as far. When their wings are spread out all the way, it's the way a moth looks, except they are a little more swept back. A moth looks triangular when it is resting its wings, but their wings seem to taper back.

If you see them on four legs, they don't look like any animals you have ever seen?

No, because when they are sitting on four legs, their wings are folded against their body, not unlike a bird's. I don't see any tail feathers, so I am not clear about how they maintain their balance. When I saw them flying, I didn't see their wings flapping. It might just be that they soar. I see them lean forward, and I'm not clear what those wings do.

We can ask Speaks of Many Truths next time just to get a little clearer. He said that their ship was alive, and its wings moved up and down like this, but that didn't have anything to do with the flight of the beings.

I can see the wings. They seem to be articulated only at the points where they meet the ship's body. They aren't moving like a bird's wings, but seem almost hinged.

Do they look similar to the wings of the beings themselves?

No. That suggests that the beings themselves, where they come from, either didn't build it or that there is somebody else that ship is patterned after. Maybe they are simply the winged ones who happen to be occupying it, but no, the ship's wings do not look the same. They look thinner and remind me a bit of bat wings, but just in shape. They are very thick as they come out from the ship.

Is the rest of the ship round? Or a bird shape?

It seems to be sort of oval or diamond-shaped, sort of a rounded diamond, front to back.

Not unlike the body of the bird?

Yes, not unlike the body of a bird. When I first saw it, I wanted to say *Star Trek,* but it's nothing like that ship at all. It looks more like a modern artist's representation of a winged being. That's how it struck me. It could easily sit in the Museum of Modern Art and be accepted.

It's interesting: I saw it flying in space giving off all this white light tinged with gold, but when it was sitting on the Earth, I saw something that looked gray and dull, like the color of steel.

He said metallic.

Yes, but it's not shiny. It's dull.

That's what he said, too. It gave off light, but it wasn't made of light. It wasn't a lightship. That's good, though; it adds to what he said.

18

Origin of the Snowmen/Sasquatch

Speaks of Many Truths
August 31, 1998

L et's see what else is worthy of mention. I think it might be interesting to talk about the ice races. There was a civilization that had some capacity to travel, but they did not use vehicles. I think they used some kind of portals around the Earth, but they lived only where there was ice. They never lived anyplace where ice and snow did not exist. I see them moving about. They remind me a little bit of the people who live on the ice today in your time, but they look a little different.

You mean Eskimos?

Yes, as you say. I think they have a different name for themselves.

The Inuits.

Yes. I think that this civilization is before their people, but it is remarkably similar, except for the usage of portals to travel from place to place. They also seem to have the ability to access the inside of the Earth. Even though they had the ability, they were not comfortable in temperatures that would melt snow. They were physically comfortable only in freezing temperatures and below, so they didn't go inside the Earth unless they absolutely had to. At such times, the civilizations inside the Earth would send what they called a cold chamber for them so that they could stay in their normal way of being.

These people, from what I can tell, did not come directly from another planet. They seem to have been seeded by the beings who live underground. As much as I can tell, the underground beings are living in an almost tropical climate. For a time they had what they considered some anomalies of birth—babies would be born who would practically die of the heat. They were frantic for a time until they discovered that the babies needed cold.

That's when they invented the cold chamber. They didn't know how long this would go on, so they established a surface group. The people who lived underground could go to the surface, but they needed to wear proper garments. They went to the surface and took care of their babies. They looked after them until they became adults and could start their own society.

For a long time they had these babies; they didn't try and stop it. They didn't consider it a disease. Some strangeness, yes, an anomaly, but they didn't consider it a problem. After about a thousand years, that stopped, and they didn't have babies like that anymore. But by that time there were already about four thousand or so on the surface. That was the beginning of that civilization.

Now, their philosophy and methods all had to do with the underground civilization, but adapted to the cold environment. Because they were so supported by the cold, they did not need shelter except during an ice storm or a strong wind. Even then they would only need something to keep the wind from blowing on them. They didn't need to be inside a house; they slept outside. They also seemed to have had a capacity, not unlike the people underground, to live off minimal nutrients. When they went from one place to another through the portals, within the portals would be the foods they needed from underground—fruits and vegetables. Because they could not grow fruits and vegetables where they lived on the surface, they always needed to be supported by the underground people.

Those underground people were here on the planet for a long time, but I don't think they are in your time. I think they moved away for a while when you started experimenting with ultrasonic devices. This was disruptive for them. They will come back, perhaps.

That civilization existed for quite a while and slowly began to evolve in such a way that, I believe, they eventually turned into the creature called the snowmen who are seen in snow places.

Like Sasquatch, you mean?

But only in cold places. There are some . . .

. . . other ones who show up in warm places?

Yes, but these beings can only be in cold places, so they are not exactly what is Sasquatch, but similar. When they originally came to the surface, they had a light coating of fur, about a quarter of an inch, but after living on the surface, the fur became longer. After a while the fur was three or four inches long and very smooth but not silky—not unlike horsehair.

So they are not related to the Eskimos? Or are the Eskimos their descendants?

I think that somehow the people of the north are not directly related to them. It is not genetic, but there is some honoring between the two societies. There is some brotherhood there, but it is a brotherhood of different species. I learn more as I speak of it, because I am not speaking from my own knowledge.

So are they still here now?

Yes, they have found some underground ice caverns, so they mostly live down there, but sometimes they come to the surface if no one is around or no one can see them. If they are picked up by a machine, they don't worry about that, because the machine or the person looking at the machine thinks it is a mistake.

"Picked up"—you mean by radar or other scanning machines for body heat?

Military machines looking for things for military purposes.

I see. So you don't want to say where on the planet they are?

They are in places that have snow and ice year-round, even places that would surprise you. They can be any place where there is snow and ice year-round. The Snowmen have adapted the portals to work only in the cold, so the portal will work only with them. They use them where there is snow year-round. It might melt a little, but they want the temperature to be pretty cold most of the time.

So how do they live? How do they get their fruits and vegetables?

In the portals. No longer do the people who live below put food in the portals, but they are still nearby and have ways of sending food to the portals. Some portals are like tunnels. You don't step into one, then step right out in the other place; sometimes you can have a space in between. It's like moving through a wide tunnel. It is usually done like that only if there is some reason to have the space, and in this case it is to provide food or anything they might need.

So what do the Snowmen do? Can you say how many there are?

I think that today there are not many more than the original number—around four thousand. They seem to have a very strong belief that it is important to maintain their numbers but not increase or decrease them. So they try to maintain the same number. I think this is mostly for ceremonial reasons.

What do they do?

They exist. I am not only going to talk about beings who make marvelous contributions; I must also talk about beings people have seen—who they are and where they are from. There is a question about them, since these beings are still with you. They are important—they are fully realized. They are simply here, and they are very advanced. They could probably go somewhere else if they felt like it, but their attitude is that they are happy here, so why go somewhere else? Fully realized means that they realize everything, that they understand everything that is part of their world, and that there are no mysteries. That's what it is to them.

Were the beings who gave them birth fully realized?

Yes.

Are they the ones we call the Founders?

No.

What dimension?

Beings like that are flexible dimensionally. They can exist in anything from the third to the ninth. They usually choose to be somewhere around the fourth or fifth, and in this way they can readily access the third if they like.

So they have to be in the third before we see them?

Yes, they like to come to the third dimension.

Because?

They like to observe other life that they associate with Earth—animals and people, peoples and machines, smells. They have a profound sense of smell. They can stand on a mountain and someone could be climbing that mountain eight thousand or nine thousand feet below, smoking a cigarette or cooking some eggs—they can smell it. They can do even more. They might be on top of a snow-capped mountain. If there is a field with flowers twelve thousand or fourteen thousand feet down, they can smell it.

Amazing. When we reach a little higher dimensional level, will we interact with them?

It's hard to say. That will be up to them. They are not social. They seem to be very happy with their own kind, and although they are not in any way hostile, they do not reach out to others, although their parent race is very welcoming of them.

You can't say when they first came, so we don't know if they have been here for a thousand years or a million years.

None of them want me to say that. I could say it, but it wouldn't be a good thing. I don't think you can understand this, but to put a time-line on it fixes your present to the past.

And we're trying to change that?

You're trying to change that. If I draw more and more lines from the past to the present, it's like throwing an anchor down and then looping the anchor chain around your time. They really have strong feelings about that. They don't want the timeline. That's why I think Zoosh resisted the timeline in the *Explorer Race* books so much—because it draped chains to the past. Someday it might be good to take that out.

19

The Electrical Beings

Speaks of Many Truths
August 31, 1998

I 'd like to talk about a very special race of beings who have had a profound effect. There are a few beings on Earth who exhibit electrical functions–fireflies, electric fish (you call them eels). I think there is also a so-called jellyfish who has an electrical capacity, and perhaps some others.

Once upon a time, as Zoosh says, there was a civilization living at the bottom of the sea. They also were living in the pyramid shape. They had a lot of interaction with the sea and its beings. They felt that someday, not in your time but about five hundred years from this time . . .

In the future?

Yes. They felt that there would be a need for natural electrical impulses in places that would not ordinarily receive them very much. When a lightning bolt hits the water, it tends to dissipate close to the surface. It doesn't go straight down to the bottom.

Because they felt that what they call pure or organic electricity would be needed, they created variations of some animals who were here and gave them electrical bodies that could produce radiations. They did this a long time ago, but in progression, and they said they would do it because there were no races of beings who would interfere with what they were doing. The project took about a thousand years, and they created about forty thousand species of electrified beings, most of which have not survived in your time, though some have. Some have proved remarkably strong. They said they would make as many as they could, and hopefully some would survive. They also created some beings you haven't met yet. I know sometimes your scientists get excited when they find beings they haven't seen before or who they have heard of or have found fossils of, but unfortunately, their way of greeting these beings is to kill them. This is definitely a sign that science has not yet found its heart.

So there are still about thirty-eight hundred of these electrically charged beings close enough to the surface of the Earth to come to the surface if necessary. If you saw them, they would look like little beings, many-leggeds or worms or something, but they have the capacity to carry an electrical charge in its purest form.

Electricity, as you know, is part of Mother Earth's body, yet even she cannot purify it as much as these creatures—the eel and all the others. They can purify the electricity, so when Mother Earth has less electricity for her use (such as in your time when you are using it), they purify what she has and it is then stronger for her.

So they are helping her. This race of beings had the idea in mind that someday, as you began to evolve toward a greater spirituality, there would need to be a means of placing in the water and air a pure form of electricity that would create a different charge in the water and the air. That charge in the water would dissipate into the air and would support life on a more spiritual plane, because electricity is felt more gently as you are more spiritual.

What now gives you a shock and feels uncomfortable would just feel like a minor, comfortable buzzing when you are more adapted to benevolent physicality. This injection of what I want to call orgone electricity will be very benevolent for Earth and all of her beings, and will greatly support your benevolence in the future (I want to say your coming of age, but perhaps that is too dramatic).

Those beings have left their housing unit. That pyramid is still there, but it cannot be seen by anyone who is not ready to see it. It cannot be detected unless it wishes to be, but it can be seen and detected by anyone whom it wishes to welcome. It has on occasion welcomed human beings.

But the people inside are far, far away. I think they may not be from this universe, because I do not see them anywhere in this universe. They left their pyramid shelter because it has something to do with keeping the Earth healthy; I think it works with the core of her being, physically speaking. This pyramid is the one they lived in and worked in under the water. I'm calling it a pyramid even though it is not shaped like your five-sided pyramid in Egypt. It is four-sided [tetrahedron] and triangular.

What is the nature or circumstance that's going to help us hold the benevolent energy for five hundred years or so? We'll need that energy then.

Yes, you'll need it, because by that time there will be lots of changes in third-, fourth- and fifth-dimensional Earth. You may or may not all be here anymore as the Explorer Race. It is not known yet how fast you will accelerate. Maybe you will be here for only a short time, maybe for a long time. It is not a path that is chosen yet. So regardless of which path you take in terms of time, in five hundred years of experiential time, based on your now time, that energy will be needed to greet the beings who are here on third-, fourth- and fifth-dimensional Earth and support them to be always benevolent for themselves and others.

I speak of these things now because it is all right for you to know. Some of these things are known and suspected and imagined by others, but I want to speak of these civilizations now because of their profound contributions to your existence today, or because they had something to do with what you've heard of or what you know about. But I will not speak of all the civilizations. Some of them came and went and had little or no impact. You'll never meet them, so why talk about them?

20

The Andromedan Origin of Stone Medicine Wheels

Speaks of Many Truths and Grandfather Many Voices
September 14, 1998

S tone circles are found all over the world. There are places where these circles were originally constructed but are no longer apparent, either because the stone was used later for something else—which is true in 30 percent of the cases—or, in the case of deserts, sands have sometimes covered them up.

Stone Circles and the Ritual of Calling

These circles were originally created to perform the ritual of calling. Calling has to do with many things. Sometimes it is for the needs of the people in the area. Sometimes it is calling home if people know they are from elsewhere. Sometimes it is to reflect a calling, meaning that sometimes you may have been told as a people that you are on a planet (Earth, in this case) for a cause. At some point, when you have fulfilled your reason to be there, you will be called by others to return home.

There are times when tribal peoples (in this case "tribal" refers to peoples all over the world), according to their culture and wisdom, feel they have fulfilled their purpose here. They might call for those who are where they come from to get them, or they might call to their god or their creator to take them home in their bodies beyond their physical

Earth bodies. After a time they might try something else, which is what I would call reflected calling.

I'm going to show a side view of a circle, so it will be elongated [draws]. In a normal calling, the energy goes out and up and the people stand in the middle. In a normal calling, one has energy such as this. People are in the circle. The calling is to be taken elsewhere, but if one has done that for a time and one has not been called, this is what you do.

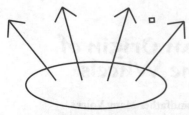

Fig. 68. Diagram showing the energy of a normal calling.

Let's say you have so many people in the circle. You do not look at the sky. You look down and you envision the stars through the planet, so the energy goes this way [draws]. It is intended that the energy go down through the planet, covering the entire energy body of Mother Earth, down to the stars where you believe your home is. You have to do this at a time of the day when you feel your home is on the opposite side of the Earth.

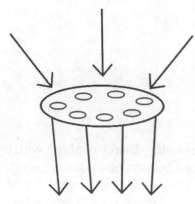

Fig. 69. Diagram showing the energy of a reflected calling.

In this case, the calling is reversed; the energy picks up energy from Earth as it goes through. She magnifies it, amplifies it, and it arrives in the consciousness of the people on your planet. The net result is that they call you.

It arrives in the consciousness of the people of the planet they are from and not this planet?

Correct. It was done in this way for a time also. It was not done simultaneously by groups of people all over the planet, because it depended whether people felt complete within their culture and their work. Of course, as time went on and modern times approached, many of these ways of calling were lost. Functions of the calling were still used to attempt to bring to the people what they needed individually or as a group or even as a clan.

One might ask how it is possible that people all over the planet should create these stone circles, even though there was clearly no communication system such as you have today. Even though mystics and visionaries could share information with mystics and visionaries in other locations on this planet, that would not be enough to create such stone circles. Some of the circles are very modest, meaning just flat stones laid on the ground and not obvious. But other circles are more profound, such as Stonehenge, which came actually after the beginning of many of these circles and other places.

We have to begin at the beginning. Who encouraged the people and why? In the beginning, as you know, there were many visitations from extraterrestrials, and the people took it for granted. Many people wanted the other-planetary visitors to come as often as possible, speak of many things, talk about their similarities and share cultures and stories and songs.

The people from other planets—the visitors, the brothers and sisters—after a while began telling people that they would not be able to come so often in the future. Everyone wanted to know why or why not. It was said that there would be changes on Earth. At first everyone was fearful. It was said by people from other planets that some of the changes would be difficult and there would be years of struggle, but that other changes would be good and would ultimately serve the purpose for their being on this planet.

So they said, "There may come a time when we will not be able to come and see you anymore, but let us recommend a way you can reach us and still talk to us. You can talk now when we are at a distance." The people and the mystics said yes.

The people said then that usually only the mystics or visionaries or shamans could hear and speak. The brothers and sisters from space said, "Yes, but we want you all to be able to hear. This is what we are going to recommend."

They said that one of the best means of communication was the stone. The planet herself is a living communicator, and her living stone body could communicate at vast distances. Many space brothers and sisters could hear communications (what you would call today "resonances") from Mother Earth, even on their home planet.

The people said, "How can we do this?"

The brothers and sisters said, "Set up some stone circles, and at first when you converse with us, each person will stand on a stone or touch a stone, then touch another stone if the stones are tall. If the stones are too far apart, put people between them and have them stand shoulder to shoulder with their arms around each other's shoulders, like this." Is this clear enough?

Both arms are stretched out on the shoulders of the persons on either side.

Yes, and the person who is closer to the rock on either side will touch the rock. These are for places where they didn't have many small stones but had big stones. Of course, some people wanted to use bigger stones because they felt that bigger would be better, but it is not like that.

The stone circles in my part of the world were not so big, and the stones were laid down flat on the ground. People could stand on them and if there was enough space between them, they would do as indicated above, then put a foot on them so that you'd have people going around in a circle.

In your time, crystal is a means of communication, and your instruments and communication devices are filled with that material. Yet, since these people were sacred people, it had to be presented to them as a sacred rite, which it was. Your people today are used to using your technology, but you would also have to be taught how to use the stone circles in order to communicate.

In the beginning, then, people would stand like that and call to brothers and sisters from space, and they could hear them. Many generations were trained, generation after generation, so that they would be heard. There would be hearing both ways, communication.

As time went on, there were wars and battles and invasions, and much of this knowledge was lost. But even in recent years it had come to be that people would stand inside the circle. They forgot about standing and touching the stones; that knowledge had been lost. So they would stand inside the circle, though it was only the mystics and visionaries, and do the calling.

The original purpose for the circles was for a unified communication device that utilized the spiritual, the physical and the instinctual energy of the people, with hearts and spirits united in this cause of communication. With the connection with the stone, everyone could hear and also see. The space brothers and sisters would sometimes want to give a picture, and sometimes the people would want to give a picture. This could go both ways. I find it interesting in your day that you still utilize a circular communication device, the old dial on the telephone that you would turn.

You might say that they used a circular dial because it was simple, but it goes deeper than that. The wisdom of the circle of communication is in the very material of Mother Earth, and your bodies are made from that material. The reason for the circle on the dial was at least 70 percent that and only 30 percent the technology. So even today you are affected by such things.

The Spherical Medicine Wheel

Is that where medicine wheels came from?

I think there may be a connection to medicine wheels. Let me check. No, medicine wheels have come from a pattern left in the ground by Andromedan ships. The pattern was placed on the ship because this ancient design has to do with balance and safety and literally the heart of God.

The medicine wheel is about different directions. It is whole and complete, the circle. It includes light, which on Earth is represented by fire. It includes warmth and heart, which is represented by the people in and around the medicine wheel and also symbolized by the warmth from the fire. The original diagram, then, had to do with ancient wisdom the Andromedan peoples shared with native peoples.

I am given the privilege to reveal more, which is that the beginnings of the medicine wheel had to do with tribal peoples who knew they were from Andromeda. When Andromedans would visit them in their ships, it was like a homecoming. They brought knowledge with them, these tribal peoples, and the contact from the ships was a family thing. I have just now been given the permission to tell this.

Could we get the story of the medicine wheels?

Let me ask the Grandfather. (Grandfather does not wish me to tell his name.) Grandfather says he will accommodate you on this project. He will speak about the origin of medicine wheels from the Andromedan perspective.

How did medicine wheels go from the Andromedan symbol to what we have today?

Let's let him begin his story. I will speak his words. Grandfather says that when the people came here from Andromeda, they did not feel comfortable with only the Earth. After a time they did feel comfortable, but in the beginning they felt that they would be more comfortable bringing some of their wisdom. They requested to do so, and their request was granted by Creator and their guides and teachers.

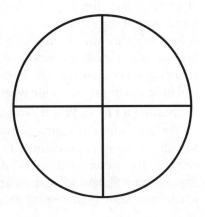

Fig. 70. Diagram of a medicine wheel.

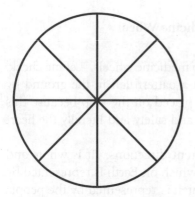

Fig. 71. Approximation of
the spherical medicine wheel.

It was, however, given only that one part of the medicine wheel be revealed. The true medicine wheel is a sphere. I cannot draw it too clearly, but I will draw what I can. One knows the medicine wheel as this, roughly. This is the medicine wheel [draws Fig. 70].

The Andromedan medicine wheel has to do not only with the inner and the outer worlds, but it also has to do with the past and the future as intended. Instead of a medicine wheel on the ground, picture a spinning sphere [draws Fig. 71]. With the spinning motion one can alter the past or the future, but only within the function of that utter and complete balance that is proclaimed by the diagram of the medicine wheel, meaning that one knows what the medicine wheel is about.

In the Andromedan sense, it has to do with beauty, with culture, with love and with the energy of life—what binds things together and nurtures them and keeps them going . . . or in a word, God. As long as the medicine wheel is fixed and on the ground, it supports and nurtures and sustains such things. But once you have that medicine wheel in a sphere and it is running two ways, like the intersection inside the sphere, it has to spin the same way the planet upon which you are is spinning.

Once you do that, it is possible to alter the past (not the present). The medicine wheel that you know now is intended to support, sustain or perhaps alter the present. But it is possible to alter the past or the future within the context of what a medicine wheel does. (Grandfather is revealing this now; I am saying his words.) Those of you who know how to utilize medicine wheels or are able to work with them for the greater good of all beings can begin to experiment gently with this original function of the medicine wheel.

Creating a Living Prayer with the Andromedan Medicine Wheel

You have all been asking, "How can we alter the past and the future so that it is more benevolent?" Because if the past is more benevolent, certainly the present will be, and if the future is more benevolent, again, the present will have to be in balance with that. This is the way: Know which way your planet spins so that when you spin this (ethereally) spherical medicine wheel, you will be able to do so in the way that honors Earth.

Now, for those of you who may have ideas to corrupt, know that even spinning it in the opposite direction won't corrupt. It won't have any effect, so it cannot be used for harm. It can only be used for good.

The great thing about this spherical medicine wheel is that you do not have to picture or structure the past. You do not even have to say that you would like this or that, because there is great responsibility in such prayers. One can so easily forget to say something, or say something in a way that later on you regret, because you think you could have said it better. Here is a system that requires no words. It only requires you to be able to envision such a thing spinning, and the balance and the nature of the wheel itself will bring about such benevolent alterations.

The most powerful way to do this is above an existing medicine wheel that has been used only for sacred purposes. For those of you who do not have such a thing available to you or do not know how to make one, then you can picture it as large or small, as you wish, but it would be best to be above the surface.

Picture for a moment what we were talking about earlier. Stand in a circle, but don't look at each other. Stand in a circle and look slightly above the tops of the heads of everybody. But begin to imagine it spinning in the center.

As if that is the axis?

As if that is the axis, yes. Wherever you are standing, and it will help if this is done over a sacred medicine wheel; it will be more powerful. If you have been unable to come to such a place or find such a place or be included in such a ceremony above a medicine wheel, then do so wherever you are. Even if you are one person and have no one else to do this with, do it. It is best if you can do it when you are outside standing on the ground. Daytime is best, because then the animals might join you in their energy. Nighttime is almost as good, but daytime is better. The night animals are more involved in the passage of spirits or the passage of wisdom. The day animals are more involved with strength, structure, or maintenance, so daytime is a stronger time for such living prayers.

Is there a particular time of month or phase of the Moon that is better than any other time?

Good question. It is best done when the Moon is full or one day before the full Moon, but not one day after. That way you have the greatest strength and support from this feminine goddess.

Is there some goddess in particular to ask for by name?

No; if you have a goddess or god who you appreciate–or any being, angelic or a great teacher–you can ask them to participate with their most benevolent and beneficial energy in the creation of this living prayer.

When you are ready to stop, stop slowly. See the sphere beginning to slow down, then come to a stop. Then gradually avert your eyes toward the ground. You may have been looking up with your eyes closed or open. It doesn't matter, but when you are done, avert your eyes toward the ground after you have seen it or pictured it coming to a complete stop. Then let it disappear on its own. Don't cause it to disappear. Just open your eyes and look at the ground; then it will disappear on its own. In this way you will be acknowledging its existence as a being. You would not have a fellow being disappear, and in this way you acknowledge the living part of your prayer.

Whether there is one or many, should they be standing on rock or within the circle of the medicine wheel?

It depends whether you can, if you have a medicine wheel that has been used only for sacred things. But if it has been damaged or not used entirely for sacred things, it is better to do it somewhere else.

If you can find that kind, do you stand on the rocks or . . . ?

You do not stand on the rocks. You stand outside the perimeter of the medicine wheel.

If there is only one person, the axis is still in front of you, you are not the axis?

Correct. You are not. It does not spin over your head; it spins above you and in front.

And there is no color involved?

You may use color if you wish, but you will probably find that the natural colors of white or gold might reveal themselves. But if there are other colors that come, do not question them. After all, some things might be in the process of transforming, and different colors might appear as you observe or as you envision it. Do not question it. If the colors are unusual or strange, do not focus on that so much. Just focus on the spinning.

Do you visualize that each individual human's past is changed in a benevolent manner?

No. You never do that. You never do anything more than visualize the spinning, only that.

You have no intent that the past be more benevolent?

You do not set an intent because of what a wheel is and what it represents–the Andromedan wheel especially, because this is what

Grandfather knows of. You do not have to set an intent. The wheel itself sets the intent. Therefore you are not required to say words or visualize or do anything. You are only urged to see it spinning. It is simpler and easier to do in this manner, and also the average person might be able to do it, not only mystics and shamans.

If done properly, the result will be that each individual who does it has a more benevolent past?

I cannot say that. It is not done for the individual per se. If you had an object in your hand that could create total balance, you might feel, while you were holding that object, more balanced than you have ever felt in your physical life. Yet if you put it down on the Earth, would not the Earth then also feel that way, and because it is touching, would not the people also feel that way?

What I am saying is that you do not ask, you just see the spinning and the object. Then you don't see it. If your life improves, so much the better. If the lives of others improve, so much the better. You might see some of it, you might hear about some of it, you might experience some of, or you might not have any of those experiences. Do it only because it is a good thing to do. It is a time-honored tradition on Andromeda today and has been changed and adapted by different cultures in beautiful ways on Earth. It is something that is good to do for its own sake.

And as far as how high the axis is, you don't visualize that. It would just be as big as it is?

Yes, for some of you it may not be much bigger than a ball you hold in your hands. For others it might be quite big. I recommend that it isn't so big that you feel overwhelmed by it. It is not good to have it so that it encompasses you or the Earth. You want it to be in front of you so that it is perhaps like the ball that goes through the hoop.

A basketball.

Or a little bigger perhaps, but not much more than that. The size makes no difference. It can be the size of the universe or the size of a pin. It works just as well either way.

So it was done then for eons and then it was lost?

It was lost. Grandfather says that I can speak only a little on this. It is still sometimes perhaps used by the wisdom people of certain tribes and cultures now here on Earth, but it was lost as a daily meditation or a daily living prayer because of the disruption of the native peoples in North America.

The First Andromedan Peoples

Can he say where on this planet the original Andromedan culture was when they first did this?

In Canada.

There is a river that goes from Calgary up to Prince Albert [the Saskatchewan River], then there is another, lower river [the South Saskatchewan] and it's on the loop of that river.

That sounds about in the area.

So that's where they first came. Were they one of the first civilizations?

They were one of the first, yes, and they shared their wisdom with others when different tribal peoples would meet, as was the case in those days. But they were one of the first peoples.

Speaks of Many Truths said earlier that the first tribal peoples came to prepare the Earth for the humans' energy. Was that their function?

No. Those peoples had already arrived, but there were not many of them. I think we could say that these first Andromedan people or tribe were the first to settle here who knew where they were from and always retained a consciousness of that, at least for the generation that started and for several generations past that. They knew who they were, and that consciousness was retained in the tribe for some time.

Some people today travel about to different countries and feel perhaps more like global citizens. They too felt more like universal citizens. They felt that they were citizens of Andromeda living on Earth, then after a generation or two that they were citizens of Earth who were also citizens of Andromeda. They were perhaps the first people who really had maintained and retained a very powerful extraterrestrial connection.

Did the medicine wheel that we know, with the animals and the directions, come much later?

It came later. It was not brought, it was adapted, if you understand the wisdom of animals. Such wisdom was united with the medicine wheel, but this came later.

By another group?

By other tribal peoples. It was a way of explaining and interpreting the medicine wheel within their own wisdom, and it is, of course, valid. It is just not the way it was originally practiced by the Andromedan people.

But there is still a sense of spinning and going out into the universe. Sun Bear said that if you could get people around the wheel who were conscious and clean and then spin it, you could go out into the cosmos.

As I said, some of this wisdom was retained or was reacquired through communications and inspirations such as this.

But there wasn't any sense in the original Andromedan wheel that you could get it spinning and travel etherically to other places?

No, but if you have observed the travel devices [UFO types invisible to most people] one sees for those who travel within a device, one will see from Andromeda and other places a clear globe with people sitting in it. This channel here [Robert] has seen that with his physical eyes, and the globe was just floating along. So for this man to speak of such things makes complete sense, and although it was not part of that original wisdom, it is wisdom that came to him.

Is there anything else that the Andromedan Grandfather would like to share?

No, he is done.

Tell him thank you very much.

If you would see him, he looks like a Native American. These garments he is wearing, his medicine shirt and other things, have to do with wisdom that he practiced when he was here on Earth.

So he had a life here on Earth. How long ago? Was he one of the first ones?

He was a second generation of the Andromedans. His parents were amongst the first generation. His parents, he said, were slow to gravitate to garments of animal skins, because they were uncomfortable with that. But his generation began to speak to the animals in such a way that the animals offered this, so they felt that when done in the most sacred and benevolent ways, it could be done. But he says that his parents would never have done so. They wore a garment that did not originate on Earth. Fortunately, it was very sturdy, because they had only what they brought with them.

They came from a technological culture and they willingly came here and lived on the Earth at a time when there was no technology?

They came, yes, but their culture was not only technological, it was profoundly spiritual. Perhaps this is how it is possible to live with technology. If you are very spiritual, you must be heart-centered, and you must know that your feelings are shared by all the beings around you, meaning that what hurts you is the same thing that hurts others, and what gives you joy gives them joy. At least you feel pain and pleasure in the same ways. If you know these things, you have heart-centered spirituality; therefore you cannot go anywhere in a vehicle that is constructed of anything other than willing particles or willing materials that desire to go with you and want to be this ship.

I believe that this is how it is possible to have heart-centered spiritual technology that, to the casual observer, would look just like a machine. But those of you who have had the privilege to be on such vehicles know the difference between, for instance, the way an automobile feels and the way it feels inside such a machine as this, just to sit in it and to approach it, a machine that is happy to be what it is, whereas the car would rather be where it was before it became a car.

Is the original group reincarnating, or does each set of souls come here only once or twice?

I think that it is the same as it is here on Earth. When they died, the original group, the parents, returned to Andromeda or elsewhere, as souls do. I believe that it works the same all over.

So there is a blood lineage, but they are different souls?

Yes.

Grandfather Many Voices
September 15, 1998

This is Grandfather Many Voices.

Welcome.

I have decided that it is all right for you to use my name.

You're the Andromedan Grandfather?

Yes. I just wanted to say that. I didn't know whether it was all right last evening of your time, but I feel now that it is.

That's wonderful. Would you talk to us again some time?

Yes. Thank you.

Thank you.

2/8/04
AA

21

Avebury, Stonehenge and Other Stone Formations

Speaks of Many Truths
September 15, 1998

This is Speaks of Many Truths. Good evening.

Oh, good evening. Welcome.

What shall we talk about tonight? Shall we continue with the stone circles?

I have pictures of a group of circles here, like Stonehenge, if you'd like to talk about any of those.

Avebury Circles Keep People Hidden

I'll speak a little bit about Avebury. Again, it had to do with the original instructions, but it started out as one circle and then became several circles. This was because the mystical people of the time in that tribe were trying to create a more powerful rhythm or signal, and they called upon a vision that was seen by one of their own. He saw into your time or close to your time. This is what he saw [draws Fig. 72]. It is, I think, nowadays recognized as a crop circle.

This is the vision this mystical person had. It was taken to mean that in order to utilize greater power (what you might call amplitude), it was necessary to use both the Sun and the Moon cycle. The crescent moon, which is how they took that shape, meant to them that they would use this circle, and they would make more than one circle within the circle.

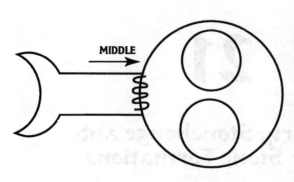

Fig. 72. Crop circle vision as seen by
mystical person at Avebury.

They would say
their prayers and do
their work both in
the daytime and the
nighttime. The vision
actually meant that
the safest time, the
time for the best work
inside the compound
circle was anytime
before that phase of
the Moon or so that
there would be the
greatest light. If the
crescent was turned the other way, it would have been any time after
that. As it turned out, they did more work than they had to do to produce results, but they succeeded.

The result was that for a long time they managed to stay undiscovered
by invaders other than the ones they could repel. Of course, the Romans
eventually found them, but before that they did not have any invaders
other than those they could repel. Although it might startle you to know
it, even that far north there were some Polynesians who were warriorlike
who came to try to settle the place. They happened to arrive at a time that
was unseasonably warm, so they thought the place might be habitable for
them. But as it got colder (and even before), the local people discovered
them and they realized that this was not a safe place for them, so they left.

In general, the workings at Avebury were useful, but you could ask,
"Why were the Romans allowed to invade?" or, "How is it that it happened?" For one thing, it was the cycle of change into the more modern age; the Roman Empire signaled the beginning of the modern age
you are living in.

Also, by that time people were beginning to use the stone circle for
personal desires, not just for the greater good of all their people. When
you do that for individual things, you are taking a chance that you might
harm somebody. One might ask to be protected, and that is all right.
But one might say, "To be protected from . . ." and then mention a name.
That is actually a misuse of the circle. These things began to happen
more often, and that drained its energy.

The circles are not only as powerful as the ceremonies done in them,
but like other places of ceremony, they build up an energy over time and

become more and more efficient. But this place was drained quickly because a few people, unbeknownst to the mystics of the time, began to use the place for their own means. That's the other reason the Romans found what is now Great Britain.

What planet did the beings there come from?

Some of them were from within the Earth and came to the surface for a time. What I am hearing is that they were of Earth.

I see. Is that what we call Celts or Druids? Was that their beginning?

I think it was. Druids came much later. I think it had more to do with the tribal peoples of Britain. What you know in your modern times of these tribal peoples is highly colored by the fact that they were described in texts. The Romans and so on described them as savages, just as your own explorers or invaders described our people [North American natives]. When one comes with a head philosophy compared to a heart philosophy, one can easily miss the culture and sophistication, and they missed it. Perhaps it was good that they did, because if they had come with a rose instead of a sword and had made friends with the people there instead of invading . . .

. . . and learned their secrets. That would have been terrible.

It would have been a very big problem, because the Roman Empire would probably still be in effect and you would not be speaking English.

Was there a circle of stones there that came from any ET culture, or was the whole pattern originated by Earth beings?

In that part of the world, it was all from the Inner Earth beings, although they, of course, had shared some knowledge with other planetary beings. The Inner Earth beings themselves are very profoundly involved. They are not here so much anymore, but they were then profoundly involved with the manner and means of mystical and cultural philosophy represented through physical expressions and acts.

They believed that the safest universal language, a language that would outlive the culture, would be physical, because physical evidence would always be of interest to civilizations that followed, such as your own when people today are fascinated by these stone circles. The Inner Earth beings felt that the best way to leave a message would be to leave a stone circle that would be sufficiently enigmatic and nonthreatening. If it had seemed complex to the Romans and if they had felt energy radiating from it, they would probably have destroyed it. Because they did not feel anything, they thought it was a curiosity, an oddity, and although they did some damage, they did not do total damage.

Did the Inner Earth beings come up and, instead of using it to call to their home planet, use it to make magic, to make their area invisible?

They did not have to do that as Inner Earth beings. They taught that to the people on the surface.

They had already gone back underground and these were now Earth people who became the British tribe?

Yes. They were taught by the Inner Earth beings the ways of such mystical circles and protection. The circles were not always used for the same thing all over the Earth, even though they all had that capacity. This shows you the versatility of such functional devices.

Sacred Symbols: The Circle and the Spiral

For example, suppose that instead of a circle, it was a square. It would not work in that shape. In your cultures, not only spiritual people but other people as well, are fascinated by the shape of the circle. This runs deep in your cultures all over the world. The circle is understood by the mystics and shamans as well as some religious leaders to have a divinity and a power of its own. The moment you take whatever you do in a circle and use it in a square, it doesn't work.

Sounds like car tires. They wouldn't go around.

And there are other things. Think of anything that is circular, not just products and devices.

Planets, orbits, star systems, amoebas, cells, protons, atoms.

So the circle is the first and the last. Do you know what that means?

It's the tiniest particle in the creation and it is the size of the creation.

Yes. It is the shape of the first form of life and also the shape of all life in its totality.

You mean if I look far enough, I'm going to find a big round circle out there that holds everything?

But you will be looking from the inside out. You see, if you could ever find the end of creation yourself, you would immediately uncreate yourself, because you cannot be in uncreation and still exist. That is why you are not allowed to find this—because you would uncreate yourself and all that you have ever done.

So I've got to watch those walls that I walk through, right?

Stick your toe through first. If you pull back and the toe is gone, then go another way.

Thanks. Back to Avebury—is the power gone now?

It is very powerful. I will reveal only a little bit, because there are those who would use it against its original purpose. The greatest power that is available for use involves what is under this place—and I am not talking about a city or a base. I have to be discreet, because the form and shape of symbols are designed to unite, sometimes to expand and other times to initiate.

The original formula for creation was spread all over Earth in different places. Now, one does not often find this symbol there in Avebury [draws], but it was put in other places. One finds this symbol often, though, in your North America.

A spiral.

If one places that shape under this place [Avebury] in any form, it immediately becomes ten times more powerful. There are three more pieces to the puzzle of creation that have to do with common symbols found in other parts of the world.

I am allowed to tell you this, because it depends on the sequence plus who is doing it and how they are doing it to cre-

Fig. 73. Example of a spiral.

ate. Nevertheless, know that the most important messages are always expressed here on Earth physically, including those messages that have been left by the great mystics and philosophers so that you would have it for sure. One of the reasons they encouraged so many stone circles is because once upon a time there were thousands and thousands and now there are just a few hundred left. But there are enough to catch your attention, and they are so unusual that you see them and say, "What is this?" Look for other symbols that catch your attention, and you will ultimately have the formula for creation on Earth.

Stonehenge Provides Stability for the Sea

What about Stonehenge?

Here's a place that was built to do something highly unusual. It was built to bring about, in its initial phase, stability and continuity of the world life of the planet at the time. Then it was added onto over the years by different groups. The main thing is that it is not so important how it looked in different stages, because there is a limit to what we can reveal.

Originally it was built to support and sustain continuity, but there came a time when it was necessary to change that. If you had something all-powerful that was supporting continuity, you could not rise up between the dimensions right now; you could not change society so easily. So stability had to be altered; therefore, what was created was literally a gyroscope. Stonehenge is now in the form of a gyroscope. If you looked at it, you might say that it does not look like one, but in a rudimentary form it does.

As a gyroscope, it can maintain stability and be flexible. Think of the spinning top: If it is in a fixed position, it tends to stabilize whatever is around it. If it is necessary for what is around it to be able to move and have more flexibility, then it might slow down and wobble.

Here you are seeing something that appears to be fixed, yet it is actually spinning faster and slower in its own right. That is why people can come and go and look at it. It is a physical example, and it is the only place on Earth like this. It is what the movie people would call a stop action. You are walking through something that is actually spinning at a great velocity, but you are seeing it in a stopped moment. It's almost like being able to walk through time. This is why sensitive people who are able to walk near the place sometimes feel dizzy, just as they would feel inside something spinning.

The dizziness is caused by that spinning. The gentle feelings are caused by the spiritual energy, but the actual dizziness people feel, whether they are spiritual people or devout or whatever, is caused by the spinning motion. This is, as you can tell, a complex, really functional thing, and all the stones are participating with their permission.

At one point, I think, some of the stones had fallen over and it was reconstructed. The reconstruction actually did very little harm to the original position, because care was taken to put them back in the way they felt they had been arranged. Because such care was taken, the actual damage to the device, if we can call it that, was only about 5 percent. Of course, when the stones had fallen over, the damage was about 45 percent. So putting it back together, even though it wasn't put back together in mystical ways, allowed it to be reconfigured almost completely.

Can you say who built it and when?

You know how I am with when, but we can talk a little bit about who, perhaps. The people who originally came to create the fixed stabilizing influence were from Sirius. This is because they had some awareness of your connection to them; this has been established. [The Earth was originallay in Sirius and was brought to this solar system.] Also, the people knew that there was a requirement with such a device. They knew that the people of the sea, the sea creatures, would be misunderstood because the planet was going through a time of difficulty.

There was an intent by the Sirian beings to create a doorway for the sea creatures, many of which originated from Sirius. The Sirian beings knew that ultimately sea creatures would be used for food and other things, and they also knew that without a strong and vibrant amount of sea life, the planet herself could not survive. The fish do not only move the water around for their own passage through it, but sometimes Mother Earth needs to have her waters moved—just this much water here and that much water there. There is a limit to what Mother Earth herself can do to move her waters around.

You now have films of fish swimming in ways that are clearly not from point A to point B. They appear to be swimming for the sheer joy of it, and they also move with one heart. They move the water around for Mother Earth that she cannot move. She can make great motions and steady motions, but she cannot do motions with finesse. So the fish, as you call them, do these things for her. If there are not enough fish to do these things, do you know what occurs? She has to do it herself with earthquakes. The typhoons do not stir up the water very far down, but earthquakes will, and earthquakes make tidal waves. So I suggest to you who fish, remember that it is for your own benefit to take only what you need and no more.

If you were a farmer, you would not go to your apple tree and cut the tree down to pick the apples. You would pick the apples and maybe leave a few for the animals. Then you would leave the tree and water it and nurture it as best you can for the next crop. When you harvest whole schools of fish, you are hurting not only the sea people but yourself, and you are certainly hurting Mother Earth. Remember this, because different sea people move the water in different ways. A school of fish not only moves the water in delicate ways, but the fish also impart their energy of joy and happiness while they are doing it, which is their unique type of energy as individuals and as a group.

There are other creatures—the whales, the sharks, the dolphins. The sharks will sometimes swim very deep and rest, sitting in a quiet place doing what amounts to a meditation. They will move the sea with their dreams. Do you know that the most powerful dreams ever dreamt on Earth by any being are dreamt by sharks? They dream the reality of the sea, and because of their dreams the sea goes on. If there is ever a time when there are no more sharks in the sea (not just in museums, but in the sea, free and wild), the sea will then begin to do many strange things. The sharks maintain continuity in the sea.

One of the original purposes of Stonehenge was to broadcast the continuity that moves around in the sea like a window, and that energy supports the sharks and others. I know that the sharks are not fun to live with. They are like any predator—and man is also a predator. They hunt to live, and humankind has transformed that in some ways. You hunt the fish to live, so you can understand why they do what they do. But a sea without sharks is a sea that does many strange and terrible things.

Right now, for instance, waterspouts are unusual, but without sharks they would be an everyday thing. They would go from the sea straight onto the land, where they are known as tornadoes or vortexes. You don't want that, do you?

Absolutely not. Did the Sirians come and build this before humans came, or was it halfway along to humans?

They had people who were there to build it, and there were also at that time British tribal peoples who worked in concert with the underground people.

So it's not that long ago, then?

It's not millions of years ago, no.

Why that particular place?

The Sirians chose that place because it was understood that it would be a safe place and not a place that would be subject to glaciers, for instance. It would not be subject to tremendous snows that might in time cause damage. It was also known that the political position of this country in time would be influential enough that such sites would be protected. Places that have been invaded constantly, such as in the Middle East, have lost many of their great structures because so many invaders have different ways of thinking and being and do not necessarily respect the ceremonies of the native people.

There are many circles all over the planet.

The advantage of the stone circles in Great Britain is that they are still there and the people there were not confused about their purpose. It was understood for years and years that this was to be considered a treasure in England, and today they are still considered to be part of one of the national treasures.

Child Initiations at Cornwall

This is Cornwall [Fig. 74]. It is often thought today that the circle in Cornwall came about as a result of citizens seeing other circles, that it is an imitation. But it is not. This was done to fit in with calling, but here you have something a little different. This circle was created for the use of children. You are all children when you are born, yet the child's heart and soul is very fragile and remains so throughout life. When any soul comes in to be born, it requires encouragement and nurturing, often

Fig. 74. Stone circle at Cornwall.

given by the family and by mother and father.

But what about before the soul gets here? How do you encourage a soul who is going to come in a form and in a place where it will be entirely helpless and dependent on others? Many souls have never been in that position. They are used to being born in places that are entirely safe and protected.

How do you do that? You do it by having such a circle and initiating the children. In this case, the children would be initiated at the age of about nine—that young. They would stand around the circle (as others had) shoulder to shoulder, touching the stones with their arms around each other.

The mystic would in this case always be a woman, because children feel more nurtured, generally speaking, by a woman than by a man. The woman would stand in the circle. If there were three women, they would face the outer ring of the children, who would start out facing in, and the three women would turn in a circle. The women would circle counterclockwise, and the children would be encouraged to move their energy clockwise.

It would take a while to get it going, and that was okay. It was intended that this would work as a balancing mechanism. The only thing the people would say in their own words and feeling was the word and the feeling, "Welcome." It would start out, as I say, with the children facing in. If there was only one woman, she would turn by herself: "Welcome." The children would look into the center, and when they had the energy going strongly enough, the mystic in the center would say, "Now." The children would then turn facing out and look up, then radiate that feeling and say quietly, "Welcome."

That circle was used for that purpose, and even today children might feel welcome there.

The Pleiadian Ship and the People of Machu Picchu

Is there any other round stone formation anywhere else on the planet that has a story that would be interesting?

Deep in the rain forest of South America one finds a few of these, but most of them have been destroyed by those who would build the square shape, whether the square shape is used for mystical purposes or otherwise. But if you look (even with instruments) at the ground, you can still sometimes make out the impressions.

Years ago there was a vehicle from the Seven Sisters that landed deep in the heart of the rain forest. Those on board asked a few of the local people to come onto the ship, and the local people, having the tradition of seeing the star brothers and sisters, did so.

After they came on board, the Pleiadians said to the people, "It would be good for you to begin moving up into the heights, into the mountains, and then live on the mountaintop, but you will have to do this gradually. Establish yourself at the lower elevation, then gradually,

Fig. 75. Machu Picchu.

every half generation, move up a little higher and a little higher." These are the people who came to be the ones who established Machu Picchu.

The circle was built where the ship had landed. When the talk to the people ended, the people brought stones and built a circle, because where ships land, there is still energy. They asked the stones if they wished to be part of the circle, and they brought only those that wished to do so, and the stones took on that energy of the extraterrestrials.

The people carefully buried the circle. The circle is still there today, because the people buried it deeply. It looks just like a hill, a small hill that nobody thinks anything about. But underneath that hill there are stones that cover the original energy of the ship from the Seven Sisters. The energy is still there, and it supported the people of Machu Picchu until they returned to the Seven Sisters.

Is that what happened to them?

That's where they went.

They were from the Earth to start with?

They were originally from the Seven Sisters. They stayed on Earth for a long time, helping to teach the local people many things. The people who live there today know that the old places are connected to the Seven Sisters, because even after the people went home, the ships continued to come. They don't come so often anymore. It's not so safe for them, but once in a while they do, and the local people know that they are coming to their old outpost.

That's enough for tonight.

2/8/04
Nel

22

Carnac in Brittany

Speaks of Many Truths

September 25, 1998

This is Speaks of Many Truths.
Welcome.

The Place of All Souls

Let's talk about a strange, rocky place tonight. This is a place of all souls. If you count the stones, you will come to a number that the people who put them there believed represented the core souls of all beings everywhere in existence. They believed that in order to create a con-

cordance, a continuous connection between the source of all individuals (they believed that all individuals in existence could trace back to three thousand core souls), it was necessary to create a grounding for these souls on the Earth, which these people believed was the source for transformational change.

Fig. 76. Megaliths in Carnac in Brittany.

The stones were put in place by more than one group. There were some people who came from the stars to talk to the local people about the souls' source and about the Earth. The people who came from the stars considered Earth to be like someone you would consider a god you might pray to. They considered Earth, then, to be this wonderful, transformative being. This was not only because they had some vague, imprecise notion of the Explorer Race that would occur thousands of years in the future from their point of view, but also, whenever they as individuals came to Mother Earth to visit, they would always experience some kind of benevolent personal transformation.

As their race accumulated these experiences, they came to perceive Earth as this magical, benevolent being, which of course it is. They would come to contact the local people to speak to them of these things. The local people also considered Earth to be Mother Earth, even Goddess Earth, if you would, but they did not have the concept for all of existence. They just thought about where they were, which is completely understandable.

These conversations took place over several generations of the Earth people but the same generation of the star people. One day the star people said, "Could we suggest that there be a permanent shrine that would anchor the soul energy of all of us, all of these beings?" The star people showed this Earth group the family tree with all the individuals relating back to one. Then they showed, in a simplified form, how all the individuals everywhere related back to just a few, and these three thousand stones would represent them. They said, "Let's do something together."

And that's how the decision was made to put these stones in that place. There was also a desire by the people of the Earth to turn it into a living prayer that acknowledges and honors water. That is why if you look at it from a distance, it appears to be almost a solid object and might be mistaken for a lake if you were flying over it.

These people of the Earth, that clan and tribe there, would fly with the birds. That was the reason they could accept the star people so easily. They took the star people to be related to the birds, because the star people flew out of the sky just as birds do. So it was a good connection. And that's why the pattern is the way it is.

Where were the star people from?

They were from a planet [draws] . . . making my usual X. I make a dot. This is where they were from. Needless to say, it cannot be seen from the Earth.

Who were they?

These people had made a study of all beings in all existence as far as they could explore them. Because these beings were special (this is the best way I can put it), they had the capacity to explore dimensions from

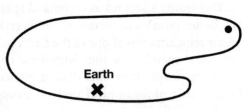

Fig. 77. Map showing where star people originated.

one and a half to thirty-two. So you know that when they talked about all beings in all existence, they were not only including this universe (they were from this universe), but many dimensions.

They also had been told by their teachers that this number was about correct. It wasn't exactly 3,000; it was more like 3,001. Anyway, they felt it was sufficient.

When they said "all souls," they weren't referring to all souls of all human beings. They were talking about all souls of *all* beings—human beings, cats, horses, snakes, ants.

Crocodiles, hippopotamuses, elephants . . .

. . . dolphins, whales and all ETs, lightbeings and so on who they were familiar with. One might think that the souls might relate along family or genetic lines, but they don't. Souls usually relate in some way along experiential lines, loosely along a philosophical or experiential theme. One might, within this concept, be a *part* of a soul—you might have animals and lightbeings and human beings and a full range of ETs and other-dimensional beings who are all part of the same root soul.

This is how these beings would explain it. Because their study had taken about the half-life of this universe, they felt reasonably certain that there was some validity to it. That's why they presented it only to this group of people. This was the only time they had ever presented this philosophy in its entirety. The family tree had to be simplified because of the time it would otherwise take. The philosophy was presented in its entirety only to this one group of people on the Earth and never to any other organized society. They felt that these particular people living in this area were the most prepared to accept this philosophy. They also felt that they had a distant familial tie with them, because when they first contacted these people, one of their (the Earth people) number was related to the soul of the leader of the star people in his soul group. That's why he sought out the specific idea to contact these people.

This leader's second in command (perhaps second in responsibility is a better term) was related more directly and was actually a simultaneous reincarnation of one of the Earth people. She wanted to meet this being and spend some time with these Earth people.

These people from this distant planet had literally dedicated their lives to this philosophical understanding. They felt that this shrine would actually function in such a way that (this is the important part) when the Explorer Race reached its zenith of creative expansion, the roots of these stones and the roots of the souls connected to this transformational planet via this shrine would guarantee growth beyond that potential. So they were really doing something that had a philosophical, a ceremonial and a practical purpose.

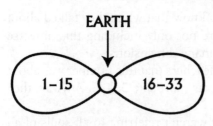

Fig. 78. Map showing Earth as the factor of transformation amplitude in the center of an infinity-shaped universe.

In your understanding, what does this shrine do?

If we pretend that the universe is actually shaped like the infinity symbol . . . you can see it from there [draws].

This represents dimensions one through fifteen. And this one, sixteen through thirty-three. Earth (a little out of proportion) is the factor of transformational amplitude that exists right in the center and that will provide this sort of in/out (I don't know how to describe this) that allows for a beneficial change.

In/out means this: picture something flat that you are flipping one way and then another. That's what Earth does. Earth is at the center point of transformation. This is probably why you as the Explorer Race find yourself here–because your job is transformation, as is your life.

Can you place this chronologically? Was it after Stonehenge?

It seems to have been slightly before Stonehenge.

Were there any civilizations such as India or China or any evolved culture?

I am uncertain of that, but I would say that the people living in the area at the time would have been perceived by a twentieth-century American, for instance, to have been native peoples, not very sophisticated. But very often what is apparently an unsophisticated culture is a culture living as gently upon the land as possible, using as little as possible of what the land has to offer so as to do the least amount of damage to a beloved and respected being. If you think about that, you can begin to have a glimmer of how so-called modern technological humans completely misunderstood Native American people when they began emigrating here.

As you said before very beautifully, you had a complex, sophisticated culture.

Very complex, very sophisticated . . .

. . . which modern humans didn't understand and don't understand even now.

They don't. We're going to get into more of that, because I think that people nowadays do not quite grasp–although there are some who are beginning to–that the reason to make do without modern technology is that technology is dependent on utilizing all forms of life in a way that disrespects their personal autonomy.

At least at our stage in development?

Yes.

Later it will change.

Yes, at some point in time when you do not require machines that have moving parts–because then you are no longer exploiting but are simply interacting–you will eventually have tiny objects that to the casual observer will look like a pebble but under a magnifying glass will resemble something like a photograph of computer circuitry. Every portion of it will have volunteered, but you don't need very much. Between your energy and the energy of all beings, you will be able to amplify a thought into a physical form. But eventually, when you get past thought, you will simply be able to manifest through your heart, and when that happens you won't even need the pebble-sized computer.

Most of the sophisticated native peoples are manifesting with their heart if they are following the old ways, but doing this is difficult in your time (and very seductive), because so many of the modern technological devices appeal to the youngsters and because methods of teaching to the youngsters have lost something along the way. The youngsters do not always have the opportunity to learn in the most benevolent and insightful way. This is partly because of damage done to the culture and also some intentional damage by those who would use the people for their own purposes.

Did these beings come here from that particular planet and interact with the beings on Earth just once?

As I said, they came for several generations. They would visit, but not be here all the time. They would come and stay for a week or ten days or so, then they would return. After a month or two they would come back. That went on for about three generations on the Earth, or roughly about one hundred years.

After that time the people on the Earth understood the star people's philosophy. Even though the Earth people still had their own philosophy, they understood it quite well, and there had been enough time to build up respect. You see, the star people understood that the Earth people needed time to build up not only that respect but also the friendliness needed to work together toward a mutually desired goal.

A New Astrology

What did these ETs do? Go back home? Do they normally travel?

No, they had done their travel in the very beginning of the universe, and they didn't normally travel. They simply made a pilgrimage. Of course, they would send the occasional person to Earth in order to experience transformational energies, but they haven't really been doing that lately. So they are no longer travelers. But the souls of the people who incarnated here, the Earth people who were the native peoples at the time of the visits and teaching by the ETs, have all gone to be with these beings on this distant planet, and they are all living there now. Once they incarnate on that planet, they are immortal, for all intents. The body that is formed there remains formed until an individual chooses to uncreate it, put it back into light and form a different body. Because there is generally satisfaction with the way the bodies look, death has yet to occur, but they could do so.

So these beings who were on the Earth are not part of the Explorer Race?

No. But they were Earth people who lived lives. When they died, some of them went on and had lives elsewhere, but now they are all on that planet.

Are their descendants now on Earth?

I think that the descendants are no longer on Earth, but their lineage went back to Mars. There used to be a surface culture on Mars, but they carefully moved it underground some time ago, and I'm not sure whether they are still there. They might not be after you have begun to send your machines up there.

Did they build this three-thousand-stone menhir shrine all at once or over the course of a hundred years, or did they build only a part of it, then somebody else built some of it?

Working together, there was about a forty-five to fifty-year period when each stone was placed in a very precise alignment. The stones not only—as some of your people today have observed—have something to do with the constellations, they also represent the signs of people as your astrologers understand them. It's just that your astrologers can know of only so many signs because you have only so many planets and star systems through which to understand the signs. There are actually *fourteen* signs represented there instead of the twelve you now have.

What are the other two?

It is not like that. Right now you have different segments of your year broken down into twelve signs. It's not a matter of adding two more signs, which would impact your calendar. I can't answer that question. It's hard to describe, but there are fourteen signs and you have twelve. I just don't know how to explain it.

So are you saying that twelve of those we have are represented there . . . or are there fourteen completely different ones from the ones we have?

Fourteen completely different ones. Thank you.

Do they relate to their home planet?

No, they relate to this part of the universe. There are a couple of influences that have been kept from you. If astrologers knew about these two influences, they would not only be able to figure out all of your past lives, but they could easily, with your records having been kept for, say, a generation and a half now, be able to tell you who you were in your past life, where you lived and what you did. They would also be able to tell you (with the other sign) what planet you were likely to be born on in the future and who, among the people you now know, you would be likely to see there again. The advantage of this in the future, of course, will be that when you know you're going to be seeing certain people again, you might make an effort to find a way to get along with them.

When do we get this information?

You'll probably start to receive this information in pieces. In about twenty-five years it will begin. There are astrologers now who will be working on what I would call the echo of these pieces, but they haven't found the exact pattern yet. When they do, they will know, and this is how (we'll give you a hint): they will look at the sign you have and see that there is a different linear arrangement in accordance with pre-dictability. It is used somewhat for predictability, but it is fallible because it is incomplete. They will notice that predictability has become more precise, and that's when the astrologers will begin to realize that they are on to something.

The people who have been doing the research to prove that there are other signs will be exonerated, because until then there will not be a lot of acceptance for this and it would naturally be difficult to prove. Your science now tries to prove that something exists by the effect that the unseen something is having on other things. This has been somewhat accepted by science, but it has not been accepted as well by astrology.

You can't talk about it now, so there's no sense asking any more questions.

No, but I have given the hint so that those who follow will know what to look for and know they are on the right track. That's important.

Pilgrimage to Carnac

So if we were to go to Carnac, to this shrine, as a tourist . . . are there certain things we could do? Would it accelerate or initiate or benefit us in any way?

It might be advantageous to have an astrologer along (particularly a sensitive who is sometimes called a psychic astrologer) if you stand in certain places among the rocks and are given a sign. If the psychic or shamanic astrologer went there first and familiarized herself with the energy of all the stones, she could take you (by your sun sign, perhaps) to one or two different stones or even a diagonal of stones. She could have you stand in a given place and be invigorated either in the best energies of that sign or, if you were having difficulty in resolving an ongoing problem, the stones of your sign might accelerate your learning of that lesson so that you could get on with your life without having that repeated challenge.

After the time when astrologers begin to understand this shrine, there will be pilgrimages with a purpose, you might say?

Yes, but even now a shamanic or psychic astrologer could do this, because it would not require mental knowledge. It would only require walking through and feeling. This is how you would do it: If you were a shamanic or psychic astrologer and had worked with people enough, you would know how you felt in the company of people of different signs. Your personality, your body and so on would react differently to a Leo or a Virgo or another sign. Then you would go to the rocks and walk slowly (perhaps it might take several weeks) and notice what you felt at each rock as you stood near it or even touched it. I think you'd get more out of its radiated field than from touching it, by your body's reactions. You would notice what sign it reminded you of most, and you'd make a diagram of all the stones. At the end you'd know which ones were Leo and which were Gemini and so on. You'd take time and research it.

It could be done only by an individual astrologer, because each person's body reacts differently to things. A group of astrologers could go in and each one of them might get a completely different reaction to a rock, just like you would meet someone and feel a certain way in your body, yet someone else might meet that person and feel something different. Both feelings are valid. It's not thoughts, but feelings.

As someone consulting this astrologer, you'd have to go with him to this stone. If you went to a different astrologer and it was a different stone, that would be all right. The main thing is that you would have to have faith in the astrologer you went with. You couldn't just sign on to somebody's pilgrimage and go with them. You'd have to know him, meet him and feel good about him so that what he told you would not be from a stranger. You would have to feel good in the astrologer's presence.

In this way you would have assimilated the comfort of your feeling and his feeling. When two people live together, there is an exchange of feeling, which is the most profound, whereas the exchange of words is secondary. After you've had time to exchange the feeling and get to know this astrologer for a while, he can take you over and do that work, provided that he has personally mapped all the stones, that is, how different stones might have to do with different signs. One stone to one astrologer might be a Gemini; the same stone to a different astrologer might be a Virgo. But if you felt comfortable with that astrologer, the energy he reacts to would be compatible with you.

That's one usage of it. Are there others? Astronomically or for any other purpose?

That is the most practical usage, because an individual could gain greatly from that right now.

How would individuals gain? They would feel an energy of transformation?

Say you are thirty or forty years old or even more, and you are continually having repeated experiences that you don't like or that are discomforting to you in some way. You are smart enough to know that you are supposed to be learning something, but it isn't happening because you keep having that experience over and over again. Then you would go to such a place as I mentioned, and the opportunity to learn the lesson would speed up. You would have the opportunity to resolve the lesson much faster, and then you could get on with your life.

And how does that work? What are the dynamics of that? Is there some radiation from that rock?

Stone is a living being. It is no less alive than you or your cat friend, yet in order to understand stone, one must understand the heart of Mother Earth. Stone is, after all, a portion of her body, and you also (at least part of you) are a portion of her body. Since she is a planet and therefore part of a constellation, it is natural that these astrological and, to some extent, astronomical relationships between different planetary bodies would have an effect upon you. These energies of relationships can be represented by individual stones, not unlike files in a computer. Astronomy is a way of understanding, not necessarily based on anything that helps people very much, whereas the intention of astrology is to help people. Your body is born at a certain time and accepts a certain energy that is understood astrologically to be your sign, along with other signs and influences and planets and all this business, and it becomes attuned to specific astrological frequencies.

When you go to such a stone, the stone will recognize that frequency in you. All the stones do, but since most of you don't know how to talk to the stone, you cannot hear it say, "Here, come over, come to me." You cannot hear it—or even if you could, you would not know which one had spoken to you, so you need a sensitive to take you. If you had a lot of exposure to different signs of people, you might be able to do it yourself, but I think this is best proved out by those who have had experience astrologically.

Well, that certainly makes it more exciting than just a bunch of stones.

Yes.

23

Egypt: Origin and ET Influences

Speaks of Many Truths

October 1, 1998

The Feline Guardian of the Underground

A long time ago in Egypt, the guardian of the underground that separated the surface civilizations from the underground civilization was the cat. This explanation has been prompted by your question before the recorder was on, about Sekhmet. The original statue of Sekhmet showed a long, lean-bodied cat resembling a Siamese, but the body was actually longer. Over the years, reproductions of these statues have accentuated the modern cat body so that the statue looks more like an acceptable cat, but the original statues showed the actual cat; however, sculptures were smaller than the size of the original cat.

The original cat would have been about the size of a yearling jaguar, but without the long, bushy tail and with more refined features, not

Fig. 79. Sekhmet.

unlike the features of the Siamese cat, though not with its blue eyes. The cat was the guardian of the passageways from underground civilizations to the surface, physical passageways. Their passage ways could be taken either way, although the usual method of moving between below ground and the surface was using light and dimensions.

But the physical passageways were there. The unusual cat we discussed was set up to guard the physical passageways. This cat was known to be a spiritual guardian. Its job was to keep people from the surface who might not be in balance from wandering down the passageway and coming close to or even entering the underground civilizations that were then numerous on Earth.

Cats could pass through worlds—they had all their earthly powers. Most of the cats you live with now do not have all the earthly powers, but about 10 percent of them do. Sometimes you call these spiritual cats, and those of you who know and live with cats know the difference. This does not mean that other cats are not spiritual. It just means that these 10 percent have all their earthly powers.

Now, the vast majority of cats you live with can still do many things. They can see things that you do not see and experience things that you do not experience. The enigma of the cat is a constant reminder of other worlds, and the average person can then ponder that and consider the reality of it. Nevertheless, 10 percent of spiritual cats have all their earthly powers.

I will give an example. The cat was the guardian in the passageway. When somebody came down the passageway and was in complete balance and harmony, if that balance and harmony was equal to or close to the cat's own or that of the underground people the cat was protecting, the cat would allow that person to pass by, even if he was a surface dweller. He had passed the test. It was not a written test, but a test of demonstrated energy.

If, on the other hand, the person became frightened because of seeing this unusual cat, the cat would challenge the person, move in front of him and stare at the person. From the cat's point of view, you would need to put yourself in balance and harmony, and then the cat would stand aside. But if the person remained frightened of the cat or the energy was still not in balance or harmony, the cat used one of its natural earthly powers, which was to appear much bigger and much more ferocious. It would appear the size of a saber-toothed tiger, very ferocious but without those teeth. That appearance alone was enough to keep most people from going any farther.

The occasional warrior would come down. What about someone

with a spear who might throw the spear? If a spear were present, the cat would first demonstrate a large, ferocious cat the size of a saber-tooth tiger but appearing like a panther. When a person approached with a spear, the cat would not immediately assume that the spear represented hostility. For some people spears were a badge of authority or a tribal custom, so the cat would not assume hostile action. The person could approach with the spear yet be in balance and harmony. The cat would come out and look, and if there was a weapon such as a spear, it would come over and sniff the spear. If the person felt at ease with the cat and was in balance and harmony in that circumstance, he would put the spear down and proceed.

If the cat felt that this spirit was not a threat, it would stand aside and let the person pass, but it would follow the person because there was a weapon. If there was no weapon and the person was in balance and harmony, the cat would stand aside or pass through the wall. The cat could pass through the solid wall because the cat had the capacity to function between all worlds—all worlds meaning not only this world but all worlds.

Does that mean all dimensions?

<u>Yes, up to dimension thirty-three.</u> Cat has this capacity because the cat sometimes must go somewhere for instruction. A spiritual cat on Earth (the cats you live with, not the underground cat I'm discussing) might necessarily pass between dimensions in your home and some other place during the activities of a spiritual cat. Some of you have seen this. In such a case the cat might go to any planet, any world, any dimension, either to receive or to give instructions, perhaps to cats, perhaps to others.

When our traveler moves past the cat and the cat brings him to the wall and goes wherever else is needed, as long as the traveler maintains balance and harmony, he is allowed to pass through the physical tunnels and chambers that lead to the underground civilization. If at any moment the traveler loses that balance and harmony, the cat will appear at once, even if it has to float in space. This would mean, "Calm yourself, come into balance and harmony and fear not." There might be challenges: you might come to something. Perhaps there is a huge dropoff, you know not how far, yet you know this is part of the path. You look for a ladder going down, but there is none, and yet you are drawn. You are a spiritual person in balance and harmony and yet you have a little fear. The cat appears, just like that. The cat looks at you. If the cat believes you are a good person, a spiritual person, balanced in harmony, perhaps invited by people from the underground civilization, it will encourage you. The cat will look at you pointedly in the face or make some gesture, then it will step out onto a hole and float in space. Then it will come back to the physical tunnel where you are standing and look at you. Then *you* get in balance and harmony. You then act with faith and step out. The cat will step with you, and you will both slowly descend to the next level.

Thus you are challenged to see how you would react if something startled you in this underground civilization. It is important that you do not become fearful and that your fear and discomfort not affect others around you. So you are tested, but not in a way that could kill you. If you became frightened or just fell in, you would be caught and then the cat would escort you out—not ferociously, but gently.

You are talking now of what period in relationship to when the civilization started? The first few generations?

I am just taking an example, but let's just say it is right around the fourth or fifth generation. The Egyptians are not totally conscious of magic but are still in pretty good balance and harmony with all life. So there would be people, of course—not unlike any civilization—who would maintain balance and train others to maintain balance and harmony, and others who would do other things. You have these people today.

The traveler would be accompanied by the cat eventually. Let's say you made it through all the tests. None of them would be frightening. They would be challenging, such as there not being an apparent place to step, but there would not be ferocious beasts chasing you. There would not be cataclysmic events around you, because it would be difficult for any surface person not to react to that. The challenges would not, then, be cruel.

It wouldn't be like Indiana Jones and the Temple of Doom?

As you say, it would not be something theatrical. As you started making it through the challenges, the cat would walk with you. This was done for a feeling of friendship, because you, the traveler, would by that time realize that the cat was there for a reason and didn't just happen to live there.

The Underground Ganymede Civilization

So the sense of companionship would form with the cat, and this friendship would prepare you to feel friendship with those you met and greeted. Therefore, after you passed the last challenge, which was not frightening but had to do with love, you would continue on and come out into the city. Perhaps it was an underground Ganymede civilization or somewhere else. Perhaps the people there looked similar to you, or perhaps they were very different.

But since you, the traveler, had proven that you could be trusted to remain calm and cheerful when called to be in balance and be benevolent and all of these things, you were welcomed like you were one of the citizens of that community.

It was okay for the ones above the Earth to know that the civilization was still down there?

This was not necessarily so. It depended on the timing. For the first generation, yes, fine; the second and third generations, maybe. That would depend on the traveler. But by the time the fourth or fifth generation came along, the traveler would be informed that this was a privilege he or she was allowed to have and that the underground people would help and support the surface people only through the traveler or others who managed to make the passage. They would provide wisdom if this wisdom could be given in a way that did not interfere with the life of the surface civilization, and it would always come through the traveler. Then the traveler would know that "This is something I could do for my people"—or not. It would depend on what the traveler wished to do in his or her life.

The traveler was often youthful, less than thirteen years old, but usually at least seven. The opening to the underground tunnel, then, was clearly apparent. It was known as a sacred place. If a young person were to enter there, parents would escort him or her, often grandparents as well. They would say, "We cannot tell you very much. Just know that if you meet the people at the other end, you will be considered a special person for our people. You will have the opportunity, if you wish, to do this again many times."

If a young person became frightened when he saw the cat . . .

. . . he would turn around and go back?

Yes, but the cat would not be the size of a saber-toothed tiger for a child, but big enough to get the child to run away. If it was a child, the cat would follow along, but invisibly. The child would not see it so that he would not fall or hurt himself. The child would be helped up and escorted to the mouth of the cave. Sensitive people (this happened two or three times) would see . . . not the cat, but the outline of the cat as it interacted with the energy around it. You would see the space where the cat was, and the energy around it would form the shape of the cat. That's how people knew the cat was there. But the initiated ones, who had made the journey before, were told not to tell much about the journey.

Did the cat have a special relationship to the Ganymede civilization? Is that how it happened to be there in the Egyptian civilization?

It had a special relationship, as any protector might have with you. But the cat was not particular to the Ganymede civilization. All cats come from their own place of residence.

We don't hear about the cat being so prominent in other civilizations as we do in Egypt, so I wondered if it started with the Ganymede people.

A reasonable question. The civilization in Egypt was known to be very important, and this type of cat would be on Earth only in very small numbers, always guarding or protecting avenues or tunnels between underground and surface civilizations, and because of this, the few cats that there are, they are still here. They are immortal in that body. There are only three over the Earth. These cats tend to support civilizations that are critically important. The surface civilization was more important, yet what the underground civilization was doing prompted a lot on the surface. The cat was helping to keep contact between surface and underground civilizations to a minimum, especially in later generations.

When did Isis come along?

After about the seventh generation came Isis.

She has a special relationship to cats.

Very special.

This one outpost from Ganymede was instrumental in starting these different civilizations, yet the resultant Earth cultures all look different. How did they become so different when they had a common basis?

The Ganymede underground civilization was not so different then in terms of your educators today. Most of the people who started the underground civilization would be what you would call anthropologists or social scientists, people who studied other civilizations all over the universe.

Which is why they were here in the first place?

Yes. As a result, the people of this underground civilization, although being from Ganymede, did not all look the same, just like Earth people do not all look the same. Some of them were dark-skinned, some were lighter-skinned; some were very short, others were very tall.

So it is possible that other civilizations came to Ganymede? It wasn't a homogeneous planet?

The focus of the civilization, the focus of their planet, had to do with the expressions of physical variety. Therefore, although the people from Ganymede lived very long lives both on their planet as well as underground, they would not choose to look the same all the time, just as you, living from life to life, do not choose to look the same all the time. The soul wishes variety. This is expected, because the Creator of this universe finds variety appealing.

So the people would not create the same nucleus of civilization in different places; they would create different forms. Sometimes people's bodies would be adapted to the environment in some slight way. Other times, people would simply be different for the sake of variety. They would not think of it as variety, but as beauty.

They could change their form.

They would not do so capriciously, but they would do so if different qualities were called from them. Different appearances of people sometimes have different qualities. Within any group of people you find different qualities. Certain peoples (at least in their core original form, as in first-generation Egypt) would represent very specific qualities. Therefore, if Ganymede peoples were having a conversation, sometimes they might change their form because a different physical form could more easily express some point of view or make the point more understandable to the listener.

Were the citizens of Ganymede in a less dense dimension at this time so that this was easier? What dimension was it?

<u>Under Earth was never more or less than the fifth dimension</u>. And the surface civilization, even at its most mystical with first generation, was 3.0.

You might ask how a 3.0 person could go down the tunnel and be greeted by a 5.0 person. The tunnel itself had a transforming effect. That's why the 5.0 cat walked through a 3.0 area easily. But at the same time, the tunnel itself was a living being and would transform a person. Of course, a person could not be transformed unless he or she was in balance and harmony. If there was an attempt to transform the person when she was frightened or out of balance or harmony, she could easily, but not intentionally, be killed. So it was done as much to protect surface dwellers as anyone else.

Ganymedians Establish Egyptian Civilization

Which came first, the Eastern civilizations or Egypt?

I am told Egypt.

So the Founders came to this incredibly important civilization. Did they know it was going to be that and what qualities it needed? Did they talk about these things to the beings from Ganymede when they invited them up onto the surface? They needed certain DNA to do these things.

I do not think that it was a meeting like that. I think that the Ganymede people were instructed directly by the Council Middle C. In this way it was easier, because Council Middle C, to use the verbal description, was just as able to communicate to the Ganymede people as to the Founders.

Did special representatives of Ganymede who could create the bodies for this function come here?

They knew that there would be a great (meaning massive and huge) project on this planet. They were told it would have a great deal to do with different forms and appearances of people. Of course, they were immediately interested. They were told that they could have a significant part to play if they chose. Perhaps most importantly for the Ganymede civilization, they were told that it would be interesting and that they would never be bored. This is very important to people from this place. If you are attracted to variety, sameness would become something you would be prepared to leave.

So they had a sense of its importance when they came here. That's exciting. Did they all come at once or were there different little groups? They started Egypt and then another group came later and started China? Is that how it worked?

No, they all came at once. First they had to set up their own civilization. They had to find the proper underground cavern. They didn't dig; they didn't change things. They were looking for a place where Mother Earth would welcome them. And of course they did not want to damage her in any way. They needed to set things up within a cavern that would be compatible with them even at their dimension. This took a little time, and when they found the best place, then they did so.

All that took a little time. This is why they all had to come at once. They had to work together to form a convenient and livable place, a culture.

So they had to agree to densify to 3.0. Was that difficult for them?

They were able to do so, but it was practically never necessary because they were able to carry with them the internal mechanism that allows them to be in 3.0 at 5.0. They could be seen and touched, but you would really be touching something that surrounded them. If you touched them, you would feel like you were touching some kind of energy envelope. In order to actually be in 3.0, they would have to traverse the physical tunnel, not unlike the surface dweller might do, and they might very gradually be changed to 3.0 in that passage.

But they had their 5.0 spiritual tools to create the Sphinx and to build things?

They had spiritual tools. They did not lose their powers.

Is there anything else we could find besides the Sphinx and this one temple [see Chapter 16]?

Most underground civilizations have made a great effort to leave nothing behind. The idea is to accomplish this yourself and not feel that there has been divine intervention. If you did, you might think that you are God's chosen people and then you don't have to do anything for the universe. That is important to avoid. In order to be in balance and in harmony, one must always feel that it is a pleasure to do for others as they do for you. Therefore, there was an effort made to leave little evidence behind. This is apparently all that is accessible.

The Ganymedians came up through the tunnel as 3.0 Egyptians and created a civilization.

Yes. Volunteers went to the surface and built the Sphinx. Everything else they built was not so durable. You can build a house now and come back in five hundred years and not know that a house was ever there.

So they deliberately didn't build anything else that was durable besides the temple and the Sphinx.

Yes, these things were meant to be enigmas.

For later civilizations.

But they were not going to leave too many traces. So volunteers came up. How do they explain this? First generation, then second generation . . .

The most important thing, you said, was to get their bodies into the soil.

Then second generation; we discussed this. The first generation—it came up that they had to experience a physical death, obviously, but their immortal personalities had the opportunity to either return to the underground civilization or to return to Ganymede or elsewhere.

So they didn't reincarnate, then. There is no history of reincarnation of the original souls.

No, they did not continue to reincarnate on Earth. They did not join the Earth reincarnational cycle.

But what they gave us was the bodies—the DNA and the blood lineage.

Yes.

ET Influences on Egyptian Culture

Then what influenced the extraordinarily unusual civilization that we call Egyptian, based on what we can find? The pharaohs, the mummies, the deities, the animals, the story of creation—where did all that come from?

Space visitors from other planets. I think they visited the area in a vehicle and brought this culture with them. They did not, however, suggest royalty; this happened because by that time people were sufficiently cut off from their immortal personalities that the idea of hierarchical culture had been born. But they did bring the artworks that were the basis for such deities.

Think about it. A vehicle lands from the stars amongst people who have a simple, benevolent lifestyle, and the people from the stars bring out their deities to show these surface dwellers not how *they* ought to be, but how the *travelers* are. But the statues, as they would appear to the surface dwellers on Earth, are magically alive.

When they brought them out and they spun to life . . . as it would appear to you if you were a surface dweller, not understanding that the statues are a temporary form of compressed light or energy in a form that pleases the travelers. The statues remind them of the deities (not necessarily deities to *them*) and of the forms of beings they have a special respect or love for.

But if you were the Earth dweller and saw something like this spring to life and become a rainbow or something like that, you might be inclined to think that there is something special about it.

Did they look like pharaohs then? Did they have the large, kohl-lined eyes, the energy coming down the chin and the snake on the forehead?

You must remember that the snake was there with one of the beings. You must remember that even in those days, the days of the pharaohs, artists existed. Look at your artists today. Do they create art that is only of the life you now have? No. They will often create their impression of this life. Thus, much of this culture and this beauty was created by the artists, but it was in terms of animals or deities, as you call them . . .

Hippopotamuses; every animal you can think of—jackals.

Of course, aside from later conquering cultures and so on, you would meet such. They are showing me a book now. This is in a book. [This means this information is available in a book on Earth now and he doesn't want to use the channel's energy to discuss topics that are available in books for humans to research.]

Okay, but did the original concept of the pharaoh, of the afterlife, of the mummies, come from this traveling space group?

No, not the pharaoh. That was already established. Look at your civilization. The leader does not wear beautiful garments and he is not like royalty, but it is a little bit like that.

There was a man who lived on Earth named Itzhak Bentov, and he would go through dimensions and beyond this orb. He said that there were levels of reality where there are beings who look like these pharaohs, and that someone went to that level spiritually and brought that image back to that civilization.

This is possible. I will inquire. I think that this occurred, yes, but the pharaoh, the leader, already existed. What they brought back was the appearance. Those beings at that level were not above anyone; they were just beautiful individuals in beautiful garments, and such beauty was natural. Your culture, then and now, and even our culture to some extent, would begin to say, "Well, he was that and she was that or those people were that or these people were this." You understand? Even in my time, mystical people would sometimes wear slightly different things than others, not to make us better than others but to inform others that we had these capacities in case they needed our services. We would not be unknown. I believe that was the original purpose of the garments of the pharaoh.

It was a spiritual position to start with, then?

I think it was a leadership position, not unlike that of any leader in your time. I don't think it was so spiritual. I think that after quite a while, the pharaoh took on the countenance of being godlike, but it did not start this way. As most royalty knows even today, royalty has less to do with luxury and comforts than with duty.

This is why the older generations of royalty in your time have no time for the younger generations who do not swear their first allegiance to serving the needs of the people in ways that are intended to uplift the people to live a higher quality of existence, emulating to some degree the way that royalty presents itself. I'm not saying that this is the way things ought to be, but this is what is recognized as the system by responsible royal persons of your time. To some extent it is admirable, but of course in your time, there are many distractions, and the younger generations just want to have a good time, yes? They are slow to accept the level of duty.

Let us discuss the English royalty, since it is most well-known. The forebear of that attitude may be the original type of pharaoh who was devoted to the people, who was allowed to be the wayshower but not considered the deity until much later. In your times the royalty is in a slightly diminished capacity. Royals are no longer considered gods or goddesses. Other than the trappings of wealth and the duty it represents—which is also sometimes reflected by wealthy people all over the world—the system is gradually changing back to what it once was, which had to do with wayshowers.

Where was this little ET traveling group from who brought the artwork that became the images of the Egyptian deities?

They were just passing by. I think that if they had to do it over again, they probably would not stop. After they left the planet, they were approached by a vehicle of friendly diplomatic people, who said, "It would have been better if you had not done this."

They replied, "Why? We showed our culture and entertained the children. They all seemed to like it so much." Then they were shown what would be the result, and they said, "Oh, my."

It is a civilization that had not (at least up to that point in time) had much experience with responsibility and consequences such as you have here every day. The civilization was from a culture influenced by the Pleiadian culture, which had a great deal to do (at least at that time) with helping other cultures they meet, helping them rise above the struggles of survival and get along and live comfortably. So at that time of their civilization, they were exploring other planets and were still childlike in many ways.

So they were not from the Pleiades but were influenced by the Pleiadians?

They were from near the Pleiades.

What particular concepts did they leave?

The people already had prayers for the Sun and the elements. It is natural. When you think of a body of people living far away from the supermarket and far away in time, they would naturally grow to think of the Sun and the rain and all the elements that made it possible for them to live as being deities of a sort.

So they did not bring that idea. The people had already developed that on the basis of their survival. After all, if it rained too much, they would pray for the Sun to return. And when the Sun returned, they would thank it. After a time this got out of balance. Around the time the pharaohs came to be regal leaders and became deities, the Sun began to be considered a deity. You couldn't have people talking to the Sun as if it were a friend; otherwise, you might get the idea that the pharaoh was a friend and not a leader. To put it shortly—it was politics.

What concepts did these little innocent travelers bring to the Egyptians that were not there before they landed?

Appearances. They brought the appearances of animals with human features, because that was the shape of the artwork they had with them. Of course, when they went to other planets with beings who did not look like human beings but looked like something else, the animals might have the features of those beings.

I don't think the people of the ship even knew this, but it was intended to be the spiritual lesson that human beings and animals are equals. Of course, just the opposite was the result. Sometimes the plan you make does not result in the desired intention.

So that is where the ideas of Anubis and Seth and all these animal deities came from?

Yes. Of course, there had been a longtime reverence for cats.

So where did the concept of mummification come from?

The people developed that. But you know, mummification is a natural process. What they developed was a way to create at least a temporary mummification that they chose. The first exposure they had to mummification came as a result of finding someone in a dry cave who had been naturally mummified. Their mystical people said, "This body is very old." And that's when they decided that this might have to do with physical immortality.

The Ship Buried under the Sphinx

Fig. 80. Ship buried near the Sphinx.

They found a ship buried at the base of the Sphinx. Is there any significance in it or anything unusual connected with it?

The ship was meant to take the pharaoh on the journey in case the other worlds were water worlds, but that was not the real purpose.

The real purpose was that such exotic vehicles—and they were considered exotic because they had been captured from other cultures that had been admired . . . you know, you can do battle with other cultures, and if you don't admire them, you think nothing of tearing down their temples and building your churches. On the other hand, if you do admire them and preserve their culture for your people to study, then you might consider their vessels to be cherished just as you cherish ancient things today.

Their intention was to make other people's admired objects available for the afterlife of leaders. Even if you did not have it to give to yourself in your own culture, you gave this other admired spiritual object to your leader. The idea was that your leader would know how to use these things, even though you did not. Obviously it was something to traverse water with, but these other people you were in battle with did more than traverse the water. You were impressed with their spirituality.

What local culture was that from?

This was a culture of water peoples. They lived and traveled by water. They never went on land—never. From the point of view of a person who lived on the land, this would be considered to be exotic, to say the least.

The Phoenicians?

I am not getting that name, but it is possible.

If they lived on the water, they wouldn't have left anything for us to see of their civilization.

No, unless you could look under water.

Under water?

Yes, because sometimes the ships would sink.

Was it in the Mediterranean or on the Nile?

On the river that went past the culture there.

The Nile River.

The river next to where I put that mark [see Fig. 61]. They show me the picture. They don't always give me the words.

I think we have given a good understanding of the origin and evolution of the Egyptian culture and its purpose for the future. Someday this will help you move to the higher dimension and also free yourself of your attraction to danger.

This is something that plagues your culture today. Many of your people are not peace-loving at all; they are attracted to danger. Sometimes this is because danger has been sold to them as being something exciting. I'm not just talking about mountain climbers here; I'm talking about the idea of thinking that war is exciting, when in fact it is actually misery.

With this kind of foolish love of suffering, which is what war is, even if you are inflicting the suffering, ultimately you will suffer. If not in that life, certainly after that life you will have to come to terms with what you have done. So this attraction to danger will someday be released, or at least its surface will be cracked. Then it will more easily fall off by what the Egyptian people will do. As that lobe that you cannot see forms on the brain to accomplish what we mentioned, there will be a temporary raising of the vibration.

If you were to take persons who have an unrealistic idea of war—such as thinking it is exciting and adventurous—to a higher dimension and show them the true effects of war, they would be devastated. This temporary increase in the vibration will help people who have this immature feeling about war to become aware of the fallacy of its attraction.

We can't put a date on that, but is it possible that it may be in the next few years or during our lifetime?

It is possible.

How long did the original Ganymedians live underground after Egypt was begun?

They left within only the past forty to fifty years.

Oh, they were here all that time.

Yes. But only in the past forty to fifty years did your development of unnatural technology begin to represent a threat—the atomic bomb and the use of sound waves as well as electrical and magnetic waves, which would disrupt anything under the surface, to say nothing of disrupting Mother Earth's continuity.

So as anthropologists, they got to stay all those thousands of years and watch the evolution of the civilizations they had started?

Yes.

Would one of them like to talk at some time? Is there a leader?

They don't have leaders, but I have been informed that someone would be interested to talk.

Great!

4/8/04

24

China: Ganymedians' Long Walk and the Influence of Sirius

Speaks of Many Truths
October 2, 1998

Chinese Culture Emulates Sirian Wisdom

China, which has a long and ancient past, is another civilization started by the Ganymede people. The people from Ganymede, again, were asked to begin the civilization, and because of their love of variety, they chose to show a different appearance. The appearance, as far as I know, was the result of their having traveled widely in the Sirius galaxy. They wished to reproduce an appearance on Earth of certain beings they had met on Sirius who had qualities they wished to impart. Of course, one can impart qualities only up to a point on the genetic level, yet it was their intention to foster and nurture these qualities.

The people on Sirius whom they were emulating in appearance were particularly interesting individuals. They were not a vast population, just a few individuals, one of whom was in charge of a hall of wisdom which, if you were to walk inside and look at it, would look very much like a hall of mirrors. The mirrors themselves, which numbered thousands and thousands, did not contain written knowledge but contained the potential for travel.

In order to study, the visitor would enter and speak to the person in charge, who looked very much like he was Chinese. The guide would ask you, "What do you want to know?" He would tell you that upon entrance to this place you would gain the knowledge and wisdom you needed. It was up to you to tell him how much experience you chose to have, because you could stay a hundred lifetimes in these places, stepping through what looked like a mirror but was really a doorway, or you could stay for only a few minutes. When you stepped back through that doorway, regardless how long you had been there, it would be to an observer as if you stepped in and stepped right back out again.

So time was suspended on one side. According to what you told the guide, he would take you to a particular doorway and encourage you to step through. He would also allow you to stick your head through first and look around to get a sense of what it was like. He would give you a means to find your way back to the doorway at any time in case you wished to come back before you had achieved your wisdom. There was no mystery to coming back.

The people from Ganymede were so impressed with this particular individual and several others on that planet who were in charge or were guides to such a place, that they wished to re-create the wisdom that it would take to know to which doorway to lead the person. They wished to create as much as possible the wisdom and timelessness of such people.

It was with that in mind that they asked for volunteers, but here, instead of what we had in Egypt, we had something different. Instead of very young volunteers to begin the Chinese culture, we had the very old, and they had to ask for some who could still have offspring to volunteer. There were many more volunteers than were needed. That's how impressed the Ganymede people were with the beings they hoped to reproduce from the nucleus of the culture.

They accepted about two hundred volunteers, most of whom were near the end of their life cycle. If they chose to, they could end their lives being immortal; they could, by that time, choose to end their lives, and going up to the surface was a perfect way to do so. They gathered up their group and discussed amongst themselves what they would like to do. When they reached the surface, they decided that instead of staying together as one group, they would split up into four groups. Some would go to the north, some to the east, some to the west and some would stay in the south of the country. They would develop the culture along similar lines, but adapt it to the geography and weather conditions of the different places in order to express this culture in reaction to conditions.

This may have something to do with the cultural expression of the Chinese people today, who are inclined . . . how can we say . . . to bend with the breeze rather than be rigid and break. I allow for the fact that the current government in China is a bit rigid, but this is in reaction to the loose-knit government that existed before that, which was very difficult for the average citizen. So this is a temporary situation and eventually, I would say within forty to fifty years, they will have a very heart-centered government, but it will still be a government that encourages people along certain pathways rather than letting everybody do what they wish.

Were any of the four groups more influential, in terms of what came to be known as the Chinese people?

The southern group was more influential. This may have to do with the fact that weather conditions were more supportive at that time. They were able to establish a culture rooted in wisdom; wisdom was revered above all. This was considered most essential in order to make people want to be wise and have appreciation for such accomplishments. This is not a predominant focus in every culture, but even today such wisdom is respected there, even though traditions are not as deeply honored as they once were.

It will come to that again, but without the rigid hierarchy that caused the current political situation there. The current government really was a reaction to a government that became too hierarchical—I'm calling the loose-knit government that existed before too hierarchical.

The Ganymedians' Long Walk

All right, they came up on the surface. In Egypt we have nothing left except two stone buildings. It took generations and generations to establish cities and rulerships and things, whereas in China it appears that they brought their technology. They had iron, they had lighting, they had cities right away. It was different, right?

They knew that the culture would eventually occupy a vast amount of land, so what they set themselves out to do was an interesting task.

Now, I'm just going to draw a shape. I need to have an outline, just a rough outline of the shape of the country, and then I will show you something intriguing that they did. You have to remember that what I am drawing here is not to scale [draws Fig. 81]. There were many more of these circles, but I am drawing enough so that the reader gets the idea. Now, what this represents is the first thing the groups started to do, each in their own territory. They formed together as immortals even though some of them were at the end of their cycle of immortality, after which they would renew themselves in a different body form. They chose to renew themselves in what you now know as the Chinese people, and now they are mortal.

Yes, but they had the ability to transform the way they looked and allow that to be reproduced? That's unusual.

Yes, but they formed up into those four groups, and then they each started to do circles like that. They were very tight circles, but eventu-

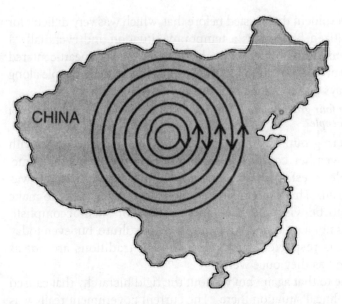

Fig. 81. Outline of China showing Ganymedians' long walk.

ally they got to be wider and wider. They would walk around this way [motions]. You see what I am doing: making circles in the air, walking around one way.

Counterclockwise.

Then they would stop after they felt they were done. Then they would all proceed out to a point a little farther away, not hundreds of miles, but just a little farther, from ten feet to forty miles. Then they would walk around in a circle the other way [motions] to the extent that they could, given the features of the land.

That's clockwise.

Yes, it would start out counterclockwise and then they would go clockwise. Back and forth and back and forth in expanding circles until they covered the general terrain. They did this on foot. Do you know why?

No.

The land of China at that time was very receptive to being influenced with the qualities the Ganymedians wished the people to have or to desire. But the land needed to be touched, so they would go around and around and around on the land, touching as much of the land as they felt they needed to touch.

Just once?

Once, but this took about forty to sixty years to accomplish. Fortunately, they didn't need to eat or drink at that time or they would have been exhausted. They did this day and night. The circles would at times overlap and they'd be walking near other groups and have a chance to see them and give greetings, but they never stopped, always kept walking, day and night, day after day, regardless of the conditions. It wasn't a hardship for them, but it was a commitment.

They had really high mountains and some difficult terrain, right?

They did it anyway. This might have something to do with the endurance of the Chinese people to this day.

Whereas in Egypt they put their bodies into the land, here they put the qualities in the land with their feet by the walking.

Yes, they were touching it—and barefoot, of course, except where there was snow; then they would walk with some covering over their feet. Of course, because it took many years, sometimes there was less snow in some places and sometimes more. But they felt they needed to cover the ground, snow or not.

Was that from Middle C's perspective? Was that their understanding?

That was their understanding. They were attempting to encourage characteristics they had observed and appreciated in the guides on that planet in Sirius. Middle C did not direct them there. This was something they were attempting on their own.

They decided what to do.

Yes. They were trusted to make the decision based on their best wisdom, so they did that.

Chinese Progenitors Choose Mortality

When they were done, they returned to the place where they began and started the culture. The difference, however, was that when they were done and they each went back to the place where they decided, "Here's where we will start," they chose to become mortals. They had lives that were fairly long, seventy-five, eighty-five years, and in one case one hundred and two. They chose to do this because they felt that they had to honor the circumstances of the land as well as the qualities that they were trying to foster in the people. The Chinese people, they hoped, would not only develop wisdom that was cosmic or eternal, but would also develop a very practical, down-to-earth philosophy and wisdom that could be used on a day-to-day basis. That is why they felt it was essential to be of the land and be mortal the moment they were done with that Herculean effort, and so that's what they chose to do.

Did they choose a central place?

If you were to examine the climate of each of the areas . . . they went to the place where the climate was best, where they would be near water and all the things that human beings need. They chose the area that was the most fertile, the most comfortable and sustainable, and that's where they began their culture.

They had knowledge. They did not discard their wisdom, even though they became mortals. But they did not immediately begin all these wonderful things that the Chinese people are known for. They decided that first they would begin a simple life, living on the land in an agrarian situation, not unlike other people all over the world. They would grow their food and only when necessary ask for animals to come to offer themselves, but not right away. They were very spiritual, yet they attempted to adapt to living conditions as mortals.

Since it was not in their awareness or experience to suffer, they did not suffer from brutal winters. They were mortals, but they had the capacity to generate internal heat when it got cold or, when it was brutally hot, cool themselves off internally. These were ancient wisdoms, some of which are still practiced today in areas that border what is now known to be China. Although China has politically taken over Tibet for the moment, this will not be permanent.

Did they build structures to live in?

Not right away, because if you can generate warmth, you do not need to get out of the rain. But fairly soon they started building simple houses, earthen huts and so on. Earthen huts are almost the first thing built on Earth. Then they used stones, but nothing fancy right away.

These Ganymedians were already old to start with. Did they have the ability to have a normal lifetime on Earth?

Yes.

Were they buried in the land?

Not buried in the land. At that time they did not feel that was a necessity. They looked around and noticed how the animals would be when they died. The body would be put outside. It was a while until the idea of wrapping the body or doing anything ceremonial came. They believed that as mortals with an Earth-provided physical body, the idea of letting the body return to Earth by natural means, whether animals were involved or not, was not only appropriate but essential to honor Earth's granting of the loan of her physical self to create the body. They did not consider the physical body itself to be anything other than a portion of Mother Earth, and therefore the body itself was not celebrated.

How did they densify to become mortal? You said that the Egyptians had to go through this transforming tunnel to get from Middle Earth to the surface—from 5.0 to 3.0.

Yes.

Did they have the same method?

No, they just went to the surface and transformed themselves into mortals. First they would go into the water, then the soil near the water. Then they were able to do this on their own. They do not wish to say how it was done.

You said the other day that the first, second and third generations could go back into Inner Earth. How could they do that if they had densified their bodies?

They could go, but they did not go very often. If they did, the Inner Earth beings would meet them very close to the surface so that they did not have to confront the guardian cat.

I was thinking that in China maybe it was a dragon.

No, not so.

So, it's always a cat. Could they communicate to Inner Earth if they wanted to?

Yes, at any moment, which is why physical contact was not really necessary.

Did they have a physical body and then go back to their immortal body, or did they reincarnate as souls?

When the body ceased to function, they would simply go on.

They didn't reincarnate later?

They could have. They just went on with their natural reincarnational cycle. As a soul being, either they would return to inside the planet or to Ganymede or wherever they wished, to re-create an immortal self. They could start a reincarnational cycle as long as it was not on Earth.

Did some of them go back into the Inner Earth and continue to guide this civilization?

Some of them went back in and would guide the continuing generation of surface dwellers based on their experience. The first twenty-one generations were still able to contact the underground beings. By that time, though, a great deal of wisdom had been accumulated. It was talking wisdom, meaning that certain individuals were responsible for certain amounts of wisdom, to know it, memorize it and pass it on to the next person to know and memorize exactly.

Language and the Separation of the People from the Wisdom

It was a while before the idea of language was firmly adapted (written down). It started out as symbols to make the wisdom easier to remember, as you use symbols today. Eventually there were words to connect the symbols. Shortly after there was print, there came to be the regular accumulation of wisdom. People didn't have to remember the wisdom. This was actually a disadvantage in some ways, because when you do not have to remember the wisdom, what happens? You don't have to practice it because it isn't consciously and constantly in your mind.

Therefore, you put the books of wisdom under the charge of individuals, and when you need that wisdom, you go to them and they tell you. That was the beginning of the separation of the people from the wisdom on a daily basis. It was not an intentional thing, of course, but that is how things work. That is why wisdom that is available when you need to know it but is not required when you do not need to know it, is so useful in what Zoosh calls vertical wisdom.

But they did not practice that for a time. By the time the twenty-second generation came, they were not practicing vertical wisdom or telepathy. There was by that time strong wisdom in the books. Some of it would remain. And there were stories, and the stories were told from generation to generation, and books of wisdom were kept. But when people do not personally remember the wisdom, if anything happens to the books, it can be lost. Even though there had been painstaking effort to retain the books of wisdom, many of them were lost, especially in later political upheavals and battles with other countries.

And wasn't there a book burning once, too?

Yes, a shortsighted experience that is now deeply regretted.

How long was it before they started having a leader?

A hierarchical system?

Yes.

At the twenty-second generation, when they started assigning others to keep the books of wisdom, it was only partway through that generation that the hierarchical system began. You can see that the keeper of the wisdom would become, if not a leader, at least an adviser, and that's when it started.

Did what they call the three sovereigns, Fu Xi, Shen-nung and Yen-Ti, live in that early time?

Now we're getting into about the fortieth generation before that.

So we have no record of anything up to the fortieth generation, because that's the earliest thing in any mythological history of China. Did they keep this division of four?

They kept the division of four until the thirty-seventh generation. By that time, enough was forgotten that if people wished to emigrate to other places or intermarry, they would move to other places. In the beginning there wasn't an attempt to segregate different groups, but rather to instill the qualities that the land had to offer. The qualities were based on not only different weather conditions, but also on different parts of the land having a different personality. One might find that the northern parts of the United States have very distinct seasons, whereas one might go to Florida, for instance, and find that seasons are either rainy or sunny.

Why did they choose such a big area?

They could see ahead. Of course, at this time they did not consider a line of demarcation to be where Thailand or Vietnam are. They felt comfortable spreading into that area. They did not spread as much then into Tibet, because their feeling was that the people of Tibet were going to be stimulated from another source. The Tibetan people would look similar to the Chinese people, but not exactly the same.

So once you have a hierarchy, then you start to have wars amongst the groups?

When you separate wisdom from the people and put it in the hands of the few, even if for the best of reasons, it doesn't take very long before some people start to say, "Let's keep this wisdom and give it only to our friends." Then you start to have resentments, and it doesn't take long before they can fester into battles.

So we have the three sovereigns and then the five emperors, then they started having the recorded history that we have been able to find and read—about 2000 B.C.?

Yes. Fortunately, they left some beautiful artwork that you can make some assumptions from, I believe.

These beings in the Inner Earth who are there to guide this civilization have to allow the wisdom to be put in books, allow the separation, allow the resentment, allow the war. They know that this will go on.

Yes. They know this because this is part of the cycle of history of the human race as it develops. They know that at some point they have to stand back, but they have their own culture and, of course, they have other activities going on.

That would still be painful.

They cannot embrace pain, so when it gets to the point that is uncomfortable for them, they step back and that's that.

The Sixteen Ganymedians

Zoosh told me that there were sixteen beings who had a particular connection from the Inner Earth to China. Was there a group of sixteen who seemed particularly interested in the Chinese civilization?

Are you talking about sixteen Ganymede people? These are the people who chose to reincarnate or regenerate their life cycles after living on the surface and went down below.

Ah, did those sixteen have an ongoing interaction with the Chinese on the surface?

Yes, they did, but once they started to feel uncomfortable, they just stepped back. When you step back, as long as other people can step forward, you can communicate. But stepping forward on the surface would mean that the people on the surface would use the old ways to communicate.

Later when we get into Lao Tzu and Confucius and some of the beings who . . .

Then they are connecting to other beings, not the Ganymede people. It was the Ganymedians' job to start things, and they chose to start them in such a way as to stimulate certain qualities in the people, but it was not their job to continue.

So all they did from that point on was watch?

They watched or did other things.

They watched but they didn't mold or nurture?

No, that would have been interference.

The Horse, the Cat and Chinese Artwork

When did artwork start? When they carved jade and bronze, was that much, much later?

Much later. Artwork, of course, comes when you have time. Artwork that is intended to please usually begins when people have time. The other way is when there is someone who has the opportunity to give time to the artist.

A sponsor.

A sponsor, so that the artist no longer has to survive and grow food. As any farmer knows, it is more than a full-time job.

This [Fig. 82] is a picture of a shaman. It looks very ancient.

This is not from this planet. This is a gift from a visitor to the planet. The visitors did not start coming until about the thirty-seventh generation. They came first to look. Then, around the thirty-seventh generation, they started to contact some of the people, and one of the people of the ship gave that as a gift to an ordinary person, not anybody in the hierarchy or anything. Eventually, as it passed through different hands in the family, it was given to a more regal personage, and that is how it survived.

The figure is intended to show a being from their planet dressed in ceremonial clothing and working in a position that today would relate to tai chi. It was presented to the people of the Earth as a form of ceremonial dance that improves the health and longevity of the person. Of course, it was considered something worthy to emulate, so the dance was taught. This is where tai chi, I believe, first began.

Can you place it in the cosmos somewhere?

I'll ask. They are showing Ganymede to me and saying, "That way," which is away from the Earth. Sometimes they are not forthcoming. This probably has to do with the potential that you will meet these people someday; therefore, the less said about them, the better.

We have to find them on our own?

Better to meet them on your own and to have your benevolent reaction with them than to form opinions beforehand.

The horse is so important in the Chinese culture. They treated animals completely differently than the Egyptians. They treated them as beautiful beings in their own right.

Fig. 82. A *wu* shaman.

They had considerable respect for beings other than ones who looked like themselves. This was initially because animals seemed to be able to adapt to all kinds of conditions and know how to keep themselves and their fellow beings safe in many different circumstances. The tendency was to look up to them and observe them to see what they did. That's why this cat carving [Fig. 83] was shown in such a way as to identify the cat as being regal, but also as having the capacity to do things the average being could not do. It wasn't just an artistic rendition.

Needless to say, the average cat could not bend like that. But the acknowledgment there in the art was to suggest that cats could do things beyond what was physically possible. In this way, respect was present for the impossible. The animal then was placed on a pedestal as having admirable qualities that the human being could strive for.

There is much all through China, old and new, about tigers. Was the tiger their symbol of the cat family?

Fig. 83. Chinese cat carving.

Yes.

What about horses?

Much, much later. They were small in the beginning, but they were greatly admired. Even in the very beginning they were considered regal. Today horses exhibit traits that royalty are expected to look up to, meaning that horses have great heart for everything they choose to do. They are dedicated and not easily deterred. At the same time they are tremendously sensitive, which allows them to know many things and react to things from a philosophical point of view, to be visionaries. These qualities are considered not only admirable but required in the proper regal circles.

Sirian Visitors Introduce the Mask

Here is a nine-foot tall-being [Fig. 84].

This is a being from another world, another visitor. Very often the very tall visitors are from Sirius. They had dark skin. This is not an exact representation of how they looked, but the figure is dressed in ceremonial garb, so the head is covered in a mask. This was when the Chinese culture was introduced to the idea of wearing masks for cultural and ceremonial purposes, in order to encourage the properties within the mask wearer that the mask itself represented.

The spiritual artist will make a mask, imbuing the mask with the energy that the artist feels when connecting with a god or a goddess. During the time the mask is being carved or created and whenever the artist has contact with the mask, he or she must feel these qualities. If for any moment the artist loses concentration, he must not only stop working on the mask, but step out of the room or out of the house. Then the artist must attain the qualities again, focus, concentrate, go in and work on the mask.

Casual persons who are aware of what their feelings mean to them could approach the mask and immediately have those feelings, even without knowing what the mask was about.

This was introduced by a culture from Sirius. Sirius has an abiding interest in cultures on this planet and has made several attempts to stimulate better characteristics in cultures (better as they see it).

Did they happen to be here, or did they come specifically?

They came specifically to visit the Chinese people. At the time of their visit they felt that the Chinese people would endure. They first came around the twenty-second generation, but they did not introduce the mask until right around the thirty-fourth generation. Then they showed it to them and danced with them, but they did not immediately show them how to make them. This happened over time. The people from Sirius are not inclined to rush anybody.

So they came many times, then?

Many times. The role of communication is interesting. If you were to meet those people today, you would say that they are very caught up in symbols, meaning the way they walk and talk (steady, high, low or sing-song) and gesture and stand or sit. Everything is

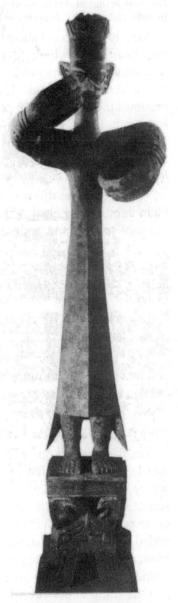

Fig. 84. Nine-foot-tall Shang sculpture.

important. In many ways it is very theatrical, and I believe it was this theatricality that may have supported the foundations of such theater as the Chinese became famous for.

Do those beings at this moment now feel good about their intervention, about their introduction of this? It seems to have had a positive result.

Yes, they feel good about it. They felt that they needed to give some people on Earth who would have a long duration these types of communications, which could be at one moment very personal and at the next affect a large group. The actor or performer puts on the mask and becomes the qualities. He gives the performance, immediately affecting everybody in the audience with those exact same qualities. They feel very good about passing this on.

When native peoples would dance around with a bear hide on or with masks of different animals, were they attempting to bring those qualities into themselves?

No. Sometimes this was for the hunt. Only at certain times would it be to imbue themselves with such qualities. This is a different subject. I cannot speak about both these things at the same time.

Early Chinese Culture and Technology

What about the beginning of some of the things the Chinese are noted for—for instance, acupuncture? That started there, the understanding of the meridians and energy lines in the body. Was that ancient or later?

It was later. Think about it. In the beginning . . .

. . . they didn't need it.

They didn't need it. They needed it only when they became more and more separated from what they could do for themselves.

Did the original Ganymedians have a written language?

No.

When they started with the symbols, did they just make it up?

Yes, they made it up. It was, "This symbol means this." Of course, the initial symbols would have been very simple. But when you built on that symbol or you wanted to say more with that symbol . . . you might have a simple symbol for "man," and then you might wish to say "man with wife," or "man with wife and children." Initially this was all one symbol or was added to the symbol that represented "man." Later, as language became more complex and nuances and subtleties were added (for which the Chinese language is well-known), many, many more symbols were added.

One thing about the Chinese language, as complicated as it may seem to the outsider, is that it is and has always been very precise. This kind of precision is not often found in other languages.

The Chinese had cities at a very early age before anybody else on the planet. They had gunpowder and iron.

I wouldn't say that they alone invented cities. They encouraged cosmopolitan cities, but many ancient cultures, even Native American cultures, had cities or colonies. They weren't cities designed to foster and encourage culture for its own sake. It would have been a culture that would serve the people in the Native American situation. One might see groups of dwellings that all emulated each other, whereas in the ancient Chinese cities one would have very artistic renditions of cities, the appearance attempting to encourage qualities within the people.

Even today, one looks at the Chinese pagoda, for example. The pagoda is intended to have a physical impact first. That's why the land is almost always cleared from around a pagoda, in order to have very little interruption to the eye. This is so the physical body will react to it first for quite a while, with the intention of fostering certain qualities or bringing them up within you. By the time you enter this place, you will then not desecrate it by bringing qualities that would corrupt or disrupt. You would be overwhelmed by the qualities you are intended to feel and would, as a result of stepping inside, simply support and sustain the qualities being intentionally fostered within you.

Were the pagodas originally teaching temples?

Yes. But you couldn't have people running into the temple feeling all kinds of different things, because it would disrupt the continuity of the energy, and continuity is the foundation of the Chinese culture.

They seem to have more technology than any other civilization. I'm wondering whether they invented it because they had these qualities, or were they influenced by someone else?

They were encouraged to be adaptable by the Ganymede people, and adaptability is expressed artistically. But ultimately, as they got further away from wisdom and spirituality and became more practical— although not without wisdom—they started looking for other opportunities. They did invent gunpowder and all the things they are known for, but that wasn't the first time they had seen its display. They were exposed again, having many visitations from people from the stars.

They were exposed to gunpowder as an entertainment; that is why they took time to get to the point of using it in any wholesale quantity for destructive purposes. For a very long time they felt that it was intended to be something of beauty, not of destruction.

Like great firecracker demonstrations?

As of today, yes.

So this planet was like an open house all the time. Off-planet people just landed and said, "Hi, I'm here." Things were shared from all over the cosmos.

Yes, but that is natural anywhere. That is normal, what one expects. One does not say, "Visitors—how unusual!"

Soon now?

Certainly not. Visitors would not be welcome if they came now, would they?

I'm saying soon, but not in my lifetime, right?

It's possible in your lifetime, but if they came right now, the other military establishments would be a threat long before the secret government had to foster anything.

Dragons, the Symbol of Good Fortune

China seems to be where the dragons come from. How did that start?

I believe that it started as a result of some voyages on ships by Chinese citizens. In those days sea creatures were more common. This was a creature of the sea, but it did not breathe fire. If you were breathing fire, you would not live very long. As a result of ocean-going voyages, fishing and so on, this creature (from sixteen to thirty-two feet long) was often seen.

A few fishing boats went out and saw one of these creatures. At first they were very frightened. But they didn't have time to be frightened, because all of a sudden there were fish everywhere, so many fish that they were jumping in the boat. The people came back with the story of having seen this creature and then being overwhelmed with many, many fish. One would make the connection right away. What happened after a while was that this sequence of events kept repeating itself.

The being looks like the dragon, but is a sea creature. It doesn't have feet. The feet were artistically adapted to the being in order to make it a land creature. This is how the being came to be known as a symbol of luck, because when it came to the fishermen, they had more fish than they could use.

They were probably running away from the animal.

No, it wasn't like that. The creature wanted to encourage humankind. It would ask for fish to volunteer to support them. So the fish who could, would jump in the boat, and the others would come close enough to be caught. This is how the dragon came to be known as a symbol of great luck. It is really known as a symbol of good fortune. There is quite a difference between good luck and good fortune. Think about it. You could be lucky and still be penniless, but good fortune brings you wealth.

Is this sea animal alive now? Does it have a name?

I suppose there is a scientific name of more letters than are necessary, but it does not have a common name.

Does it still exist at this moment?

It does not exist on the surface of the planet because it does not feel safe. Humans of today would just consider it an oddity and would not care for it. It lives inside the Earth in underground oceans. There are still some underground oceans and beautiful places inside the Earth. As far as I can see, they are not peopled by humans or humanoids, but by plants and animals. They look very much like Gardens of Eden. They may not be at this dimension, but I am not certain.

Many of the beings who used to populate the oceans took off, you said, because of the bombs and radiation and the sonic weapons.

Yes, radar and sonar have been very devastating to sea creatures. The sad thing is that humankind does not understand that even if the radar signal does not bounce off of something, the signal continues on. It blankets people every time the signal comes around. Radar and sonar signals continue well past their target. Even though they may not be able to use the signal past a certain point, it continues on and is destructive to all life. "All life" includes human beings.

Every time a weather radar spins around and sends out its energy, it is cumulative. A human being today is exposed to more artificial electrical technology than is healthful. It is excess electrical energy exposure that causes fully 40 to 50 percent of disease. Chemicals that you ought not be exposed to prompt another 20 or 30 percent, and the rest is caused by unresolved feelings.

Can you describe this sea creature? Does it have a head?

Yes.

It actually has a head like in the pictures?

Its head is not quite like the pictures, but very similar, and it has a body. It is not a smooth body like an eel. It starts out bigger at the head and gradually tapers to the tail, not unlike a snake. But it is quite massive, and it exudes a very benevolent energy, so it has no enemies. Wherever it exists, life does better—all life. It exudes something that is good for all beings.

How long is it?

Sixteen feet would be a young one. At maturity it might be thirty-two feet long.

Thank you very much. Good night.

Good night.

25

Tibet's Origin
and
Indomitable Spirit

Speaks of Many Truths
October 3, 1998

The Underground Light Cavern

Good evening. When the beginning of life as we have come to know it took place in the place that birthed star systems, there was a directional beam of light that split into twelve equal portions, aimed outward in twelve equal directions. One of those places centered into the space that would one day receive the planet upon which the country of Tibet would be known.

The light resided for a long time on the exact place where the planet would orbit and where the country would be. When the planet took up its position where it now exists, the beam of light started to activate underground caverns deep within the mountains of Tibet. These caverns are so deep and so sheltered by the light energy that no weapon, thought or sorcery can reach them. In this space came to be developed the foundational spiritual enigmas and plans for all religions, all philosophies and all mystical functions of plants, animals, planets and humans that would occur on Earth as well as in this part of the universe.

In time certain portions of that light began to solidify and take form, but only briefly. These forms would be seen by the sensitive eye. Sometimes it would look like a human being and sometimes like some other kind of being, but not an Earth person. Sometimes it would look like an animal. Sometimes it would even look like a place or a scene on the planet. At this time the light was exercising its attempt to manifest any form of life that might someday encounter that cavern. This was the place from which the Tibetan civilization would one day be launched.

The people would come later, but first there had to be the indomitable spirit from the center of the creation of galaxies. This is because the spirit of the Tibetan people as well as the mountains, which radiate this spirit unstoppably, must be the place where absolute wisdom, allowance and the pursuit of knowledge applicable to all peoples are broadcast.

This cavern, with its light-shell protection, is still in existence. It does not look much different today than it looked when it began. However, today one finds that the light has had enough experience with visitors—both in their spirit form and the occasional physical visitor who has come for a time to communicate in some way—to be able to quickly adopt an acceptable form of the wise teacher in both appearance and energy that would be graciously accepted by any visitor. It is this place that is often seen, in meditations and prayers alike, all over this planet and on other planets in this area, this cave of light and beauty of fragrance and form that is loving, endearing and totally accepting of all beings.

This place, then, is temporarily in residence on this planet at this dimension. It is at home on this planet, but in the ninth dimension, so one has to bring that ninth-dimensional reality into the third dimension and on let it move with you on your passage to the fourth. In this place one often finds that a person who is having a meditational experience or even a creative visualization will often pass through without realizing it is the same space for almost everyone on the planet who has these experiences.

It is a place where all wisdom can be attained. It is a place where total love and harmony exist and where all beings who pass through it physically will become total love and harmony regardless of their mindset when they enter. From this place was launched the beginning of the Tibetan people.

The people did not come from China, as is the current assumption by many social scientists. The people have a greater connection to India and Siberia than they do to China. Although they are not connected directly with the underground Ganymede civilization, there is a link of friendship with that civilization.

The people did not come from underground to the surface as they did with the Ganymede civilization. It was not like that. Rather, the light formed the original people, utilizing a composite of the appearance of people who either existed in the geographic area of the time or would come to exist there. This composite intended to cause these individuals to look similar to others around them but have their actual roots in the heart of native peoples all over the world. This is why a strong kindred spirit was felt when native people occasionally visited in spirit or when the occasional physical visitor came in the past when Tibet was still honored by its neighbors.

In my time I have experienced this place and these people on the surface, and I feel the kindred spirit very strongly. It is as if they are my brothers and sisters. It is a feeling as if they could walk into my village, the place where my people are, and fit in without having to learn or know our customs. This means that we are united through the heart.

So the Tibetan people were created by the beings in this light cavern, who represent the light from the center of the place that creates galaxies. This, then, came to be a place that sustains Earth. If anything ever happened to Earth, which is very unlikely . . . they showed me a dot and many, many zeros and a one as being the possibility of Earth's complete destruction. This is by way of saying that it is a remote possibility.

However, because the possibility exists, however remote, this place would continue to exist and by that existence acquire your souls. You would then be able to pass into the cave, really a floating atmosphere within the cave, gradually through the end of your journey as it is set up for you as the Explorer Race. This is probably not going to happen that way, but in case it is necessary, it has been set up.

The Four Original Beings in Tibet

So the forms of the Tibetan people moved through the solid mass up to the surface, and when they arrived there were four. The original beings in Tibet were four people. They were granted physical existence with a complete connection to all that was known inside that cavern and the capacity to communicate with any peoples inside the Earth or on its surface for their lifetimes, granted to them as twenty-five hundred years. It had to be this long so that they could people the place, because the very next generation had no greater lifetime than anyone in that region has today.

Although the mysticism and wisdom were taught to these four beings, because of the limited capacity of the human mind to retain information, it was not possible to teach all that wisdom, even only what would be applicable or useful to Earth citizens. But as much as was possible was taught.

The original four then showed people that they must in time find their own cave inside their mountain, and that there would be three places waiting for them because they must develop their own emulation of the place from which the original four came. By the time the original four passed over at the end of twenty-five hundred years, they did not go into the Earth, as in Egypt, but simply passed as their physical forms changed into their original light forms and then went back into the ninth-dimensional atmosphere inside the Earth. This took as many generations as twenty-five hundred years would encompass.

You might ask, "By that time, had the succeeding generations found their way in through one of the three openings?" By that time they had found their way into two of the openings, and when the four turned back into light and returned to where they came from inside the Earth, the third opening was permanently sealed.

The people were taught how to disguise the natural opening, which was inside the mountains. There was no mining or drilling at any time. Not a single rock was moved, not a stone, although the dust was swirled up. The people went inside and established an underground civilization as well as the one on the surface.

About six hundred years ago, the underground civilization, with all its numbers and accomplishments and wisdom and knowledge, was transported in its entirety to another planet at a slightly higher dimension, near this galaxy but not in it. This was done to preserve the Tibetan civilization—their wisdom, humor, stories, everything—and also the original religion, which was not Buddhism as it came to be known, but had more to do with mysticism and the honoring of all life. Buddhism also has mysticism and it honors all life, but it is an adapted form of the original philosophy. Buddhism has much greater flexibility due to the knowledge, experience and general activities of the time in which Buddha lived.

So there exists in a nearby galaxy a population that is now about eighty-three thousand strong. These individuals will repopulate Tibet on Earth if the entire Tibetan civilization is somehow lost due to the current Chinese government's embrace of a rigid political system, which is largely in reaction to something that they feel caused great suffering for the Chinese people in the past. The current Chinese form of communism has not differentiated between the exclusive religion from the past, as they see it in China, and the inclusive religion of Tibet. They have not seen the difference. They have seen only the surface similarity and reacted with violence toward it as a result. This is not an excuse but an explanation.

The Tibetan culture and civilization is considered to be very important, because not only is it the thread that will, in time, allow you to feel your heart connection to all beings, but it is also the source of wisdom and stories that will allow all beings to notice their similarity. Many scholars of your time have studied the history, the stories, the myths, the religions and the fictional formats for stories, and have found, of course, great similarities. There are certain types of stories that are told in certain ways all over the world. For example, someone finds something valuable and intrinsically useful and then has to do battle and deal with conflict in order to maintain it in its originality and other variations. These types of stories were all created and originally generated from this place, even the love lost story, as in Romeo and Juliet.

All these forms of stories are designed to encourage you to look beyond the limits of your daily life, beyond what you feel can be attained, to reach for something that seems impossible and desire to attain it, which requires the mystical. In my experience, regardless of how hard something might be to attain in your time, when you utilize the mystical it is possible to attain it, to grow from it and be enriched by it. Even if you do not have to possess it, you can experience it long enough to have those other valuable legacies. This is the origin of the Tibetan peoples.

How did the four souls come into the bodies that were created?

The energy that existed in the cave, that light that comes from the center of the place where galaxies are created, ensouled those beings. It was like one soul and four beings, if you look at it that way. This is the only time I'm aware of where one soul is functioning as four beings living concurrently in the same place at the same time in Earth's history.

Why was that choice made?

This was done so that there would not be any deflection from the common purpose.

Did that being or that light ever reincarnate again on Earth?

This is not a being so much as it is a place, a source. I believe that a previous book discussed a creator who created galaxies. It didn't experience an end of life. It had twenty-five hundred years of a physical life, but even though it bore beings, it did not consider that incarnation any different from its existence as it had always been. Thus we cannot use the terms "incarnation" and "reincarnation" as exchangeably as we might with ourselves.

Communalism versus Communism

Well, there are not many people left now in Tibet. Is there a high probability that those beings taken to the other planet from Tibet would come back?

If it is necessary, once the Chinese people have come to see the original purpose of communalism. It has come to be known as communism, but its original purpose and inspiration, not necessarily as written by Lenin and Marx and Trotsky, was communalism, which is common amongst other planets and benevolent societies that have existed on Earth as well. In communalism, no one is forced to do anything, but your abilities are noticed and encouraged. If you are not good at something, you are not forced to become good at it. This is the route of communalism. Then different people do different things well and support a common goal, which is to live together in harmony on the land in the most gentle way possible for all beings.

This is the original purpose of communalism. It is likely that a certain part of what is now China will begin to demonstrate this. Although those in the government will be slow to accept this as their form of communism, they are unlikely to interfere with it, because they will quickly see how this practice will be adapted and will not interfere with their influence as a country.

What was the original territory that the four beings inhabited, felt responsible for or sought to populate? Was it as large as it is now?

It was where the mountains are, not so much anything else. Most of it is mountain. But where the valleys were, the outer perimeters of the original line that was the boundary, was not part of it. It was all the mountain place, the mountain people.

When did it start?

Before China.

After Egypt but before China?

Yes.

So they always maintained this insularity?

Their job was never to go out into the world and teach anything. Their job was to survive in some way, and at some point apparently someone decided that there would be a threat in the future, as is now being experienced. That is why the other eighty-three thousand or so are in existence on the other planet.

Who decided that?

I have to assume that it was the original lightbeing, light creator being.

So they went in their human bodies and their human DNA. Are they humans?

They are human beings; they went in a ship.

Do they know who they are and that they may return?

Yes. It was about six hundred years ago. That's when they went in a ship to the other planet.

That's about the time the beings on the surface became Buddhists, about six hundred years ago. They were warriors and they expanded their territory. Then they suddenly changed and became totally peaceful for six hundred years. Is there a connection between the two events?

I will ask. [Pause.]

Buddha Comes to Tibet

It seems that the surface population was visited by someone who knew all about Buddhism and its value. Also the surface population was reminded of the beings (it was told to them as a story) who lived far away and who were just like them. They would meet in their soul travels someday. Stories were told to them about this. The speaker who was telling this went to all places at once and spoke of these things to all peoples at the same time.

You might talk to your neighbor and say, "I had an interesting conversation with this man who came to visit." "Well, so did I," the neighbor would say. "And what did he look like?" And everybody would describe the man in the same way. This is the sort of thing that gets your attention.

Who was the man?

Who would know a lot about Buddhism?

Buddha. What was the purpose of this?

To create stability so the surface dwellers would not destroy their civilization.

Through war?

Yes.

So Buddha was asked by this light spirit. Was it the original light spirit?

Yes.

And this area underground is still there, but sealed off?

Which area underground?

Under Tibet, the cavern that had the soul of the light.

The light cavern? You will never enter that. It is at the ninth dimension. How could you?

But is it still there, resident inside the Earth?

Yes.

All of this came after the planet was here from Sirius?

It was here, then the planet arrived and then it was sent into the planet. But the light was here first, not the planet.

Was it also in the planet that got blown up? [See introduction of The Explorer Race *book.]*

Yes.

Those first four beings . . . how did they get DNA? If they were the progenitors of all Tibetans, did they gather up DNA and blood qualities or something? How did that work?

If you are a creator . . .

You can create anything you want.

Yes.

What can people do now to aid these refugees? They can't do anything for the ones who are still in Tibet.

If the refugees wish to settle in your country, welcome them. What else can you do? You cannot go over and take Tibet back from China. So welcome the refugees as your country has welcomed them ever since the first ones arrived here from Europe.

If the first ones were so familiar to native peoples, their existence was shamanic before the Buddhist conversion.

By the time they became warring tribes, many of the people were no longer mystical or shamanic. So Buddhism came as a welcome relief.

From that lack of spirituality?

Some had been lost, although not from the underground civilization, but on the surface.

Was there contact between the underground and the surface? Did they know about each other?

The surface did not know about the underground.

But the underground knew about the surface?

Yes. That's why when the surface people were told in this story form about the other people who were just like them, it was explained to them that these other people were far away, not that they were underground (and they were *far* away at the time the story was told).

Did they develop in a parallel way? Aboveground is a completely different type of life, from the one underground, right?

I can't exactly say that it was a parallel way. The underground civilization gleaned all that was the best—not took it, but emulated all that was the best from the surface civilization and carried that on—but they did not take on that which was the worst, such as the impatience and anger and violence.

Did they become Buddhists?

They are not Buddhists. They are the original mystical people.

And are you talking tens, hundreds, thousands, millions?

As I said, eighty-three thousand plus a few, who went to the other planet.

Tibet has always been the spiritual mecca for the planet. Are there other caverns that are tucked away spiritually in Tibet besides the light cavern?

Not that I know of.

The Light That Created the Tibetans

Who is telling you this story? It's not Middle C anymore, right? Is it the original light that created the Tibetans?

Yes.

And was he asked to do this by the Creator?

It, not a he or a she. It was not asked to do this by the Creator of this universe, but by that portion of the Creator of this universe that it has not come into contact with. That which is more than that Creator, which is referred to in previous books, asked this being to do that, and because it came that way, the Creator of this universe could not say, "Don't," but could just sit back and watch, as you might say.

That's the first intervention we have heard of from the total beingness of this Creator. Have there been others?

I do not know. Perhaps this is a better question for Zoosh.

Interesting. We have never heard that the other portion of Creator was anything except just absent.

If one exists someplace but not in another place, one is not absent. One is are simply not there. There's a difference. I'm not splitting hairs; I'm mentioning this because often human beings are striving for something more than they are now, but that greater thing they are going to become is not absent or missing. It might be there even though *you* are not there yet. This paradox can exist in higher dimensions but here it is a paradox.

Let's talk just a bit about this light that created the Tibetans. Is it in Love's Creation?

Yes.

And you say it created galaxies.

Yes, that's all it does. It creates galaxies.

In everybody's creation?

Yes. I am told now that it creates prototype galaxies. Perhaps it does not create them all, but I think the being is trying to suggest that it would not be offended if somebody else created galaxies.

I see. I remember when we talked to that being. He's from the future.

Mystical Tradition and Shamanic Leaders

The little we know of Tibet before the Chinese takeover is that really courageous souls would somehow manage to go there and try to meet one of the lamas for their spiritual teaching.

But lamas have to do with Buddhism, see.

So they never really got to the old Tibetan way.

No, and perhaps that's just as well. You do not have to go to the mountaintop to learn mystical tradition. It is available in your backyard. Just notice what the plants do and what the natural animals do. I differentiate animals who live with you because they might have to be demonstrating certain lessons to you. But notice what the natural animals do, the little ones.

Who live free outside.

They live free outside. Or the bigger ones. Just observe, not as a scientist. Notice how the animals and the plants interact. Notice how different plants interact and different animals interact. Just notice this, and you will begin your mystical training. Do not notice it as a scientist, for there is no heart in science in your lives at this time, but notice it as a heart-centered being. How are they like us? How are we like them? What are our heart connections? This is the beginning of any mystical training. To believe that mystical wisdom comes from one person is to wear blinders to all that lives around you.

Supposing that Tibet was once a seabed, was it raised as these incredibly high mountains before it came to this position? Was it like this when it came here?

It says that the mountains grew as mountains do.

They were raised up by pressure?

This is possible. Mountains are like people; they grow. When they are young and vigorous, they grow quickly, by their mountain time. When they are old and tired, they shrink slowly and become a little more rounded, as old ones often do.

Well, these must be pretty young mountains, then. They're rather pointed.

It is safe to say that if they are pointed, as you say, they are still youthful, in mountain terms.

There is no archaeology. There's no anthropology. There's no knowledge anywhere that I can find quickly about these beings.

Although it seems sad but true, often the most advanced cultures are despised by those who desire those very same advances but do not recognize it in the culture they are destroying. This is what is going on again with China in Tibet, but China did not invent this.

The American people did a pretty good job of it with the American Indians.

Yes, and others. The new Americans came over and repeated that. They had mystical desires and they proceeded to destroy those who were in a position to teach them. This is the way of polarization, but it is also a demand of Creator School, because without consequences and mistakes, you can never test your plan for creation. This is the place where things like that are tested to see if they will remain benevolent regardless of a change of circumstance.

Every government that has unnatural technology (which is most of them) wants to explore the stars and the planets sooner or later. Some of the governments and the people want this desperately, yet those who could speed you on your way to these great adventures are often treated in the most hostile fashion—extraterrestrials and, yes, some shamanic and mystical people. When a mystical man or woman tells you that he or she has touched the Moon, he or she does not mean strictly imaginatively or as a dream. They mean that they have physically touched it, because if you know how, you can extend your physical touch and know how something feels. But as is the paradox here, one tends to destroy what one wants the most.

Since your great teacher Jesus lived on the planet, there have been three more just like him, born and raised on Earth. One was in that area, though not of his kind of people—that area would now be called Syria. All three of them were very different from the people they were raised with, so they were rejected and eventually killed because they were different.

Pay attention to those amongst you who are different. If they are different in a beneficial and benevolent way, embrace them. If they are different in a self-destructive or hurtful way, try to help them in some way that does not harm you or others.

Can you say more about these three? That's never been talked about.

This man Jesus felt very strongly about giving you a chance. He decided at the end of his life that he would encourage you by putting a portion of himself in a human body once every five hundred years, and he did so—twice in a woman's body and once in a man's body. The end of another five hundred years approaches.

Have we ever heard of any of these historically?

No, I do not think that any of them lived past nine years. When Jesus was young, he was no different than these young people. But he was in a culture at that time that was a little more flexible, and that culture was able to suggest that he was learning mystical ways because it has a mystical tradition. The people who thought him strange tolerated him. That's how he lived as long as he did.

So five hundred years later, it was in Syria in a male body?

Yes.

And five hundred years after that, where was it?

Turkey.

In a female body?

Yes.

And in 1500, where?

Iceland. It is a special place. It has had many opportunities and will have many more.

26

The Sirian Japanese Progenitors

Speaks of Many Truths
October 3, 1998

The beginnings of the Japanese people were from another planet. These people came, again, from Sirius.

The Japanese people did not come from Zeta Reticulum, as seems obvious by their appearance; they did come originally from Sirius. Many of the people of the sea also came from Sirius, some who are still with you—dolphins and whales and so on.

At that time many volunteers were coming from Sirius to emigrate to Earth temporarily as a species. I am told that because the beings were coming to the oceans, when they arrived they said, "We would like, if possible, more beings from Sirius" (there were already African peoples from Sirius). "We would like it very much if there were beings from Sirius in this part of the world," because it was quite a ways from Africa.

So there were some volunteers on an outer planet in the galaxy Sirius, a scholarly group. They were most interested in the usage of symbols, not only intellectually, but also on the feeling level and in the full range of subtleties that could be represented by language. These people were also very mystical, and they had a profound connection with all life, as most beings from Sirius do.

These were the people who volunteered. They came originally as a group of ten in an automated ship to fly them directly to what is, I believe, the island of Honshu. The ship landed, and everything the people would need for a thousand years, including that which could manufacture food, if necessary, shelter—everything, including things people had not thought of—was unloaded from the vehicle and put in a special chamber that would keep it safe. The people also went into the chamber. You would say it was like a sealed city, but it was on the surface. It did not sit right on the land, but was hovering. The beings unloaded the ship while it was hovering. The people respected all life and didn't want to crush any life beneath the supplies. Then the ship left and returned to where it came from.

For the first five hundred years, the people did not step on the land physically. They took a small device with them that could carry one or two people and they would float above the land, using amplified magnetic energy from the Sun or Moon and amplified magnetic energy from the Earth. It was essentially a device that floated, and if they leaned in a certain direction, it would go that way. But it did not have a motive force of its own.

It could travel frictionless about three feet above the surface of the land. It took them a long time to come to terms in their hearts with the fact that walking on the land would necessarily harm other beings—plants and animals, small or large—and that the nature of life in the human form necessitated destruction just to exist. They did not come to terms with that for five hundred years, which for them represented ten generations. Their life cycle then was approximately fifty of your now years.

By the eleventh generation there had been enough time after the arrival that people began to leave the ship. First they swam in the ocean or in freshwater places, because they believed they could do so without harming life, which is as close to true as possible. You can step, as it were, on the water, and when you do, of course you are swimming without harming the water or, if you are careful, the water beings. The eleventh generation swam, but the twelfth generation was the first one to step on the land—very carefully.

What did they do on Sirius? How did they live there?

There the land was different. There were not plants everywhere; it was like a desert planet. You would find little places where plants would grow or where the little beings would be. The people who emigrated to what is now Japan felt that they could step on dirt or sand as long as there were no living beings on it they could see (ruling out microscopic beings).

I think that this was the original reason that in the very early days of the Japanese culture, before it came to be known as Japan, people were very careful to step lightly and put as little of their foot as possible on the land.

They came from a desert planet in Sirius?

Yes. There was water on the planet, but it was in one place and the desert was in another. You did not find rivers running through the desert. There were lakes and desert, but that was it. One does find desert planets in Sirius as well as other kinds of planets; they are not all water planets. One simply finds more water planets there than anywhere else.

Did they show you their physical characteristics from that time and place? Is that what they looked like on their home planet?

Yes, that is what they looked like, including the height. The height on that planet was, for a mature adult, anywhere from four foot eight to about five foot three. In recent years people have gotten taller (different diets and so on), but that's how it was originally.

They came because the sea beings asked them to. Did they bring a culture, a technology?

Remember that they had a machine that could produce everything, including their food, but the machines would be active for only a thousand years. By the time the twelfth generation began tiptoeing around on the land, they were almost six hundred years into that cycle. They knew how much time they had with the machines, so they spent the next three or four generations learning how to walk gently on the land. It is not only Native Americans who walk on the balls of their feet. It is a gentler way to walk on the Earth.

Then they had to prepare to live off the land and plant and grow food.

And all this education was provided. They knew that at some point the device, the thing they were living in—which looked like a triangle but was not an equal-sided triangle—would become inactive. It had more of a point on top, but it was a triangle on the bottom. It wasn't like the Great Pyramid; it was an elongated triangle, tall.

Was it translucent? Could they see out, or was it like a building?

It was like a building.

What happened to the building?

If you approached it, you could tell that there was a light inside, but the people couldn't see out and you couldn't see in.

So it disintegrated along with the machine at the end of a thousand years?

It didn't disintegrate. At the end of the thousand years, when the people had established themselves gently on the land and had begun growing crops for several generations and were living at peace with each other, it went home just like the ship did a thousand years, to the exact moment, before.

And it was gone.

It was gone. By that time the people had acclimatized, as you say, accustomed themselves to the land.

The Development of the Shinto Religion

When those thousand years were up, they didn't have any technology?

No, none, but they had their philosophy. They had the qualities they held dear.

Talk about those a little.

I mentioned them before, but the qualities they came to adapt to on the Earth were the joy of preserving all that is beautiful and the rejection of that which was in disharmony with life and existence around it. That is the appreciation of beauty that is the foundation of the Shinto religion, quite a beautiful religion.

Did they have that with them?

No, they adapted it. They did not bring Shinto with them. That was developed by generations to come.

But from within the society, not from outside, as from a visiting ET?

Correct. With this respect and honoring of nature, they were able to extrapolate that philosophy from this, I believe.

Is someone from that civilization telling you this now? Who is communicating?

I am seeing this civilization with my long vision and I am hearing the words. I do not know who is talking.

Can you ask?

I never do. Do you know why? When you ask who is giving the information, it is a challenge, just like the cat in the tunnel. You ask to justify your existence. You don't say that, but it is considered poor manners to ask. How do you know, then, that you are hearing from a benevolent being, one you can trust? You know by the way you feel physically.

I'm not challenging anybody. I'm just lining up people to talk to.

Excuse me. I am speaking my truth. You do not have to live my truth, but I must. Do not be insulted, please. It makes things very difficult. You must remember, personally speaking for a moment, that what you admire does not have to be better. It is only different. That which you are may be greatly admired by others, but that does not mean they give up their way of life to be just like you.

It's just that sometimes things are so illogical.

Yes.

You love that word. I know.

In reality, in my world and in the mystical world, practically nothing is logical because logic always requires straight lines and precision. In my experience, straight lines and precision are a rarity in the mystical world, although they do exist, since the mystical world embraces all form.

27

Siberians Emigrated from an Ice Planet

Speaks of Many Truths
October 5, 1998

L et's talk tonight about the Siberian people.

Beings from the Ice Planet Emigrate to Earth

The Siberian people originated on another planet, but they had an unusual journey to the land where they now live. In the distant past—I think it was about forty thousand years ago—there were people on an ice planet quite far from here. I do not think it is in a part of the universe that is known here.

They had the glimmer of an inspiration on that planet, that it might be possible to increase their growth rate spiritually and intellectually if they could live on this great school planet that would be open to receiving them in about ten thousand years. There was great excitement over that. This planet they lived on (and it is still their home planet) was very responsive to the people.

When the people would get excited about something, areas of the planet would suddenly be filled with a gold doorway, a gold circle, and one could go from the surface to inside the planet and enjoy great beauties and comforts within, but this would be available only when the people became more excited and happy than usual.

They took this understanding of this intimate relationship between the people and the planet with them when a few (<u>about thirty</u> origi-nally) emigrated to Earth, to the northern areas of Siberia. When they arrived on the Earth, they tried that. They told stories and laughed, but it didn't work and they were a little sad, so they talked to their teachers and guides. The teachers and guides said, "We know you miss that, but let us show you where you can have that."

They got everybody back on the ship again and flew to the North Pole, which wasn't very far away, and their teachers and guides said, "Now tell your stories and laugh." And sure enough, there was a beau-tiful golden glow at the North Pole. The ship flew down inside and there was a beautiful world there, warm and tropical, and everyone shed their warm garments and visited with the people there. The people inside Earth welcomed these recent arrivals and said, "We are so happy that such spiritual people as yourselves are going to be touching the land in this place that will come to be known as Siberia, and we wish you well. Please bring your ship and come see us anytime you want our support or companionship."

The people stayed for a few days and then returned to the area now known as Siberia. They are the ones who began the population. They did not send the ship back to their native planet; the ship required a pilot. Instead they caused the ship to sink inside the Earth; it went into its ninth-dimensional energy and sank easily into the Earth, just as water soaks into the soil. <u>The ship is there today and someday might be discovered.</u>

How did they start a civilization?

The ship had the capacity to express itself, meaning to be focused in anything from slightly less than the third dimension to about the eleventh. The people made the trip from this ice planet to Earth slowly, considering time travel, and when they came into your solar system, they slowed down their transit and traveled in space rather than in time. This allowed them to slowly and gently densify so that by the time they and the ship got to Siberia (or what the people then called it, which was the Golden Land) and landed the ship, the people inside were at 3.0 dimension. Therefore, they had offspring in the same way you do.

The people were from the third to the eleventh dimension also?

No, the ice planet itself, which was the surface civilization, was at about the fifth dimension, and the subsurface civilization could be any-thing between the third (believe it or not, third dimension is not always about tough times) to the seventh dimension. So it was the surface peo-ple who went, because the people inside the planet (on that ice planet) would not be comfortable with a cold place. The surface people were at about fifth dimension, so it wasn't such a major task to condense to the third dimension.

Spiritual Respect for Animals and the Totem Pole

Since they came from an ice planet, they had the skills for surviving and living in that environment here?

That's right. They had everything they needed to know. They did bring their spirituality, which had to do with complete and open communication with all animals, plants and flying creatures, fishes, everything. When they hunted or fished or did anything involving the acquisition of food and drink, they would always pray first. When they needed to hunt or gather water, they would ask for the animals who would volunteer their bodies, then they would eat them with great respect. They would honor them and remember them in their lifestyle and show them to their young ones.

This may have become the beginning of what is now seen in various north-country societies as the totem pole. The totem pole in the beginning was just like a tree trunk, but it did not have anything horizontal across it. This came later. The artist's impression of the animals they consumed were carved in the totem pole and the totem was honored and loved and appreciated. In this way the animals were never taken for granted.

Did they live a nomadic life on their home planet?

No, there were quite a few people on their home planet. You could be nomadic, but you would see other people. No, they just liked the cold. On their home planet it was windy and cold, but it wasn't what you would call a brutal cold. It would get down below zero and one might have a twenty- or thirty-mile-an-hour cold wind, but that would be the coldest it would get on the surface of the ice planet. They were willing to accept a little colder on Earth, which they did. Nevertheless, it was not burdensome to them.

So they came basically to focus on their spirituality?

Yes, and to increase their capacity for growth, because the ship had another function once it was buried under the Earth and that is that the ship is seen as a living entity by the people. It would acquire a sample of the growth, such as the growth stream the people were experiencing on Earth, as well as their adaptation of spiritual life, such as the totem pole, and broadcast all this back to the home planet to be revealed in a form of a hologram. The people on the home planet could go up and touch it and feel the feelings.

If you didn't want to feel the feelings at that time, you didn't have to touch it. You could just see it and get the idea. So the spirituality and the growth were stimulated on the home planet as well.

Is it still broadcasting?

It will broadcast only that which will uplift the intellectual growth and the spiritual celebration of life. It is a very narrow focus. It will not broadcast everything. If people ask, for instance, why there hasn't been a broadcast for a while, they will receive the cryptic reply that there is nothing new or beautiful to share. This does not offend, yet it tells the story. Sometimes, however, the ship would broadcast what was happening in nature, as with the animals, and the people would enjoy this, so this happens today as well. (Not just wild animals—sometimes even domestic animals, a pet or different animals who help you.)

Are there different animals in that area than on the home planet?

Yes. On the home planet there are more flying creatures. They don't look exactly like birds; they are very sturdy. Their feathers look to me like they are more substantial than the feathers of birds here. Birds are the majority of the creatures on the home planet.

By the time these beings got to Siberia, what animals were still there—caribou, elk?

There were other animals. At first they did not consume them, but after a while they did. They felt it would be all right, because their teachers and guides informed them that if done in a ceremonial and sacred way, it would be acceptable.

Did the original thirty beings who came reincarnate on Earth?

They reincarnated on Earth in that area for about ten cycles. This is unusual. Usually people do not reincarnate in the same place or even in a general place (a planet) more than three times in a row. But they did ten times in a row because they felt it was necessary to make such a commitment and because they were given the privilege of remembering those ten lives and all the experiences in those lives. As a result, they were able to offer a great deal of wisdom to others for a time.

So by the third life, they remembered the other two? They remembered all ten lives while they were here?

Yes, the second life remembered the first and so on, all the way through until the tenth life—and of course some of them got to the tenth at different times. They then revealed that this would be the last time there and that the people would have to absorb as much knowledge as they could from them, because they would be going home at the end of that life.

They went home without the spaceship?

No, it wasn't that way. I see the ship coming, but it wasn't for them. Another ship came to sing the ceremony of returning the lightbody to the home planet, which is a rare but occasional occurrence in that culture. Often they would not go anywhere, but this was an exception. Every once in a while one or more of their members would go to other planets and their life cycle would come to an end, and the ship would come and sing. The people inside the ship would sing. They would sing the soul back, so it wasn't necessary to transport them. They went back.

Of course, the ship would have to come and go because not everybody died at the same time. So over a period of seventy-five years, the ship came and went several times.

If we were to look at the myths of these Siberian people, do they have stories about these original elders?

I don't think they do. But I think they do have some knowledge that they came from the stars. Understand that because there has been so much strife in the area, the original bloodline has been altered a lot.

Did the progenitors travel and did they colonize any other areas?

No.

They stayed in what is called Siberia.

But in the far north by the sea.

Beings of the Inner Earth

Who were those beings they visited when they first came?

Oh, those Inner Earth beings. This is the same place that was seen by Admiral Byrd. They are not there anymore, but they were there for a long time. I think an underground civilization may have been the original source of many of the native peoples who originally lived in Mexico, Central America and South America. If you were to go there in that time, looking at the civilization and the way it looked, in my long vision it reminds me very much of the way certain Central American places used to look in my time.

So when these tribal beings have stories of the beginning of creation, of coming out of a hole in the ground from inside the Earth, that's accurate?

Yes. These are emergence stories. Emerging does not always mean for all peoples that they originated inside the Earth, but it might mean that they lived there for a time.

The Hopis say that this is the Fifth World. There is a cataclysm and they go inside the Earth.

It's not just that they go, but they also are invited. Certain members of the people will know when it is time to go, if that should ever occur again; where to go and who will lead them; who will support them; what to bring and who to bring. All these are important things.

So there are other entrances into this civilization other than the North Pole? There are many entrances, as you talked about with the Ganymedians?

There are other entrances. Sometimes the entrances are not there, but if they need to be, they can be temporarily. Those kinds of entrances are the safest because they cannot be detected beforehand and they are not there afterward.

Where was this civilization from that was inside the Earth—the civilization the Siberians went to and that Byrd saw?

It seems that they were there when the planet was in Sirius, and so they are, you might say, from Sirius, but they traveled with the planet. I don't see any ships.

Do the tribes in Central and North America have the same source?

I don't think they do. I think they have the same heart but not the same exact source. The same heart is not just the organ, but the energy.

That's the origin of many of the native tribes of North and South America?

Not North America so much.

Central?

As I said, Mexico and Central America and South America. There may be some in North America, but they do not want me to say so.

Siberians Followed the Ice

The Siberians stayed close to the land. There must be cities there, or were they started by somebody else?

The original peoples stayed close to the land. They are showing me a book, so the material must be available. [This means this information is available in a book on Earth now and he doesn't want to use the channel's energy to discuss topics that are available in books for humans to research.]

Although you said that the bloodline is diluted, there is still some left?

There is still some, yes—some of the original bloodline but not 100 percent pure, which one would not expect at this time.

It is interesting that they basically stayed there. Everybody else on the planet seems to have wandered all over the planet, right?

Yes, they stayed there partly because they knew that if they wandered too far, they would be somewhere that was not an ice planet. They wanted to be where the ice was. It was what they knew and liked. They weren't looking for something that was going to be too warm, so they tended to follow the ice rather than the Sun. They moved around only to follow the ice.

Is there a connection between the Eskimos and the Siberian people?

Yes. Originally the people from Siberia crossed over to Alaska. I think that some of this was done by boat and some of it was done some other way. I see people rowing.

So they are the originators of the Eskimo people—Inuits is what they were called?

That's one of the tribe names, I believe. They are the originators, and they also have some relatives farther south in North America.

In Canada somewhere?

Yes, Canada. Not all over Canada. They have some of their bloodline in some Canadian tribes and some North American tribes. Only some, but they are there.

You don't want to say which ones?

Definitely not, because a certain amount of tribal secrecy must be honored. Remember that tribal peoples have managed to survive as long as they have in these complex times you are living in because they have maintained the continuity of their wisdom and have not been distracted by contemporary knowledge. This requires great discipline and oftentimes secrecy.

So the original thirty beings had a shamanistic understanding when they came?

Yes, that would be the word that the average person would use.

They lived that way on the original planet?

Yes. The original thirty were all mystical people. Only much, much later did people start specializing, but even then everyone had a lot of mystical knowledge. Even if you or your family or your friends were separated from the tribe, you were never far from the hearts of all beings.

Earth's Original Bloodlines

Each of these separately—Egypt, China, Siberia, Japan and all the rest we haven't talked about yet—set up a bloodline and a culture so that the Explorer Race would have all these different stage settings to incarnate in, right?

Yes, that is one way to say it. The things they focused on, such as mysticism and totems, all came to be things that the following generations, regardless of their heritage, would have available to them.

Look, for example, at the most widely seen totem in the United States today, one that is seen around the neck of people who call themselves Christians. This would be considered a totem, meaning that it intends to honor the man who died on the cross. One would not say that this is a heart-centering/honoring totem, but you can see how totems led to the wearing of a symbol and the proclaiming of one's allegiance to this religion and, in some cases, philosophy. So these cultural developments would be contributions to the mainstream, available as ways of being.

Most planets have a predominant culture only because most planets usually do not test the cultures as severely as they are tested here. Survival is more of a guarantee on other planets, whereas on Earth it is iffy. Developing a homogeneous civilization is almost easy on other planets, whereas maintaining the continuity and traditions of any given tribe, clan or people on Earth is a great challenge. There are disease and early death—compared with what an extraterrestrial might say, "Seventy-five years old, and you're already *dying*? I don't understand."

They also don't understand disease and discomfort and simply wearing out. Friction, for example, as you know it here on Earth, doesn't exist the same way on other planets, especially in other dimensions, so one doesn't have the wearing out of the physical self.

And there's a lot of emotional friction here, too.

Yes, indeed, and that also takes a toll on one's endurance.

How many different original bloodlines do we have on this planet?

I am not sure, but I am told over forty. They might be more specific later, but right now that is all they will say. Creator seems to be very enthusiastic about variety.

That's why our mythology is so rich and varied.

Yes.

What about these beings from Siberia? They went back to their home planet? Do ships come and check on the civilization?

There was some visiting early on. I think the visits stopped about five hundred years ago, but they were still coming occasionally. I think they stopped when more and more people from other places came to discover this land, and of course the land and the weather conditions on the land itself tended to keep many people away. That was a protection in itself.

So then these original cultures that came from other planets are on this planet now. How many? Look at how many dialects there are just among the North and South American natives.

Yes, and most of the tribes in North America do not even exist anymore because of the disaster—the invasion, we call it.

But surely several of them had a common heritage. There's a lot of splitting off and separate evolutions.

Yes, people get different visions and they interpret the culture's stories differently. If it comes to be seen that the different vision stands on its own, then some people follow that path, not unlike the way the Christian religion has many, many different branches of the same tree.

It seems that there are hundreds of languages and dialects. So over the course of ten or twenty or thirty thousand years, that's what happened?

Sometimes language is simply the best you can do. Sometimes dialects have to do with adapting, such as when people move from one place to another. Even though they speak their language, maybe they move to a place where there are already people there and they end up living in some part of the area where those people are all around them. The language they brought with them becomes affected by the language already there, and that is how a dialect might begin.

Some languages reflect the homelands of the people who originally came here. Because the culture and the interactions might be different on Earth, the language adapts and changes to the conditions of Earth. The original people might not recognize the language later because the words the people arrived with didn't fit the new conditions.

Look at English and American.

Yes, some English people, especially if they were given a proper scholastic education, as many of them are, come over here and have a hard time understanding American slang, as they call it—just like you go over there and can't follow what they are saying, but the language root is the same.

Thank you. Good night.

28

The Middle East and the SSG

Speaks of Many Truths
October 8, 1998

In the country of Israel, as it is now called, where the western border meets the Mediterranean sea, to about sixty miles north of the southern border that also meets the sea and about, I think, just a few miles south of their northern border, which meets the sea, there is a fold in the energy of continuity that supports Mother Earth as a planetary being. This fold (it's the best way I can describe it) would look very much like you folded over a piece of cloth, then folded it back toward yourself. It would look like a lap in the cloth, as they say in some craft circles.

This fold is very difficult for Mother Earth to comprehend, much less deal with. It is not of her making and is a direct result of the sinister secret government's attempt to hold the spiritual psyche of that region in check and bind it to past rivalries. It is a current success, or challenge, depending on your view of the sinister secret government, that has so far defied many spiritual attempts to resolve it.

It has been in effect for about eighty-five hundred years, which would suggest, naturally, the question of what the sinister secret government has to do with it. It is one of their time-travel successes. They haven't had many, but that's one of them. As a result, if you went back in tribal history in that part of the world, you would find that about ten thousand years ago, even nine thousand years ago, most of the tribes were at peace with one another. They shared resources, water and so on.

In 1985 the SSG Time-Traveled to 7000 B.C.

But right about eighty-seven hundred years ago, people started to get nervous. They didn't know why they were nervous; they didn't even know that they were nervous. They didn't have words for that then. This nervousness was their anticipation of the secret government's attempt to go back in time. The SSG had started, right around nine thousand years ago, to try to poke a hole in the spiritual rhythm of that place, and people started to feel it about eighty-seven hundred years ago. About eighty-five hundred years ago, the SSG was successful, and they tore a hole in the spiritual fabric. Then, in order to confound other spiritual beings from repairing the hole, they folded it over on itself. They tied its resolution to the peoples in the area having to return to the peaceful state or condition that preceded their attack on the area.

In this way they were able to confound the attempts to resolve it. From their point of view, they were being reasonable. Of course, the damage they did to the spiritual fabric has been largely the cause of strife in those areas.

What year in our time did they go back and do that?

I am told it was between 1985 and 1987. Their first attempt was in 1985. They lost about 457 people in the project and damaged a great deal of their equipment, but they didn't care about that. Through the utilization of their time field, which uses electricity, magnetics and some radioactive elements, they ruined a natural underground cavern they were using. They also utilized sorcery to pull in certain soul energies, without permission, from human beings living on the Earth. (They did this to disguise what they were doing.) I cannot say more about their process without putting weapons in the hands of people who might misuse this information, but those who understand such things will know what I am talking about.

Was it done underground in Montauk or somewhere else on the planet?

No, this was done underground in South America, very deep under the country known as Argentina, about eighty miles underneath the surface. Needless to say, this was done without the knowledge of the surface population.

Down at the tip of the continent? At the very tip?

Down at the southern end, yes.

Is that what Zoosh says is the office from which the secret government runs the planet?

No, because this is a natural cavern, but it is close to that place. Their base is something they dug, but this is a natural cavern. Now it is not safe for life. It has been damaged, and it is not possible for Mother Earth to repair it, but it will be repaired in time by higher beings, most likely not for another five or six thousand years.

Mideast Conflicts Result from Damage to Spiritual Fabric

So is the fighting and lack of peace in Israel and in that area now a result of what the SSG did?

As I said, the tribal warfare had not really begun before they did this, and the battles up to this time, including now, of this whole area are a result of the SSG's activity. The damage and the radiation create a tension. If one puts an artificial tension in any construction . . . an analogy is that if a tension is artificially placed in, say, a bridge or a road, that bridge or road will fail in considerably less than its expected lifetime.

In this case we have a tension compounded upon itself. Imagine, those of you who get chiropractic adjustments or even massage, if you have a tight muscle that needs to be released and it isn't, it gets worse and worse and worse. It is like that. To the degree that this fold is under tension, it radiates more of what I would call the feeling of agony. If you show me a map, I will show you how far it radiates out of that fold.

The center point, where the radiation is most extreme, is right here, a big city—Tel Aviv. This is where the tension is usually the most extreme in the area. This is usually the tension, but it does not stay only there. What I am told is that this is where the energy is, but there are some little tendrils everywhere. These are temporary and move around.

But what about to the east? Is it getting into the eastern countries or south to Egypt?

No, it doesn't go that way, only where I have shown it. This is the center of the fold. If you

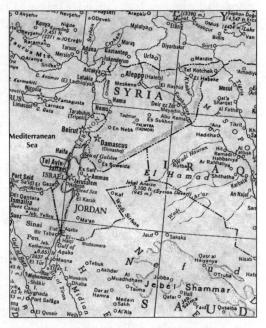

Fig. 85. Map of tension radiating in the Middle East.

were to look down at it, you would see it as a smoky area. Now, I am also told that this energy, if the sinister secret government wants to make trouble, can be concentrated like one concentrates a light ray; it can be momentarily focused or beamed for a second or maybe a half or three quarters of a second.

Like a laser.

Not that tightly. No, it would be condensed down to about fifty miles wide. It can be aimed, but only in the general direction of its current radiation.

Toward the east.

I am told that this has been the cause of a great deal of strife that has been stimulated in recent years in Afghanistan, Pakistan, India and other countries (the presence of Russia or the then Soviet Union in Afghanistan, for instance). The people in these countries have suffered because the energy is so powerful and it is used to keep the area disrupted.

It goes almost through Baghdad.

The Mideast Was Originally the Greatest Influence for Unity

You might easily ask (and I did the first time I heard of it), why did they do this in this area? They did this because the most influential religions and philosophies consider this area to be sacred; their members do not make up all the people of the world, but they are, together, an influential group.

It was originally intended that these religions—Christianity, Islam, Judaism—form three portions of a single circle of influence and that this circle of influence would support a united world. If the SSG had not been successful in this attack on the spirit of peoples, that area would have united completely and formed this circle of influence. Your establishment of the United Nations and its encouragement would have been followed by a one-world benevolent society ten years after the foundation of the United Nations.

That is why the SSG considered this so imperative. They were willing to pay any price in order to cause this calamity. Now let me tell you what you can do.

Practical Homework to Change the Energy

For those in the area, if you should hear of these things we are speaking of today, here is your practical homework. I know that it is difficult to live there. If you are Islamic, it is very difficult right now. If you are Christian, it is also difficult. If you are Jewish, it is not only difficult but confusing. So I'm going to give you an assignment: In the next three to six months from when you hear about this, please go out and make one new friend of each of those religions, which includes your own religion. Then the four of you make it a point to get to know one another and do something socially at least once a month. That's the homework for you who are living in this area. If you cannot do this because you do not know people of the other religions or it is not easy to meet them, then try to make friends with people who live near you, people you never see and have nothing in common with. This will help.

Now, for those of you who do not live in the area but are of one of these religions, you can also do that homework. When I say you are of these three religions, I mean that you practice one of these religions, not just that you were born to it. For those of you who practice something else or do not practice a religion as it is understood in your time or who maybe have a philosophy you live by, I encourage you to do whatever ceremonies of love and companionship and friendship you can.

If you are at a wedding, a christening or a celebrated holiday where there is happiness, just once during the celebration say, "Peace and brotherhood" (and you can say sisterhood if you prefer) "is natural to this area." So know the map. You can say Israel. You can say Syria. You can name these countries, but try to have a picture. You might not believe it, but just say it. Others of you, put it in your prayers; do something to soothe the area. Try to contribute to the peace there, because the people who live there are having a very difficult time.

When the people who live in the area affected by the folded energy have friends who practice another religion or even friends in their own religion, sometimes they are at such complete odds that they almost (and sometimes do) come to blows. But I will tell you the biggest challenge: It's not just the different languages (that's enough, yes), but that people are so overwhelmed by this fold of energy that makes the communication of people's feelings into words that are understood by others much more difficult.

Communication by Feelings

Those who have the greatest passion to communicate with their feelings are the Islamic people. Those (I am generalizing, you understand) who have the greatest command of words and who trust words more than feelings are the Jewish and Christian people. If you know that as a general rule (not for everyone), then understand that feelings and mental words do not directly communicate.

If someone is talking to you and has strong feelings that you are not understanding, you may not have perfect communication language-wise, but normally it's good enough to understand. If you don't understand, ask the person to touch you physically, gently, in some way. Reach over and touch that person's arm or hand while she is talking to you; then you will feel the person's feelings and understand. Do the same when you talk to that person, because passionate feelings are most easily understood by the feeling body.

Equally, if you are a person of words and a person of feeling cannot understand your words even though he understands your language, if he does not know what you are trying to say, reach out and touch that person in some socially acceptable place. (These touches should be all right. I am saying the arm or the hand, but you know in your part of the world how or where to touch each other.) If that is acceptable, do that and then talk. Even if that person does not understand what you are saying at first, he will in time, especially if you get into the feelings of what you are saying. Ultimately, all people communicate with their feelings, but those who rely on words are more apt to have misunderstandings.

That's something everyone can do. So the history of the past eighty-five hundred years has changed as a result of this interference by the SSG?

Yes.

Is what we're seeing in the Middle East the result of that change?

Yes. If that attack by those negative peoples (the SSG) had not taken place, the area would be beautiful. It would be the place people would come to when they want to go somewhere to have a good example for getting along with one another. If people were having trouble . . . let's say that you are a father and you are having trouble communicating with your son and your son cannot make you understand. You would then go to that place, and after a few days there you would be able to understand each other. That was how it was meant to be.

History Changed for Everyone Alive in 1985

It happened in 1985, so things were changed in our lifetime?

They went back, you know. It took them two years, from 1985 to 1987, to succeed in their cruel goal. I mention that because it was in 1985 that they began and it was in 1987 when they decided to say, "This is enough." They felt that they had accomplished their purpose.

What we know of Israel and the formation of their state, the wars, our modern history . . .

. . . has all been affected by that. I am told that I have to explain this. When this kind of change is caused, in 1985 you should have been able to read a history book printed in 1945 and the history would be accurate. But no, when this intervention in past time takes place, it changes the memories and the reality of all beings. So even if you were born in 1935, you would remember what has taken place coming forward from eighty-five hundred years ago, not the past you lived before 1985.

When you go back in time and change something, it changes the present as well as the past. It changes memory; it changes everything. That's why we have to fix it so that you can recapture your true memories.

The Remedy

Why can't the dimensional masters or the spiritual teachers go in and undo it?

They have all told me that this is something that the people of the area must begin, that if the people of the area become convinced that they must have peace so that they can discover what they like about one another, then they will be able to do it. But it must begin that way. It doesn't have to be that the people there have to make this conversion to this society. But they must begin of their own desire, not because someone like Speaks of Many Truths tells them they ought to.

I think that in time it is going to happen. I wouldn't be surprised if it happens in your lifetime, because all the work is in place by all the spiritual teachers and benevolent beings to immediately change it. The only thing they are waiting for is the action of the people in the area, and when that takes place the energy will change.

The first thing that people all over the world will notice is that they won't seem to be able to remember the history of that area, and no one will be able to find any history books that say anything about it. That will last for a while, then people will begin to remember this different history that was supposed to have taken place. Then they will find it in the history books.

That's wonderful! I didn't understand that back when Zoosh told us about the time-track removal of the peace avatar U.S. President by the SSG. [See Shining the Light I.]

Science, Sorcery and Shamans

It's very scientific. The SSG has to use science and sorcery because they are doing things that are against the natural flow of energy, and only science and sorcery can do this. When science is reengaged in your time with its natural heart and finds its god, as Zoosh says, then science will no longer be used by them and they will have only sorcery. By that time you will have enough mystical people and shamanic people to combat that sorcery. Even as I speak in your time, many mystical people are training. Some of them do not know why or what for, but they are training to combat sorcery.

The need for people with shamanic training is probably why there is so much of it out there today?

Yes.

In the United States people are remembering the Native American teachings, and there are other countries of the world where the people are looking for their shamanic heritage.

When times are unknown and uncertain, this is part of the reason people are almost always attracted to the permanent, natural ways.

The Aborted Meeting and Shamanic Training

You said that there was a meeting of native elders not too long ago and that they were supposed to disclose all their secrets, which would have created new interest in the shamanic way of life.

They were going to disclose these things, yes, but they didn't because they needed to have two other groups, I believe.

One group was the Mormons—what was the other one?

It was going to be certain scientists, and one was going to say, "This is our story." They wouldn't say, "This is our vision." They would say, "This is what we believe." Then the Latter Day Saints religion would say, "This is what we believe, and here are our proofs." Then the scientists would say, "We know of these things. We have found all these proofs, and here they are."

But because the other two groups were not prepared or did not show up, the elders wisely decided to say nothing or to say only things that people had heard before. They knew that if these other groups were not prepared to talk, something was out of balance and they would have to wait.

In spite of that, the people who need shamanic training are going to get it, whether or not these secrets are revealed. Is that true?

Yes, people are getting that training now all over the world. Some of them have been misunderstood, and people think they are crazy and put them in institutions. If you are practicing and are being taught to be a mystic or a shaman, when you are doing your practicing, your teaching, your studies, as long as what you are doing is benevolent (not harming you or anyone else), it might look very strange to someone else.

If you think they can accept these words, you say, "This is part of my mystical training, and it is a step on the way. I don't understand it completely yet, but there will be more revealed to me in time." But if you think they would not understand those words, then you can say, "It's part of my religion and I feel inspired to do it." Most people can accept that.

The people in that area . . .

It is difficult to talk about their origin because of this corruption. That's why I'm not talking about it. I can't talk about their origin when I can't see the slightest demonstration of their origin. Their origin is clouded, so I have to skip over talking about the people's origins there. Maybe we can talk about it some other time, but I am guided to say nothing about it at this time. My feeling is that if the SSG knew of the people's origins, they might find even worse ways to attack them.

Please do not feel that this difficulty with the SSG is a permanent situation. I have faith in your resolving this, because I have seen the future of Earth in third and fourth and fifth and other dimensions, and I see people in this area getting along and doing well together, even forming a mutually shared philosophy.

So I feel that you will succeed, but you must make the effort. Some of you will have to make the effort as if success is not guaranteed. I have seen this future, but my feeling is that it will take a great deal of work and commitment, especially by the people in that area. It's awfully hard, you know, to make a friend out of someone you don't trust, but sometimes, if you go slow enough with it, you'll find things you like, and you can share and do things together. Maybe you both like to play the same game and get to be friends because of that game. You do these things now. I feel that you will resolve it, but it will take a little time. So make the effort, please.

LIFE WITH A
COSMOS CLEARANCE

Daniel M. Salter as told to Nancy Red Star

. . . IF THE GOVERNMENT DOES NOT COME FORWARD WITH THE TRUTH, THEN THE ALIENS WILL TAKE A MORE PUBLIC ROLE IN DISCLOSURE.

On May 9, 2001, the Disclosure Project hosted a major event at the National Press Club in Washington, D.C. This historic event had witness testimony from twenty to twenty-five military, intelligence, government and corporate individuals, involved with UFO projects over the last fifty years, who presented their information before a worldwide group of media correspondents.

Those of us who were military witnesses of UFO history showed **OFFICIAL GOVERNMENT DOCUMENTATION** with our detailed testimony. Our focus was and is on the facts and documents. Our purpose was and is to get the mainstream media and government officials to hear those facts and move us toward an honest congressional inquiry.

We who came forward want to **BAN WEAPONS FROM SPACE** and stop aggressively shooting down these space vehicles and their extraterrestrial occupants. We need to declassify the advanced electromagnetic propulsion systems in use by the secret government, start producing them for the world to use and thereby help save this planet.

The people who had been employed in agencies within the military and knew **THE TRUTH ABOUT UFOS** had been sworn to secrecy. Now I am finally relieved to speak the truth. We military men who hold on to this knowledge are getting old and dying, and we want the truth to come out. We will either do it ourselves or leave it for our children and wives to do.

Personally, I have told those on Capitol Hill that I am being led to do it by the aliens themselves. They have convinced me that it is time. They have been waiting on the government, and if the government does not come forward with the truth, then the aliens will take a more public role in disclosure.

—Daniel M. Salter ISBN 1-891824-37-6 $**19.95**

Highlights Include

- The Kalahari Retrievals
- Weaponizing Space
- From Void to Mass: Wave Particlization
- Vienna and the Black Sun
- Germany's Advanced Technologies Prior to WWII
- The Brotherhood Lodges
- Secret Deep Underground Military Bases and Advanced Earth Craft
- Star Wars
- Russian UFO Files for Sale
- Approaching the Millennium Shift
- The Wingmakers and the Ancient Arrow Site

Agent Daniel M. Salter is a retired former counterintelligence agent for the Scientific and Technical Unit of Interplanetary Phenomena in Washington D.C.. He was a member of the Pilot Air Force, NRO (National Reconnaissance Office) and DCCCD (Development of Conscious Contact Citizenry Department) with the United States military. He was a CON-RAD courier for President Eisenhower, with a clearance far above Top Secret (Cosmos) and a member of the original Project Blue Book. His expertise was in radar and electronics, his field of investigation UFOs, Aliens and Particlization. Now seventy-five, Salter has both Comanche and French ancestry.

P.O. BOX 3540 • FLAGSTAFF • AZ 86003 PHONE: (928) 526-1345   1-800-450-0985
FAX: (928) 714-1132   1-800-393-7017 www.sedonajournal.com

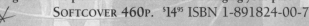

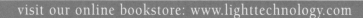

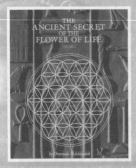

SPEAKS OF MANY TRUTHS AND ZOOSH THROUGH ROBERT SHAPIRO

SHAMANIC SECRETS for MATERIAL MASTERY
Learn to communicate with the planet

This book explores the heart and soul connection between humans and Mother Earth. Through that intimacy, miracles of healing and expanded awareness can flourish.

To heal the planet and be healed as well, we can lovingly extend our energy selves out to the mountains and rivers and intimately bond with the Earth. Gestures and vision can activate our hearts to return us to a healthy, caring relationship with the land we live on.

The character and essence of some of Earth's most powerful features is explored and understood, with exercises given to connect us with those places. As we project our love and healing energy there, we help the Earth to heal from man's destruction of the planet and its atmosphere. Dozens of photographs, maps and drawings assist the process in 25 chapters, which cover the Earth's more critical locations.

$19⁹⁵ SOFTCOVER 498P.
ISBN 1-891824-12-0

SHAMANIC SECRETS for PHYSICAL MASTERY

COMING SOON

The purpose of this book is to allow you to understand the sacred nature of your own physical body and some of the magnificent gifts it offers you. When you work with your physical body in these new ways, you will discover not only its sacredness, but how it is compatible with Mother Earth, the animals, the plants, even the nearby planets, all of which you now recognize as being sacred in nature. It is important to feel the value of oneself physically before one can have any lasting physical impact on the world. The less you think of yourself physically, the less likely your physical impact on the world will be sustained by Mother Earth. If a physical energy does not feel good about itself, it will usually be resolved; other physical or spiritual energies will dissolve it because it is unnatural. The better you feel about your physical self when you do the work in the previous book as well as this one and the one to follow, the greater and more lasting will be the benevolent effect on your life, on the lives of those around you and ultimately on your planet and universe. SOFTCOVER 600P.

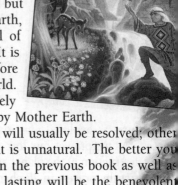

Shamanic Secrets for Physical Mastery

SPEAKS OF MANY TRUTHS AND ZOOSH THROUGH ROBERT SHAPIRO

$19⁹⁵ ISBN 1-891824-29-5

Chapter Titles:

- Cellular Clearing of Traumas, Unresolved Events
- Cellular Memory
- Identifying Your Body's Fear Message
- The Heart Heat Exercise
- Learn Hand Gestures
  - —Remove Self-Doubt
  - —Release Pain or Hate
  - —Clear the Adrenals or Kidneys
  - —Resolve Sexual Dysfunction
- Learning the Card Technique for Clarifying Body Message
- Seeing Life as a Gift
- Relationship of the Soul to Personality
- The New Generation of Children
- The Creator and Religions
- Food, Love & Addictions

- Communication of the Heart
- Dreams & Their Significance
- The Living Prayer/Good Life
- Life Force and Life Purpose
- Physical Mastery
- His Life/ Mandate for His Ancestors/ Importance of Animals/ Emissaries
- Physical Mastery
- Talking to Rain/ Bear Claw Story
- Disentanglement
- Grief Culture
- Closing Comments

SONG OF FREEDOM

My Journey from the Abyss *by Judith Moore*

Judith Moore knew she'd been sick a lot more than most people—but it wasn't until she joined an incest survivors' group to help one of her adopted daughters that the memories began surfacing.

At first she feared for her sanity, for these recollections were of painful medical experiments, torture and sensory deprivation at the hands of the United States government.

In this brave and groundbreaking work, Judith Moore shares her shattering revelations of the reality of **HIGH-LEVEL MIND CONTROL**. She opens the pages of her journal and the innermost feelings of her heart to share with the reader her **JOURNEY TO WHOLENESS** and to healing. As memories flood her consciousness, she struggles to make sense of what is happening, to process the information in accordance with her lifelong worldview of love, intellectual curiosity and deep respect for nature.

Her early environment, rich in **NATIVE AMERICAN FOLKLORE**, helps her in her quest. She researches, travels, investigates and meditates in an effort to set herself free, to reclaim her very sense of herself as a person. Her search leads her into terrifying unknown territory and **ILLUMINATING DISCOVERIES** about her own psyche and that of today's society as a whole. **$19.95**

JUDITH'S MEMORIES BEGAN TO BRING TO THE SURFACE
- **PAINFUL MEDICAL EXPERIMENTS**
- **TORTURE**
- **SENSORY DEPRIVATION**
- **HIGH-LEVEL MIND CONTROL**

AT THE HANDS OF THE UNITED STATES GOVERNMENT!

Song of Freedom is a wake-up call to Western civilization! Moore's gripping account of her extraordinary life takes us to extremes of human experience—from depravity beyond comprehension to the triumph of one child's unassailable spirit. Song of Freedom dares us to take off the blinders we wear to what lies buried in our societal closets. Those who dare to look are taken on a transformational journey through the horrors of mind control and ritual abuse to Judith's amazing experiences of healing. The book is strewn with insights and gems of wisdom which prove that although fear often seems to have the upper hand, it is always love that triumphs in the end.

CHRYSTINE OKSANA, AUTHOR
Safe Passage to Healing: A Guide for Survivors of Ritual Abuse

JUDITH K. MOORE No longer a victim, Judith Moore now leads a productive life, teaching, sharing and channeling the truths that helped her in her journey to freedom.

LIGHT TECHNOLOGY PUBLISHING
P.O. BOX 3540 • FLAGSTAFF • AZ 86003
PHONE: (928) 526-1345
1-800-450-0985
FAX: (928) 714-1132
1-800-393-7017
www.lighttechnology.com